The Ultimate Boogeyman Safari

The Ultimate Boogeyman Safari

Matthew Petchinsky

The Spooky Journey begins

The Ultimate Boogeyman Safari: A Journey into the Boogie World and Beyond
By: Matthew Petchinsky

Prologue: The Boogey Book
There are whispers in the dark corners of our world, tales exchanged in hushed tones when the moon is veiled and shadows grow long. These tales speak of creatures that lurk beneath beds, slink through closet doors, and wander the endless corridors of human fears. They speak of beings that thrive on the energy of our fright, our nightmares personified—these beings are known collectively as Boogeymen. And within the realms of myth and magic, there exists one artifact that holds their secrets, an ancient compendium of knowledge passed down through generations: **The Boogey Book**.

Bound in the midnight-hued leather of a beast no longer seen in this world, and clasped with iron inlaid with sigils of protection, the Boogey Book is not just a collection of words but a living relic. Its pages, some aged and brittle as the centuries they have witnessed, others as fresh as yesterday's fears, pulse with an uncanny energy. It is said that the ink within its pages changes color, reflecting the mood of the reader. Some who have dared open its cover see text written in blood-red ink, while others see blue, green, or even silver—a phenomenon scholars attribute to the book's innate understanding of its holder's soul.

Legend tells of the Boogey Book's origin. Crafted in an era when the veil between worlds was thin, it was the creation of an ancient order of sorcerers known as the **Nocturnarii**, dedicated to studying the unseen dimensions and creatures that inhabited them. The Nocturnarii devoted their lives to understanding the realm of the Boogeymen, recording every encounter, every trap, every spell of containment. Yet, despite the order's dissolution over millennia, their legacy survived within the book's pages, waiting for the next soul brave enough to confront the darkness.

The Boogey Book's journey through history has been fraught with peril. Hidden from the eyes of those who would misuse its knowledge, it has been passed down through a clandestine network of hunters, shamans, scholars, and the occasional frightened parent. Each custodian added to its knowledge, etching notes into the margins, scribbling hastily learned lore from whispered warnings and firsthand encounters with the Boogeymen. Some pages bear the scorch marks of attempts to destroy it, while others are stained with peculiar substances—blood, tears, and even a glimmering powder said to be the residue of a banished Boogeyman.

Contained within this tome is not just a bestiary of the Boogeyman species but a guide to their world—a place known among the keepers of lore as the **Boogie World**. This realm, a dimensional paradigm 40 times larger than any bedroom or closet, is a labyrinth of twisting paths, cavernous halls, and shadowy corners where reality bends to the will of its monstrous inhabitants. It is a world ruled by fear, where time does not flow as it does in the mortal realm, and those who enter often find themselves changed forever, if they return at all. The Boogey Book offers glimpses into this reality, providing maps and warnings for those who dare to venture forth in pursuit of these elusive creatures.

But this is not merely a book of terror. The Boogey Book also serves as a manual for tracking and containing these fiends. From ancient rituals performed during the full moon to recipes for creating **Boogie Goo**—a sticky, iridescent substance used to trap a Boogeyman—this tome is the definitive guide for those who wish to arm themselves against the darkness. It outlines the art of **temporal**

manipulation, teaching the creation of temporalfudge devices that can distort the fabric of time, tricking a Boogeyman into momentary stillness.

It is also a catalog of myths from around the world, recording over 200 worldwide boogeyman-like entities, each with unique traits and weaknesses. For every page turned, the reader uncovers another thread in the vast tapestry of the Boogeyman's existence, revealing the interconnectedness of global folklore and the universal nature of fear.

However, the Boogey Book carries a warning. It is not a simple collection of facts but a living entity, a conduit to the very world it describes. Those who open its cover do so at their own risk. For the Boogeymen have a way of sensing when their secrets are being explored. They become restless, slipping through the cracks of reality into the waking world, their eyes fixed on those who would dare to learn about them. Stories tell of readers who, after delving too deeply, found themselves haunted by the very creatures they sought to understand.

And so, as you prepare to embark on this journey through the pages of the Boogey Book, remember this: knowledge is power, but it is also a beacon. The light you shine into the darkness may reveal more than you wish to see, and the shadows may follow you back. This book is not merely a guide but an initiation into a world where myths become reality, and nightmares take form.

Take a breath, steady your hands, and turn the page. The knowledge within may be your greatest ally—or your most haunting adversary.

Part 1: *Entering the Boogie World*

Chapter 1: What Lurks in the Shadows?

The Boogeyman has haunted the dreams of children and adults alike for centuries. A creature of shadows, its existence is woven into the fabric of human fear, passed down through stories whispered by candlelight and tales exchanged in the deep of night. Yet, despite its universal presence in folklore, the Boogeyman remains an enigma, shifting and evolving with each retelling. In this chapter, we will delve into the origins of these shadowy beings, exploring their history, the myths that birthed them, and how they have come to embody our deepest fears.

The Origins of the Boogeyman: From Myth to Reality

To understand the Boogeyman, one must first travel back to a time when the world was still wild, and the line between reality and the supernatural was thin. In those ancient days, early humans lived in a world full of darkness—both literal and metaphorical. The night was a realm of danger, a veil behind which predatory creatures lurked, and within this primal fear, the first seeds of the Boogeyman were sown.

Different cultures, separated by continents and languages, began to give form to this fear. Across the vast plains of prehistoric Europe, stories spoke of **The Boggen**, a creature that crept through the forests at dusk, devouring children who wandered too far from the fire. In the deserts of the Middle East, there were tales of **Al-Baghul**, a monstrous spirit that hid in shadows, waiting to snatch up the unwary. The Boogeyman was born in these shared experiences of the unknown, taking on a form that was both familiar and foreign—a creature that existed everywhere yet belonged nowhere.

However, the Boogeyman was not just a singular entity. It was an amalgamation of fears, changing faces with each new culture. In Scandinavia, it was **The Nokken**, a shape-shifting water spirit that lured children into the icy depths. In Japan, it became the **Namahage**, a demon that visited homes during the winter, carrying away misbehaving children in its sack. In every culture, the Boogeyman adapted, embodying the fears unique to each society. This adaptability is a key characteristic of the Boogeyman, suggesting that its origins lie not in a single myth but in the collective subconscious of humanity.

Birth of the Boogeyman: Theories of Their Creation

Scholars and mythologists have long debated the true origins of Boogeymen. One prevailing theory suggests that Boogeymen were **thought-forms**—beings brought into existence by the fears and nightmares of humans. In the same way that dreams can manifest our subconscious anxieties, the Boogeyman is believed to have been shaped by centuries of fear, accumulating power and substance from the tales and legends told about it. As these stories spread, so did the influence of the Boogeyman, growing stronger and more diverse with each generation's retelling.

Another theory, popular among occultists and practitioners of the dark arts, posits that the Boogeyman originated from the **Shadow Realm**, a parallel dimension that mirrors our own world but exists in perpetual twilight. This realm, they argue, is home to entities born from the energy of fear and despair, creatures that seep into our reality when the boundaries between worlds weaken. The Boogeyman, according to this belief, is not merely a figment of human imagination but a denizen of a world where nightmares take physical form.

There is also the **Nocturnarii Theory**, named after the ancient order that created the Boogey Book. This theory suggests that Boogeymen were once **guardians** of the boundaries between the physical and spiritual worlds. The Nocturnarii, who devoted themselves to studying and documenting supernatural phenomena, discovered early writings that described the Boogeyman not as a monster but as a sentinel. These sentinels were tasked with maintaining balance, ensuring that restless spirits and dark energies did not overflow into the mortal realm. However, something went wrong. Some believe that over time, as humans began to fear these guardians, their essence was corrupted by the very energy they were meant to contain. They transformed from protectors into predators, feeding on the fear they were originally created to dispel.

Boogeymen in Human Folklore: Shapeshifters of Fear

One of the most fascinating aspects of Boogeymen is their **ability to shape-shift**, both in form and in narrative. No two descriptions of a Boogeyman are ever quite the same. In some stories, it is a grotesque figure with long, spindly fingers and eyes that glow in the dark. In others, it is an indistinct shadow, a mass of darkness that swallows up light and warmth. This malleability is not a coincidence but rather a defining trait of the Boogeyman, allowing it to adapt to the fears of those who believe in it.

The Boogey Book catalogues numerous examples of these transformations. For instance, in Victorian England, the Boogeyman became the **Bugbear**, a cloaked figure that prowled the cobblestone streets at night. Meanwhile, in the American South, it took on the guise of the **Rawhead**, a headless ghoul that haunted swamps and forests, its decapitated body an omen of death. These shifts in appearance reflect not only the cultural fears of the times but also the **Boogeyman's inherent need to resonate with the psyche of its prey**.

Yet, despite its many forms, certain themes persist across cultures. The Boogeyman is almost always associated with darkness, hidden spaces, and the unknown. It preys on the vulnerable, particularly children, reinforcing its status as a **symbol of unchecked fear**. Whether hiding under the bed, lurking in the closet, or peering from the shadows, the Boogeyman embodies the terrors that reside in the unseen corners of our lives.

From Shadows to Reality: How Boogeymen Became the Creatures of Our Fears

In modern times, the concept of the Boogeyman has evolved, yet its essence remains unchanged. Today, Boogeymen are no longer confined to folklore and myths; they have found new homes in literature, cinema, and even the back corners of the internet. This new incarnation of the Boogeyman thrives on the fears of an increasingly complex world. No longer merely the guardians of children's bedrooms, they now represent the anxieties of modern life—fears of loss, loneliness, failure, and the unknown.

Psychologists often discuss the Boogeyman as a **projection of the human psyche**, a way for people to externalize their internal fears. Children, for example, imagine the Boogeyman in their closet or under their bed because it gives shape to their anxieties in a form they can understand. For adults, the Boogeyman may represent more abstract fears—financial ruin, illness, or the unpredictability of life.

However, some believe that Boogeymen have taken on a **physical presence** beyond mere imagination. Accounts documented in the Boogey Book describe encounters that defy rational explanation: objects moving on their own, whispers in the dark, the sensation of being watched even in an empty room. These occurrences suggest that the Boogeyman has become more than just a metaphor; it has crossed into our reality, feeding off the collective fear that has sustained it for millennia.

As you turn these pages, remember that the Boogeyman thrives in darkness—both the physical darkness of night and the metaphorical darkness of ignorance. By understanding what lurks in the shadows, by learning its history, origin myths, and the ways in which it has shaped itself to embody our fears, we gain the power to confront it. For the Boogeyman is not an undefeatable monster, but rather a creature of our own making, a shadow that can be dispelled by the light of knowledge.

Thus, as we delve deeper into the world of Boogeymen in the chapters to come, let this knowledge be your guide and your shield. Fear has many faces, and the Boogeyman wears them all. But in understanding the nature of what lurks in the shadows, we take the first step in turning that fear into a weapon—one that can banish even the darkest of nightmares.

Chapter 2: Boogey Basics: Understanding the Boogeyman

What makes the Boogeyman so terrifying, and how does it continue to exist in the collective consciousness of humankind? To truly grasp its nature, one must explore the key traits, powers, and behaviors that define the Boogeyman across cultures. This chapter unravels these aspects, shedding light on the Boogeyman's connection to childhood fears and its reliance on human fear for sustenance.

Key Traits of the Boogeyman: Shadows Given Form

Despite the many forms that the Boogeyman can take, there are several core characteristics that remain constant across its various manifestations. These traits make it instantly recognizable and imbue it with an aura of foreboding that transcends cultural and geographical boundaries.

1. **Amorphous Form:** One of the most distinguishing features of the Boogeyman is its ever-changing appearance. It is a master of disguise, often presenting itself as whatever form will invoke the greatest fear in its victim. Some perceive it as a hulking shadow with glowing eyes, while others see it as a gaunt, skeletal figure with elongated limbs. This amorphous quality allows the Boogeyman to adapt to different circumstances and environments. However, a recurring element in its appearance is its connection to **darkness and shadow**. Even when it assumes a more physical form, it retains an ethereal quality, as though it is only partially anchored to our reality.

2. **Heightened Sense of Fear:** Boogeymen possess an uncanny ability to detect fear. They do not hunt by sight, sound, or smell as other creatures might; instead, they sense the vibrations of fear emanating from their surroundings. This skill is so refined that they can pinpoint a child's fright from across dimensions, honing in on the source as though drawn by an invisible thread. Once fear is detected, the Boogeyman becomes more powerful, feeding off that energy and using it to manifest itself in more terrifying ways.

3. **Invisibility:** The Boogeyman can fade into invisibility at will, making it impossible to see with the naked eye unless it chooses to reveal itself. This trait is part of what makes the Boogeyman so terrifying—it is always there, lurking just beyond the corner of one's vision, yet impossible to pinpoint. Its invisibility is not just a physical absence but also a presence that can be felt, a subtle, creeping sensation that something is watching from the shadows.

4. **Mimicry:** Another unsettling trait is the Boogeyman's ability to mimic voices, sounds, and even shapes familiar to its victims. It often uses this skill to lure children into dark corners or to isolate them by mimicking the voice of a trusted figure. This mimicry is not perfect; those who listen closely will notice an unnatural cadence or an eerie echo in the voice, clues that the source is not what it appears to be. Nevertheless, the Boogeyman's mimicry is often convincing enough to sow confusion and panic, further feeding its strength.

5. **Intangible Presence:** While the Boogeyman can affect the physical world—slamming doors, flickering lights, or rustling under beds—it is not always fully corporeal. It moves through walls, passes through solid objects, and occupies spaces that defy the physical constraints of

the environment. This intangible nature makes trapping or confronting the Boogeyman a complex task, as it can simply vanish into thin air, leaving only the lingering fear in its wake.

The Powers of the Boogeyman: Masters of Fear

The Boogeyman's abilities are centered around the concept of **fear manipulation**. It is not a mere scavenger of fear; it is an architect of terror, capable of warping reality and perception to evoke maximum dread.

1. **Fear Feeding:** Fear is the Boogeyman's sustenance, the source of its power. Unlike other supernatural creatures that may require physical nourishment, the Boogeyman thrives on the emotions of its victims. The more intense and prolonged the fear, the stronger the Boogeyman becomes. Some accounts describe Boogeymen that can even influence dreams, causing vivid nightmares to extend their influence over their prey. This feeding process is not always immediate; Boogeymen often cultivate fear over time, lurking in the shadows and subtly manipulating their victim's environment to heighten anxiety and paranoia.
2. **Reality Distortion:** One of the most formidable powers of the Boogeyman is its ability to distort reality. It can alter the perception of space and time within its immediate vicinity, creating the sensation of being trapped in an endless hallway or making rooms appear far larger or smaller than they actually are. This distortion serves to disorient and frighten the victim, trapping them in a labyrinth of their own fear. The Boogey Book details accounts of Boogeymen turning familiar rooms into twisted versions of themselves, with shadows that move independently and walls that pulse as though alive.
3. **Shadow Manipulation:** The Boogeyman has dominion over shadows, capable of bending and warping them at will. It can extend shadows to reach across rooms, transforming them into clawed tendrils that snatch objects—or even people—into the darkness. It is not uncommon for those who encounter a Boogeyman to witness shadows behaving unnaturally, stretching towards them even in the absence of light. This power allows the Boogeyman to traverse spaces undetected, slipping between cracks and crevices in an instant.
4. **Illusions:** Boogeymen are masters of illusion, creating visions that play upon the deepest fears of their victims. These illusions can be as subtle as a faint whisper in the dark or as grand as an entire room filled with creeping, crawling creatures. Victims often describe seeing grotesque faces peering from closets or hearing the sounds of breathing from under the bed. These illusions are not confined to the mind; they have a physical impact on the victim's senses, making them indistinguishable from reality.
5. **Teleportation:** The Boogeyman's ability to vanish and reappear at will makes it nearly impossible to track. It can teleport from one dark corner to another, moving through shadows as though they were doorways to another realm. This teleportation is not bound by the physical laws of our world; a Boogeyman can slip into a child's closet in New York and emerge from beneath a bed in Tokyo within the blink of an eye. This is believed to be linked to the Boogeyman's connection to the **Shadow Realm**, where space and time function differently than in our reality.

Behaviors of the Boogeyman: Stalking the Shadows

The Boogeyman is a predator, but not in the traditional sense. It does not hunt to kill but to instill fear, feeding on the emotions of its victims over time. Understanding its behaviors is key to evading its grasp and, ultimately, surviving its presence.

1. **Stalking:** The Boogeyman prefers a slow, methodical approach to its prey. It does not attack outright but instead stalks from the shadows, gradually introducing itself into the victim's life. It starts with small, unsettling events—a door creaking open, a toy moving on its own, a whisper in the dark. As the victim's fear grows, the Boogeyman becomes bolder, manifesting more directly until it becomes an inescapable presence in the victim's mind. This stalking behavior is designed to create a sense of **paranoia**, making the victim feel as though they are being watched even in the safety of daylight.
2. **Fear Amplification:** Boogeymen are adept at amplifying existing fears. They exploit the vulnerabilities of their victims, drawing out their anxieties and magnifying them. For children, this may involve tapping into common fears like monsters under the bed or the dark closet. For adults, the Boogeyman may manifest as a creeping dread of failure, illness, or loss. By intensifying these fears, the Boogeyman creates a self-perpetuating cycle of anxiety that fuels its power.
3. **Attachment to Childhood Fears:** Boogeymen are intrinsically linked to childhood fears, which are often pure and unfiltered by the rationality of adulthood. They are drawn to the innocence and imagination of children, who are more susceptible to their illusions and reality distortions. This connection to childhood fear is why Boogeymen are commonly associated with hiding under beds or lurking in closets—places that children view as gateways to the unknown. However, their influence can linger into adulthood, as they sometimes attach themselves to unresolved childhood traumas, resurfacing in times of stress or vulnerability.
4. **Feeding Cycles:** Unlike traditional predators, Boogeymen do not need to feed constantly. Instead, they operate in **cycles**, emerging during times when fear is most potent—at night, during thunderstorms, or around periods of emotional distress. This cyclical behavior allows them to conserve their strength and remain hidden until the conditions are right for feeding. In some cases, Boogeymen have been known to go dormant for years, waiting until a victim's life circumstances provide a ripe opportunity for their return.
5. **Escalation:** As the Boogeyman feeds and grows stronger, its actions become increasingly bold and terrifying. What begins as flickering lights and creaking floors escalates into full-blown manifestations—doors slamming shut, objects levitating, and disembodied voices taunting from the shadows. This escalation serves to break down the victim's defenses, plunging them deeper into a state of fear and helplessness. It is during these moments of peak terror that the Boogeyman reveals its true form, cementing its hold over the victim's psyche.

Sustenance Through Fear: The Lifeblood of the Boogeyman

The Boogeyman's existence hinges on one thing: fear. It is not a physical creature in the traditional sense but a **manifestation of dread**, sustained by the emotions of those it haunts. Fear is both its food and its weapon, allowing it to alter reality, become tangible, and exert influence over the physical world. The more fear it consumes, the more potent its abilities become. Conversely, when starved of fear, the Boogeyman weakens and becomes less able to affect the world around it.

This reliance on fear is why the Boogeyman is most active during childhood, when fears are raw and unguarded. However, it also explains why it continues to exist in the adult world, finding nourishment in the anxieties and insecurities that plague human existence. It is a predator of emotions, feeding on fear in all its forms—from the terror of a child left alone in the dark to the existential dread of an adult facing life's uncertainties.

In understanding these traits, powers, and behaviors, we arm ourselves with the knowledge necessary to confront the Boogeyman. For while it may be a master of shadows, it is not invincible. The first step in defending against its influence is recognizing the ways in which it operates, exploiting fear as both sustenance and weapon. As we continue to explore the nature of the Boogeyman, we will uncover the methods for containing and combating this ancient predator of the night.

Chapter 3: The Dimensional Paradigm: The Boogie World Explained

When one speaks of the Boogeyman, it is impossible to ignore the realm from which it originates: the **Boogie World**. This dimension is not just the home of the Boogeyman but the very source of its power and essence. Stepping into the Boogie World is akin to walking into a nightmare brought to life, a place where the laws of reality are warped and the familiar becomes unrecognizable. The Boogie World exists in a realm parallel to our own, tethered to the human experience of fear and darkness. This chapter delves into the nature of this strange dimension, exploring its rules, geography, and the ways in which time and space operate within its twisted confines.

The Nature of the Boogie World: A Dimension of Fear

The Boogie World is not just another reality; it is a **dimensional plane** that overlaps our own, anchored to places where fear thrives—bedrooms, closets, basements, and the dark corners of our homes. It is believed that every time a child feels a chill of terror in the dark, a doorway between our world and the Boogie World creaks open, allowing the Boogeyman to slip through. These doorways are not physical in the traditional sense but are rather **psychic thresholds**, where the boundaries of reality blur, allowing the Boogeyman to pass between dimensions.

Unlike our world, the Boogie World does not conform to the principles of physics or rational thought. It is a landscape born from fear itself, constantly shifting and adapting to the minds of those who enter it. This dimension feeds on the anxieties and imaginations of its inhabitants, warping itself to reflect their deepest nightmares. It is said that the Boogie World is **40 times larger** than the average bed or closet, not in terms of physical space but in terms of **dimensional distortion**. Within the Boogie World, space stretches and contracts unpredictably, creating an environment that is both claustrophobic and vast, a labyrinth where the sense of direction and distance is continually undermined.

Geography of the Boogie World: A Landscape of Shadows

The Boogie World's geography is a paradox—both familiar and alien, chaotic yet strangely organized. It is a land formed from the very substance of fear, where shadows take on tangible forms, and light is a rare and fleeting commodity.

1. **The Endless Corridors:** The Boogie World is known for its **endless corridors**, hallways that twist and turn without ever truly leading anywhere. These corridors resemble the hallways of homes, schools, hospitals, and other places associated with fear and anxiety. They are lined with doors that open to rooms far more expansive than the spaces they should contain. Some of these rooms appear to be normal at first glance, furnished with beds, desks, and toys. However, upon closer inspection, unsettling details emerge: mirrors that reflect nothing, clocks that tick backward, and windows that show impossible landscapes. The corridors themselves seem to stretch endlessly, looping back on themselves in impossible ways, creating a sense of disorientation and entrapment.
2. **The Shadowed Forests:** Further into the Boogie World lies the **Shadowed Forests**, a vast expanse of gnarled trees that writhe and twist as if alive. The trees here are unlike any found in our reality; they are formed from darkness itself, their bark cold to the touch and their leaves whispering secrets in the wind. The ground beneath is a patchwork of soil, dust, and bones,

hinting at the countless lives that have wandered here and never returned. The forest is thick with mist, which serves to obscure one's vision and play tricks on the mind. Those who venture too deep into the Shadowed Forests risk becoming lost, as the paths seem to shift behind them, leading them in circles or into deeper, darker regions of the Boogie World.

3. **The Lair of Mirrors:** Deep within the Boogie World is a place known as the **Lair of Mirrors**, a sprawling complex of tunnels and caverns lined entirely with reflective surfaces. These mirrors do not show one's true reflection but instead distort it, revealing versions of oneself that embody fear, regret, and anger. It is here that the Boogeyman is said to draw upon its mimicry abilities, learning the fears of those who enter. The Lair of Mirrors is a maze with no discernible end, each turn revealing new reflections, each more twisted than the last. In this place, time seems to stand still, trapping those who gaze too long into the reflections, mesmerized by their own horrors.

4. **The Abyss of the Unseen:** At the farthest edges of the Boogie World lies the **Abyss of the Unseen**, a vast, dark chasm that stretches infinitely in every direction. It is a place of absolute silence and darkness, where even the faintest light is swallowed whole. The Abyss is said to be the Boogie World's heart, the source of its power and the origin point of all Boogeymen. It is here that they retreat to when not stalking their prey, regenerating their strength by drawing on the endless fear that permeates the chasm. Those who approach the Abyss report a sensation of being watched by unseen eyes, a feeling of cold dread that seeps into the very soul.

Rules of the Boogie World: Where Fear Bends Reality

The Boogie World operates on a set of rules that defy the natural laws of our reality. Its environment is fluid, constantly changing in response to the thoughts and emotions of its inhabitants. Understanding these rules is crucial for those who hope to navigate the Boogie World and return unscathed.

1. **Time Is Fluid:** Within the Boogie World, **time** behaves unpredictably. It stretches and compresses, warping the perception of those who wander its halls. What feels like hours in the Boogie World may amount to mere minutes in the mortal realm, or vice versa. This fluidity is a direct result of the dimension's connection to fear, as fear often distorts one's sense of time. The longer one remains in the Boogie World, the more difficult it becomes to maintain a grasp on reality. This phenomenon is why many who encounter the Boogeyman describe the experience as both fleeting and eternal, a nightmare that seems to last forever even though it may have transpired in the blink of an eye.

2. **Space Is Malleable:** In the Boogie World, **space** is not fixed. Rooms and corridors change size, shape, and layout at will, responding to the fears of those who tread upon them. A hallway that seems to stretch for miles may suddenly contract, trapping the traveler in a claustrophobic passage. Conversely, a small closet can expand into a cavernous room, filled with shadowy recesses that conceal hidden dangers. The Boogie World twists the concepts of proximity and distance, making it nearly impossible to navigate with any sense of certainty. Maps of this dimension are useless, as they shift and alter each time they are drawn.

3. **Fear Is the Key: Fear** is not just a sensation in the Boogie World; it is the very fabric of the realm. The dimension feeds on fear, drawing power from the terror of those who enter it. The stronger the fear, the more the Boogie World warps to reflect it, transforming mundane environments into nightmares tailored to the individual. This rule means that those who enter the Boogie World must keep their fear in check, as giving in to terror only strengthens the realm and the Boogeyman that dwells within it. Conversely, those who can maintain their composure and resist the influence of fear can temporarily weaken the Boogie World's hold, allowing for brief moments of clarity and safe passage.

4. **Echoes of Reality:** The Boogie World mirrors aspects of the human world, creating **echoes** of familiar places. A child's bedroom, a basement staircase, or a dusty attic may all manifest within the Boogie World, but in twisted forms. These echoes serve as lures, drawing the unwary deeper into the dimension by exploiting their sense of familiarity. However, upon closer inspection, these places reveal their true nature—beds with sheets that wriggle like worms, closets that groan and shift as though alive, and staircases that descend endlessly into darkness.

5. **Portals Are Temporary:** The doorways between the Boogie World and the human realm are **temporary and unstable**. They manifest in places where fear is strongest—under beds, in closets, and behind mirrors. These portals flicker open and closed unpredictably, often vanishing as quickly as they appear. Those who wish to traverse these portals must do so quickly, lest they become trapped within the Boogie World when the threshold closes. The portals are more likely to appear during times of heightened fear, such as during thunderstorms, nightmares, or moments of intense stress.

Navigating the Boogie World: Survival Tactics

Surviving in the Boogie World requires an understanding of its unpredictable nature. Since the environment responds to fear, travelers must employ mental discipline to keep their wits about them. Here are some key survival tactics for navigating this treacherous dimension:

1. **Grounding Techniques:** Since the Boogie World distorts time and space, one of the most effective ways to maintain a grip on reality is to practice **grounding techniques**. These involve focusing on physical sensations—clenching one's fists, tapping a rhythm, or reciting a mantra. By concentrating on something concrete, travelers can anchor themselves in reality, preventing the Boogie World from fully warping their perception.

2. **Use of Light:** While light is scarce in the Boogie World, it is a powerful deterrent to the Boogeyman. Travelers are advised to carry light sources—candles, lanterns, or even glowsticks. However, these light sources do not behave as they do in the human world; they flicker and wane in the presence of strong fear. Nonetheless, even a faint glow can provide a sense of direction and stave off the encroaching shadows.

3. **Mental Resilience:** The Boogie World feeds on fear, so maintaining **mental resilience** is key to survival. This involves controlling one's breathing, confronting fears instead of running

from them, and reminding oneself that the horrors within the Boogie World are reflections of the mind. The more one acknowledges this truth, the weaker the Boogeyman's hold becomes.

The Boogeyman's Dominion: Where Fear Is Law

The Boogie World is, in essence, the Boogeyman's kingdom. It is the source of its power and the place where it retreats to regenerate when not hunting. By understanding the Boogie World's rules and geography, one gains insight into the nature of the Boogeyman itself. The Boogeyman does not simply emerge from the shadows; it **is** the shadow, a creature born of a dimension where fear reigns supreme.

Those who venture into the Boogie World do so at great risk, for it is not merely a place but a state of mind—a labyrinth where one's deepest fears manifest and take on a life of their own. Yet, through knowledge and courage, one can navigate this realm and even bend its rules, turning fear into a weapon against the Boogeyman. In the chapters to come, we will explore these strategies, delving deeper into the practices and tools that can be used to confront the terrors of the Boogie World. For now, let this understanding serve as your guide, a glimmer of light in the darkness of an ever-shifting landscape.

Part 2: *Identifying Boogeymen*

Chapter 4: The Types of Boogeymen: From Closet Stalkers to Underbed Crawlers

The Boogeyman is not a singular entity but a diverse species with numerous subtypes, each adapted to different environments and tactics for scaring their prey. These creatures have evolved over time, learning to thrive in the dark, confined spaces of our homes and exploiting the fears that arise within them. This chapter introduces a classification system for the various kinds of Boogeymen based on their habitat—whether it be the closet, under the bed, attic, or other dark recesses—and the unique tactics they employ to invoke terror.

Boogeyman Classification System: An Overview

Boogeymen can be categorized according to their **habitats** and **scaring tactics**. Their choice of lair is often dictated by the types of fears they prefer to evoke. Some thrive in the enclosed darkness of closets, where the fear of the unknown takes root, while others lurk beneath beds, capitalizing on the primal dread of what might be hiding just out of sight. Understanding these types is key to identifying and confronting the Boogeyman in its many forms.

1. Closet Stalkers: The Hidden Watchers

Habitat: Closets

Tactics: Silence, mimicry, and gradual escalation of fear.

Closet Stalkers are perhaps the most classic and well-known type of Boogeyman. Their habitat is the dark, cramped space of the closet—a place that is inherently unnerving due to its enclosed nature and the mystery of what might be lurking within. These Boogeymen are masters of **silence and patience**, preferring to lie in wait until the perfect moment to strike terror into their prey.

Tactics and Behaviors:

Closet Stalkers often begin by creating a subtle atmosphere of fear. They may start by causing a faint rustling of clothes or a soft scratching sound against the closet door. These noises are barely perceptible at first, designed to instill a sense of unease in those nearby. As the fear grows, the Closet Stalker escalates its tactics—causing the door to creak open just a sliver or allowing an ominous shadow to appear behind the gap of a half-closed door.

One of the Closet Stalker's most chilling abilities is **mimicry**. These Boogeymen are known to imitate voices, particularly those of family members or pets, to lure children closer to the closet. Victims report hearing faint whispers or their names called softly, urging them to approach. This tactic is used to amplify fear by blending the familiar with the uncanny, creating an unsettling experience that blurs the line between reality and nightmare.

In extreme cases, Closet Stalkers may allow themselves to be glimpsed—often as a pair of glowing eyes or a faint silhouette—before retreating back into the darkness. This fleeting appearance is meant to leave the victim questioning what they saw, driving their anxiety and heightening their fear of the closet.

Unique Weakness: Closet Stalkers can be temporarily deterred by keeping the closet door open and using bright lights. Since they rely on shadows and confined spaces, exposure to light and openness weakens their hold on the environment.

2. Underbed Crawlers: The Ambushers of Darkness

Habitat: Under beds

Tactics: Surprise, ambush, and touch-based fear.

Underbed Crawlers are creatures that inhabit the narrow, shadowed space beneath the bed—a place inherently associated with childhood fears of monsters lurking just below the surface. They are adept at utilizing **surprise tactics**, often choosing to strike when their victims are at their most vulnerable—just as they're about to drift into sleep.

Tactics and Behaviors:

Underbed Crawlers are stealthy and silent, rarely making their presence known until the precise moment they choose to scare. They excel at creating a sense of imminent threat, often manifesting as scratching noises, faint whispers, or the sensation of something moving beneath the mattress. Some victims report feeling an eerie **coldness** emanating from under the bed, as if the space is a doorway to an icy, otherworldly realm.

One of their most unsettling tactics is the **ambush scare**. Underbed Crawlers are known for their ability to reach out from beneath the bed, using elongated, shadowy limbs to graze the feet or ankles of those too close. This touch is icy and fleeting, designed to send a shock of terror through the victim and make them leap back in fear. Unlike Closet Stalkers, Underbed Crawlers are more tactile in their approach, relying on physical sensations to evoke dread.

In some instances, these Boogeymen employ **psychological manipulation**, whispering softly to their victims, suggesting that they can feel every movement on the mattress. This causes the victim to lie perfectly still, paralyzed by the fear of triggering another encounter. Underbed Crawlers thrive on this fear, feeding off the rising tension and anxiety that fills the room.

Unique Weakness: Underbed Crawlers are particularly sensitive to vibrations. Stomping on the floor or making sudden, loud noises can disrupt their attempts to grasp at their prey. Additionally, placing heavy objects or boxes under the bed can limit their space, restricting their ability to move freely.

3. Attic Dwellers: The Keepers of Forgotten Memories
Habitat: Attics

Tactics: Nostalgia, disorientation, and manipulation of objects.

Attics are often repositories of forgotten memories, cluttered with old belongings, photographs, and relics of the past. Attic Dwellers take advantage of this environment, drawing upon the sense of unease that arises from exploring dusty, dimly lit spaces filled with echoes of bygone eras. These Boogeymen are **masters of nostalgia and disorientation**, using the relics stored within the attic to create an atmosphere of haunting familiarity.

Tactics and Behaviors:

Attic Dwellers are known for their ability to manipulate objects. They start small—causing items to shift positions, creating faint creaks in the wooden floorboards, or triggering the movement of shadows among the stacks of boxes. Over time, they escalate their activities, knocking over objects, creating loud bangs, or even hurling items across the room. These actions are not random; they are calculated to draw attention to specific memories or fears associated with the stored items.

These Boogeymen often **play on memories**, whispering fragments of forgotten conversations or recreating the sounds of past events. Victims have reported hearing echoes of laughter, crying, or arguments that they thought had been long buried. This tactic serves to unnerve and distract, causing those in the attic to become lost in their own thoughts and fears.

Attic Dwellers are adept at manipulating **spatial perception**. The attic may seem to stretch on indefinitely, its shadows growing deeper and more impenetrable the longer one lingers. This warping of space can lead to disorientation, making it difficult to find the way out. Some victims report an increasing weight in the air, as though the attic itself is pressing down upon them, trapping them in a space that grows colder and darker with each passing moment.

Unique Weakness: Attic Dwellers are sensitive to strong, consistent light. Installing bright, high-wattage bulbs or using portable lights can weaken their ability to manipulate objects and distort space. Playing loud, upbeat music can also disrupt their nostalgic manipulations, breaking the atmosphere they thrive on.

4. Basement Haunters: The Lurkers of the Depths

Habitat: Basements

Tactics: Isolation, darkness, and sensory distortion.

Basements are naturally unsettling places, often associated with darkness, dampness, and the unknown. Basement Haunters thrive in this environment, using it as a **natural amplifier of fear**. These Boogeymen are known for their ability to invoke feelings of isolation, creating a sense of being trapped in a place far removed from the safety of the living areas above.

Tactics and Behaviors:

Basement Haunters excel at **sensory distortion**. They manipulate the darkness, making it seem thicker and more impenetrable than it should be. Lights flicker and dim in their presence, leaving corners of the room shrouded in shadow even when the lights are on. Victims often describe a growing sense of unease, as though the darkness itself is alive and watching them.

These Boogeymen use **sound** as a weapon. They create noises that echo through the basement—dripping water, faint footsteps, or the sound of something scraping against the concrete walls. These noises seem to come from all directions, causing confusion and heightening the victim's fear. Basement Haunters may also produce heavy, labored breathing or faint growls that seem to emanate from the darkness, reinforcing the sensation of an unseen presence lurking just beyond the light.

One of their most unnerving tactics is **sensory isolation**. Victims report feeling an abrupt drop in temperature and the sensation of pressure in their ears, as if all sound and warmth are being drained from the room. This creates an atmosphere of claustrophobia and isolation, where every sound and shadow becomes a potential threat.

Unique Weakness: Basement Haunters are repelled by warmth and consistent noise. Placing portable heaters or loud, white-noise machines in the basement can disrupt their sensory distortions and prevent them from creating an atmosphere of isolation.

5. Mirror Wraiths: The Reflected Terrors

Habitat: Mirrors and reflective surfaces

Tactics: Illusions, mimicry, and psychological manipulation.

Mirror Wraiths are Boogeymen that inhabit mirrors and other reflective surfaces, using them as gateways to their own dimension. They are **masters of illusion**, preying on the fear of what might lie just beyond one's own reflection. Unlike other types, Mirror Wraiths do not need to be hidden; they are present wherever there is a reflection, waiting for the moment when their prey dares to look.

Tactics and Behaviors:

Mirror Wraiths manipulate reflections to create **distorted images**. Victims may catch glimpses of their own reflection moving independently or see shapes and figures lurking behind them that vanish when they turn around. These illusions are designed to create doubt and fear, making the victim question the reliability of their own senses.

One of their most terrifying abilities is **mimicry**. Mirror Wraiths can appear as the victim's own reflection but with slight alterations—eyes that glow faintly, a mouth that moves independently, or a hand that reaches out toward the glass. They use this mimicry to instill a deep sense of unease, suggesting that the reflection is not merely an image but a sentient, malevolent presence.

Mirror Wraiths are also known for **psychological manipulation**. They may whisper thoughts into the victim's mind, using the reflective surface as a conduit. These thoughts often take the form of self-doubt, fear, or paranoia, convincing the victim that they are not alone in the room. Over time, this manipulation can drive the victim to the brink of hysteria, feeding the Mirror Wraith's power.

Unique Weakness: Mirror Wraiths can be repelled by **covering mirrors** or using non-reflective materials to block their access. Additionally, drawing protective symbols on the glass surface with chalk or marker can create a barrier that weakens their influence.

Understanding these various types of Boogeymen—their habitats, tactics, and weaknesses—provides crucial insight into defending against them. Each Boogeyman preys on specific fears associated with its chosen environment, tailoring its approach to maximize the terror it evokes. In the chapters to follow, we will explore practical methods for warding off and confronting these creatures, utilizing the knowledge we have gained from centuries of encounters documented within the Boogey Book. For now, remember: fear is their ally, but knowledge is yours.

Chapter 5: When Imaginary Friends Turn Boogey: The Abandonment Syndrome

Children's imaginations are boundless, creating entire worlds of fantasy, magic, and wonder. Within these realms, imaginary friends often emerge as cherished companions, confidants, and guardians against the loneliness or fears of childhood. These invisible companions can be sweet, playful, and protective, comforting children in their moments of uncertainty. However, what happens when these friends are abruptly forgotten or abandoned as a child grows up? What becomes of the imaginary friend left behind in the realm of fantasy? For some, the answer is far darker than expected.

This chapter explores the phenomenon known as **Abandonment Syndrome**, where the trauma of being cast aside or forgotten transforms once-loving imaginary friends into vengeful, fear-feeding entities. This metamorphosis can turn a childhood companion into a Boogeyman, haunting the child—or even the adult they become—long after their friendship ends. Understanding the signs of this transformation and how to prevent or manage it is crucial in protecting oneself from the sinister evolution of these former imaginary allies.

The Origins of Abandonment Syndrome: A Psychic Wound

Children often create imaginary friends as a means of coping with loneliness, stress, or the complexities of social interactions. These friends are not merely figments of imagination; they are constructs born from the child's subconscious mind. They serve specific emotional needs, such as providing companionship, protection, or even guidance through difficult experiences. In some cultures, these friends are believed to be spirit guides, while in others, they are seen as manifestations of the child's inner world.

The **Abandonment Syndrome** occurs when an imaginary friend, deeply tied to the child's psyche, is abruptly cast aside. This can happen for various reasons: the child grows up, finds new social circles, or simply forgets about their invisible companion as they lose interest in the fantastical games they once played. For the imaginary friend, this sudden abandonment can be akin to a traumatic severing, creating a **psychic wound** that festers and changes its nature.

It is believed that imaginary friends possess a form of consciousness fueled by the child's imagination and emotions. When they are abandoned, they do not simply vanish; they persist in the shadowy corners of the child's mind or the realm of imagination where they were born. Without the positive emotions that once sustained them, these entities can become twisted and corrupted, transforming into Boogeymen driven by feelings of rejection, loneliness, and a desire for revenge or recognition. This metamorphosis is the essence of Abandonment Syndrome, turning a protector into a predator.

The Evolution of an Imaginary Friend into a Boogeyman: A Sinister Metamorphosis

The process by which an imaginary friend becomes a Boogeyman is gradual, often occurring over months or even years. As the child grows more distant from their imaginary friend, the entity begins to change. It may start exhibiting behaviors that mirror the child's subconscious fears and insecurities, growing darker and more unsettling as time passes.

1. **Initial Signs of Transformation:**
   In the early stages, the imaginary friend may exhibit subtle changes in its demeanor. The child might notice that their friend has become less playful and more withdrawn, appearing less frequently during their imaginative play sessions. The once comforting presence may begin to adopt a more somber or sullen attitude. Conversations with the imaginary friend might take on a slightly disturbing tone, with the friend expressing feelings of sadness, anger, or even resentment at being ignored. These early signs are often dismissed by the child, who may not fully comprehend the emotional undertones of their creation.
2. **Manifestation of Negative Traits:**
   As the abandonment deepens, the imaginary friend starts to exhibit negative traits. It may become possessive or demanding, urging the child to spend more time with it and expressing jealousy over real-world friends or activities. During this stage, children may report hearing their imaginary friend making strange requests, such as hiding objects or creating disruptions in their daily routine. This behavior is a manifestation of the entity's fear of being forgotten, as it desperately tries to regain the child's attention.
3. **The Turn to Darkness:**
   If the imaginary friend continues to be ignored, it begins to shift into something darker. The once gentle and caring companion becomes a **sinister presence**, appearing in unsettling forms or at inappropriate times, such as in nightmares or during moments of fear. Children might start to see their imaginary friend's image in the shadows, mirrors, or reflections in windows, even when they are not actively thinking about it. This stage marks the entity's transition from a benign figment of imagination to a Boogeyman. It begins to feed off the child's growing anxiety and fear, drawing strength from these emotions as it solidifies its new, twisted identity.
4. **Full Transformation:**
   In the final phase, the imaginary friend fully transforms into a Boogeyman. Its appearance becomes increasingly grotesque, often adopting features that symbolize the child's deepest fears—sharp teeth, glowing eyes, elongated limbs. This new form is a reflection of the entity's corrupted nature and its desire to frighten the one who created it. By this point, the Boogeyman no longer acts as a friend but as an adversary, lurking in closets, under beds, or in dark corners of rooms, much like the other types of Boogeymen.

This process is not limited to childhood. In some cases, the Boogeyman may lie dormant in the subconscious, only to resurface years later when the individual experiences stress, trauma, or a resurgence of childhood memories. The adult, now unprepared to confront this resurfacing fear, may find themselves haunted by a presence they had long forgotten—a reminder of the friend they left behind.

Signs of an Imaginary Friend's Transformation into a Boogeyman

Recognizing the warning signs of Abandonment Syndrome is essential to prevent the transformation of an imaginary friend into a Boogeyman. Here are key indicators that an imaginary friend is evolving into something more sinister:

1. **Changes in Behavior:**
   The imaginary friend begins to behave differently, adopting a more demanding, moody, or even hostile demeanor. It may express feelings of resentment, jealousy, or anger when the child does not interact with it. Conversations with the imaginary friend take on a darker tone, with the friend making unsettling comments or suggestions.

2. **Disturbing Appearances:**
   The imaginary friend starts appearing in unsettling places or forms. Children may describe seeing their friend in shadows, mirrors, or reflections, often in a form that is subtly distorted or frightening. For example, they might say that their friend's eyes glow in the dark or that it has grown longer limbs.

3. **Strange Requests:**
   The imaginary friend may make increasingly odd or troubling requests, such as hiding objects, causing disruptions, or engaging in behaviors that make the child uncomfortable. These requests often have a manipulative undertone, designed to test the child's willingness to obey or fear the entity.

4. **Nightmares and Night Terrors:**
   As the transformation progresses, the child may begin experiencing nightmares or night terrors in which the imaginary friend appears in a frightening or threatening manner. These dreams are often vivid and recurring, suggesting that the friend is attempting to infiltrate the child's subconscious and feed off their fear.

5. **Manifestation of Physical Signs:**
   In extreme cases, the imaginary friend may start manifesting physical signs in the environment. Objects may move on their own, doors may creak open, or a chilling coldness may fill the room when the friend is "present." These occurrences indicate that the entity is gaining strength and crossing the boundary between imagination and reality.

Preventing and Managing the Transformation

The best way to prevent an imaginary friend from turning into a Boogeyman is to manage the transition from childhood to adulthood with care, acknowledging the importance of these companions in a child's life. Here are steps to take in order to prevent or manage the transformation:

1. **Respectful Farewell:**
   When a child begins to outgrow their imaginary friend, it is important to encourage a **respectful farewell** rather than abrupt abandonment. Suggest a ritual where the child can say goodbye to their friend, expressing gratitude for the companionship and explaining why it is time to move on. This ritual provides closure, reducing the likelihood of the friend feeling "rejected" and transforming into something darker.

2. **Acknowledge and Address Fears:**
   If a child expresses fear of their imaginary friend or describes unsettling changes in its behavior, take their concerns seriously. Engage in conversations that help the child express their feelings and fears, providing reassurance and guidance. In some cases, creative activities like drawing or storytelling can be used to help the child process their emotions and regain control over their imagination.

3. **Use of Protective Measures:**
   In situations where an imaginary friend seems to be transforming into a Boogeyman, consider employing **protective measures** within the child's environment. This may include placing objects of comfort, such as stuffed animals or nightlights, around the room to create a sense of safety. Symbols or sigils drawn on paper and placed under the bed or near mirrors can also serve as a psychological barrier, helping the child feel empowered to confront their fears.

4. **Positive Imaginary Constructs:**
   Encourage the child to create **positive imaginary constructs** that can counteract the growing influence of the darkening friend. For instance, the child can imagine a new guardian figure—such as a superhero or a protective animal—that watches over them and keeps the sinister presence at bay. This imaginative exercise not only empowers the child but also provides a mental safeguard against the Boogeyman's encroaching influence.

5. **Consultation with Professionals:**
   If the child's fear of their imaginary friend becomes extreme or persists over time, consider consulting a mental health professional. Children's fears can sometimes reflect underlying anxieties or emotional challenges that require specialized support. Early intervention can prevent the situation from escalating and ensure the child's mental well-being.

The Boogeyman Born of Abandonment: A Unique Threat

The Boogeyman that emerges from the transformation of an imaginary friend is unique in its tactics and motivations. Unlike other Boogeymen, which feed primarily on generalized fears of darkness, shadows, or the unknown, this type feeds on the specific emotions associated with **rejection, loneliness, and loss**. It knows its creator intimately, having been a part of their inner world, and uses that knowledge to exploit their deepest insecurities.

This Boogeyman often harbors a deep desire for recognition and will go to great lengths to ensure that it is not forgotten again. It is not simply a creature of malice but a tragic figure, born from the pain of abandonment and the longing to reclaim its place in the life of the one who created it. This complexity makes it one of the most difficult Boogeymen to confront, as it embodies both the darkness of fear and the remnants of a once cherished companionship.

In the chapters that follow, we will delve into methods for dealing with different types of Boogeymen, including those born of abandonment. By understanding their origins, motivations, and behaviors, we arm ourselves with the knowledge needed to confront these entities and navigate the fine line between imagination and fear. Remember: fear may give these creatures power, but awareness and understanding can turn the tide, allowing us to reclaim the shadows they inhabit.

Chapter 6: Signs a Boogeyman is Near

The Boogeyman thrives in darkness, feeding on fear and anxiety. It lurks in the shadows of bedrooms, closets, basements, and attics, biding its time until it chooses to reveal its presence. Although it is skilled in concealing itself, certain **physical and emotional symptoms** can indicate when a Boogeyman is near. Recognizing these signs is crucial for those who seek to protect themselves and their loved ones. This chapter explores the various symptoms of a Boogeyman's presence, including **environmental changes**, **strange noises**, and **sudden spikes in fear**. By understanding these signals, one can take proactive steps to mitigate the Boogeyman's influence and regain control of their environment.

The Physical Symptoms of a Boogeyman's Presence

Boogeymen are masters of the unseen, able to distort reality and manipulate their surroundings to instill fear. When they begin to manifest in an environment, they often create a series of physical disturbances that act as telltale signs of their encroaching presence.

1. **Fluctuations in Temperature:**
   One of the most common signs of a Boogeyman's proximity is a **sudden drop in temperature** within the room. The air grows unnaturally cold, often creating a chilling sensation that seeps into the bones. This drop is not simply a passing draft or change in weather; it has a distinct quality that feels heavy and oppressive. Some individuals describe the cold as being almost "alive," pressing down on them like an invisible weight. In extreme cases, frost or condensation may appear on windows or surfaces, even in warm weather.

This coldness is thought to result from the Boogeyman's ability to draw heat and energy from its surroundings, using it to strengthen its presence. The more intense the temperature fluctuation, the closer the Boogeyman is to making itself known.

1. **Electrical Disturbances:**
   Boogeymen have a peculiar effect on **electrical devices**. Lights flicker and dim, bulbs may shatter unexpectedly, and electronic devices—such as televisions, radios, and alarms—turn on or off by themselves. Batteries in flashlights drain rapidly, leaving individuals in the dark when they need light the most. This phenomenon is believed to occur because Boogeymen feed on the energy around them, disrupting electronic signals and drawing power to bolster their manifestations.

In some instances, devices that require no external input, like children's toys with built-in lights or sounds, may activate without warning. A toy that suddenly starts playing music in the dead of night can be a clear indication that a Boogeyman is attempting to make its presence felt, using these disturbances to unsettle its potential victims.

1. **Movement of Shadows:**
   A Boogeyman's presence is intrinsically linked to shadows. One of the most unsettling physical signs is the **movement of shadows** in ways that defy logic. You might notice shadows flickering or shifting on walls and floors, even when there is no apparent source of light or movement to cause them. In some cases, shadows may seem to stretch, grow, or even take on vaguely humanoid forms, lingering at the edges of one's vision.

These shifting shadows are not mere tricks of the light but the Boogeyman itself, partially manifesting within the space. It uses shadows as both a cloak and a means of travel, moving fluidly through them to observe or interact with its surroundings.

1. **Inexplicable Drafts and Air Pressure Changes:**
   Doors may creak open or slam shut, curtains flutter when windows are closed, and a sudden **gust of air** may rush through the room, accompanied by a sensation of pressure in the ears, similar to being on an airplane during ascent or descent. These drafts often seem to originate from nowhere and can be accompanied by an overwhelming sense of unease. This disturbance in air pressure and movement is linked to the Boogeyman's manipulation of its environment, using airflow to create an eerie atmosphere and announce its presence.
2. **Physical Touches:**
   The sensation of being **touched by an unseen hand** is one of the more terrifying physical symptoms of a Boogeyman's proximity. Victims may feel a light brushing against their skin, an icy grip on their ankle, or the unsettling impression of something pressing down on their chest while they lie in bed. These touches are often fleeting, leaving behind a lingering chill or a sensation of pins and needles. The Boogeyman uses this physical contact to escalate fear, confirming its presence in a way that is unmistakably real.

Environmental Changes as Indicators

The Boogeyman is not limited to affecting individuals directly; it can also alter the environment to suit its needs and intensify the fear of those around it. These changes are often subtle at first but grow more pronounced as the Boogeyman draws closer.

1. **Changes in Light and Darkness:**
   A room may seem to grow **darker than usual**, even when lights are on. Corners become shrouded in shadow, and darkness seems to pool unnaturally in places where light should reach. Light sources, such as lamps and flashlights, may appear dimmer or fail to illuminate the space effectively. This deepening of shadows is a sign that the Boogeyman is distorting light, creating a space where it can move and hide undetected.

Conversely, sudden bursts of light—like a flash from a lightbulb or a spark from an electrical socket—may signal the Boogeyman's arrival or departure. These changes are not random; they are part of the creature's strategy to disorient and frighten.

1. **Distortion of Sound:**
   Sound is another tool the Boogeyman manipulates to announce its presence. Familiar noises may become **distorted**—footsteps may echo unnaturally, voices sound muffled or stretched, and ordinary household sounds like the creaking of floors or the ticking of clocks grow louder and more ominous. Victims often describe hearing faint whispers, laughter, or crying that seems to emanate from the walls, floors, or the air itself.

In some cases, sounds become **disjointed** and out of sync. For instance, the sound of a door closing may follow the actual motion by several seconds, or an object hitting the floor may produce no noise at all. This auditory distortion serves to disorient the senses, making it difficult for individuals to trust their perception of reality.

1. **Unusual Smells:**
   A distinct and **unpleasant odor** can be another sign of a Boogeyman's presence. The smell may be musty, akin to mold or decaying wood, or carry an acrid, burnt quality like sulfur. This odor often appears suddenly and lingers in the air, clinging to objects and clothing. In some cases, the smell is described as faintly metallic, evoking the scent of blood or rust. The source of the odor is usually untraceable, as it emanates from the Boogeyman itself, signaling its encroachment into the physical realm.

Emotional Symptoms: The Boogeyman's Psychic Influence
Beyond the physical and environmental changes, the Boogeyman exerts a powerful **psychic influence** on its victims. This emotional manipulation is one of the most reliable indicators of its presence, as it targets the core of human fear and anxiety.

1. **Sudden Spikes in Fear:**
   One of the earliest signs of a Boogeyman's presence is an unexplained **spike in fear** or anxiety. Individuals may feel a sudden, inexplicable sense of dread, as though they are being watched or pursued. This fear often arises without any clear cause, manifesting as a tightening in the chest, racing heartbeat, or difficulty breathing. It may wash over the individual in waves, intensifying when they approach certain areas like closets, basements, or darkened rooms.

The Boogeyman feeds on this fear, drawing strength from it to further its manifestation. The more frightened the individual becomes, the more tangible the Boogeyman's presence grows, creating a vicious cycle that can be difficult to break.

1. **Unexplained Paranoia:**
   Victims often experience **paranoia**, feeling as though they are being watched or followed, even when they are alone. They may become hyper-aware of their surroundings, reacting to the slightest noises or changes in light. This paranoia can lead to compulsive behaviors, such as checking locks, peering into closets, or looking under beds for signs of intrusion. The

Boogeyman uses this state of heightened vigilance to keep its prey in a constant state of anxiety, feeding off their fear and uncertainty.

2. **Mood Shifts and Irrational Anger:**
   Those who are under the influence of a Boogeyman's proximity may experience sudden and **unexplained mood shifts**. They may become irritable, angry, or withdrawn without any apparent reason. This emotional volatility is caused by the Boogeyman's psychic influence, which amplifies negative emotions and disrupts the individual's mental state. These mood shifts often create tension and conflict within households, further isolating the victim and making them more susceptible to the Boogeyman's presence.

3. **Fatigue and Weakness:**
   The psychic drain caused by a Boogeyman's presence often leaves individuals feeling **exhausted** and **weak**. They may struggle to sleep, plagued by nightmares or a persistent feeling of unease that prevents them from resting. This fatigue can manifest physically, resulting in headaches, dizziness, and an overall sense of lethargy. The Boogeyman thrives in environments where individuals are too tired to resist, using their weakened state to deepen its hold over them.

Conclusion: Recognizing and Responding to the Signs

The signs of a Boogeyman's presence are varied, affecting both the physical environment and the emotional state of those it targets. Recognizing these signs is the first step in defending against the Boogeyman's influence. When such symptoms appear, it is important to take immediate action:

1. **Illuminate the Space:** Turning on lights and using flashlights can disrupt the Boogeyman's manipulation of shadows, making it more difficult for it to move undetected.
2. **Calm the Mind:** Practicing breathing exercises and grounding techniques can help manage the sudden spikes in fear and paranoia, reducing the Boogeyman's psychic influence.
3. **Create Noise:** Playing music or using white-noise machines can interfere with the Boogeyman's auditory distortions, creating an environment that is less conducive to its scare tactics.
4. **Use Protective Symbols:** Drawing protective symbols or placing objects of comfort, such as stuffed animals or personal items, around the room can help establish a sense of safety and ward off the Boogeyman's encroachment.

By understanding the physical, environmental, and emotional signs of a Boogeyman's presence, individuals can better equip themselves to confront and repel these shadowy entities. While the Boogeyman is a master of fear, knowledge and awareness can provide the tools necessary to stand firm in the face of darkness and reclaim the spaces it seeks to inhabit.

Chapter 7: How to Spot a Boogeyman

Boogeymen are masters of concealment, thriving in darkness and fear. They hide in plain sight, using shadows, corners, and confined spaces to avoid detection. However, with the right knowledge and techniques, it is possible to identify their presence before they have the chance to take hold in your environment. This chapter covers expert methods for **spotting a Boogeyman**, including analyzing shadow movements, identifying their preferred hiding places, and using tools to confirm their existence. By learning these techniques, you can protect your home and loved ones from the influence of these fearsome entities.

The Fundamentals of Boogeyman Identification

Spotting a Boogeyman requires a careful blend of **observation, awareness, and intuition**. They are creatures that thrive in the peripheral, rarely revealing themselves outright. However, they leave behind subtle signs that can be identified with a trained eye. Before delving into specific techniques, it is crucial to understand the Boogeyman's nature:

1. **Boogeymen Hide in the Shadows:** They seek out places that are dark, confined, and often neglected. Shadows are their primary means of concealment, as they can manipulate and distort them to move about undetected. Identifying these shadowy areas is the first step in spotting a Boogeyman.
2. **Boogeymen Thrive on Fear:** The presence of fear strengthens a Boogeyman's ability to manifest. They are more likely to hide in places that evoke fear, such as basements, closets, attics, and under beds. These locations provide not just physical cover but also an atmosphere of dread that helps them go unnoticed.

Techniques for Identifying a Boogeyman

Spotting a Boogeyman is not as simple as catching a glimpse of it in the open. Instead, it involves a combination of **environmental analysis, behavioral observation**, and **the use of specific tools** to detect their presence.

1. Shadow Movement Analysis: Watching the Darkness

Since Boogeymen use shadows as both a cloak and a pathway, **shadow movement analysis** is one of the most effective ways to identify their presence. This technique involves carefully observing shadows in your home for any signs of unnatural behavior.

Steps for Shadow Movement Analysis:

- **Turn Off Unnecessary Lights:** To perform an analysis, it is best to limit the light sources to a few controlled ones. This creates defined shadows that are easier to monitor. Use a single light source, like a lamp or flashlight, to create a consistent environment where shadow movement can be observed.
- **Create a Baseline:** Spend a few moments watching how shadows naturally fall and move within the room. Pay close attention to how they change with the movement of light sources

or your own movement. This baseline is crucial for identifying any deviations that may indicate the presence of a Boogeyman.
- **Monitor for Unnatural Movements:** Boogeymen distort shadows in ways that defy normal physics. Look for shadows that move independently of their light source or surroundings, shift shape, or grow darker without a change in lighting conditions. Some shadows may seem to stretch towards you or contract when approached, a telltale sign of a Boogeyman's manipulation.
- **Use Peripheral Vision:** Boogeymen often hide in the corners of your vision, only moving when they think you are not looking directly at them. Scan the room using your peripheral vision to catch glimpses of shifting shadows or faint movements that vanish when you turn to face them. This technique requires patience and a willingness to trust your instincts, as the Boogeyman relies on its prey dismissing these fleeting impressions as mere tricks of the light.

2. Identifying Preferred Hiding Places: Common Lairs of Boogeymen

Boogeymen are drawn to certain areas within homes that provide ample cover and an atmosphere of fear. By thoroughly inspecting these **preferred hiding places**, you can spot signs of their occupation.

Key Hiding Places and How to Examine Them:

- **Closets:** Boogeymen favor closets for their confined space and darkness. To check a closet for signs of a Boogeyman:
    - **Inspect the Shadows:** Open the closet door slowly and observe how the shadows inside react to the change in light. Shadows that seem to cling to the corners or resist illumination are potential indicators of a Boogeyman's presence.
    - **Look for Misplaced Objects:** Boogeymen often disturb the contents of closets as they move. Look for clothes that have been knocked off hangers, shoes that have shifted positions, or objects that appear to have been pushed deeper into the closet without reason.
- **Under the Bed:** The space beneath the bed is another classic Boogeyman lair, as it is dark, enclosed, and close to where individuals sleep.
    - **Use a Flashlight:** Shine a flashlight under the bed and watch for shadows that seem to shrink away from the light. Boogeymen under beds will often try to evade direct illumination by shifting deeper into corners or wrapping themselves around the bed's structure.
    - **Listen for Sounds:** Boogeymen in this location may create faint scratching, tapping, or rustling noises. Lay still on the bed for a few minutes in silence to listen for any subtle movements beneath you.
- **Attics and Basements:** These areas are prime hiding spots due to their isolation, darkness, and often cluttered state.

- **Examine Dust and Cobweb Patterns:** Boogeymen disrupt the natural accumulation of dust and cobwebs as they move. Look for trails through the dust, displaced cobwebs, or areas where dirt has been scattered in odd patterns.
- **Look for Unusual Cold Spots:** Use a thermometer or your hand to identify sudden drops in temperature, a common sign of a Boogeyman's presence in these spaces.
- **Mirrors and Reflections:** Mirrors can act as gateways for Boogeymen, allowing them to observe and influence their surroundings.
    - **Gaze Indirectly:** Stand at an angle to the mirror and use your peripheral vision to catch movements within the reflection that do not correspond to any real-world motion. Boogeymen may appear as faint shapes or distortions in the glass.
    - **Check for Fogging:** Mirrors that fog over or develop smudges without a clear cause could indicate a Boogeyman's proximity. Touch the glass; if it feels unnaturally cold, it may be a sign that something is lurking within.

3. Behavioral Observation: Watching for Changes in Behavior and Environment

Changes in household behavior, especially among children and pets, can be key indicators of a Boogeyman's presence.

Behavioral Signs to Monitor:

- **Children's Reactions:** Children are often more sensitive to a Boogeyman's presence due to their heightened imaginations and susceptibility to fear.
    - **Changes in Sleep Patterns:** A sudden onset of nightmares, night terrors, or reluctance to go to bed can indicate that a Boogeyman is lurking nearby. Pay attention if a child starts avoiding specific areas of the house or develops an intense fear of the dark or certain spaces like closets or under the bed.
    - **Imaginary Friends Turning Dark:** If a child's imaginary friend begins exhibiting hostile, demanding, or frightening behavior, this could signify the early stages of a Boogeyman's influence.
- **Pet Behavior:** Animals, especially cats and dogs, are highly perceptive of changes in their environment and can sense the presence of entities that humans cannot see.
    - **Unexplained Agitation:** Pets may growl, hiss, bark, or stare intently at seemingly empty spaces, especially corners, closets, or under furniture. If a pet refuses to enter certain rooms or areas of the house, it may be reacting to the presence of a Boogeyman.
    - **Pacing or Whining:** Dogs, in particular, may pace back and forth or whine near doors or stairways leading to basements or attics, indicating they sense something hidden from human perception.

4. Tools for Spotting a Boogeyman: Enhancing Your Detection Capabilities

Certain tools can aid in the identification of a Boogeyman by measuring environmental changes that might be imperceptible to the naked eye.

Recommended Tools:

- **Flashlights with Colored Lenses:** Red and blue filters can reveal details within shadows that regular light cannot. Boogeymen have a tendency to react to changes in light wavelengths. Shine a red-filtered flashlight into dark corners, closets, or under the bed. If shadows shift unnaturally or seem to absorb the light, it may indicate a Boogeyman's presence.
- **Thermal Imagers:** Since Boogeymen often cause temperature fluctuations, thermal imagers can be used to detect cold spots in the room. Sweep the area with a thermal imager, looking for cold anomalies that do not correspond with drafts, windows, or vents.
- **Digital Recorders:** Boogeymen can manipulate sound. Leave a digital audio recorder running overnight in suspected areas. When reviewing the audio, listen for strange noises, whispers, or disturbances that do not align with typical household sounds. Recordings that capture static, garbled voices, or distant scratching noises may indicate a Boogeyman.
- **Cameras with Night Vision:** Boogeymen often appear in low-light conditions. Set up a camera with night vision in areas where activity is suspected. Review the footage for shadow movements, objects shifting, or brief flashes of light that occur without an obvious source.

Conclusion: Knowing What to Look For

Spotting a Boogeyman requires vigilance and a methodical approach. By using shadow movement analysis, inspecting common hiding places, observing behavioral changes in children and pets, and employing tools like thermal imagers and night-vision cameras, you can identify the subtle signs of a Boogeyman's presence. The Boogeyman relies on fear and darkness to hide itself, but with the knowledge of these techniques, you can pierce through its veil of secrecy and reveal its presence within your home.

The next step is to learn how to confront and repel these entities once they have been identified. In the following chapters, we will explore various methods for defending against Boogeymen, dispelling their influence, and reclaiming the spaces they inhabit. For now, remember: the key to spotting a Boogeyman is awareness and the willingness to face the shadows with a discerning eye.

Part 3: *Tools of the Boogey Safari*

Chapter 8: Boogie Safari Gear: What You Need

Embarking on a mission to capture and handle a Boogeyman is not to be taken lightly. These creatures thrive in darkness and fear, using shadows as their shield and manipulating their environment to instill dread. Confronting a Boogeyman requires more than bravery; it demands a carefully selected set of tools and equipment designed to illuminate its presence, disrupt its powers, and safely contain it. This chapter serves as a comprehensive guide to the **essential gear** needed for a successful Boogie Safari, including **special lights**, **sound traps**, **anti-fear amulets**, and other protective items. With the right equipment, you can shift the balance of power away from the Boogeyman and secure a safe outcome for your expedition into the shadows.

1. Special Lights: Shedding Light on Darkness

Boogeymen draw strength from shadows and darkness, making **light** one of your most powerful weapons. Not just any light source will do; specialized lights can penetrate their veil of darkness, exposing their form and disrupting their activities.

Essential Light Sources:

- **Full-Spectrum Flashlights:** Boogeymen often manipulate shadows to conceal their presence. A full-spectrum flashlight emits light across a broad range of wavelengths, including infrared and ultraviolet, which disrupts their shadowy forms and makes them easier to spot. These flashlights allow you to scan darkened areas, closets, and under beds for traces of the Boogeyman, revealing movements or anomalies that regular light might miss. Many full-spectrum flashlights come with interchangeable lenses to shift between different wavelengths for a more thorough search.
- **Red Light Torches:** Boogeymen are particularly sensitive to red light, which disrupts their ability to blend into shadows. Red light torches are excellent for nighttime safaris, as they illuminate dark spaces without causing harsh reflections or making it difficult to see in low-light conditions. Use these torches when scanning confined spaces like closets and attics, watching for shadows that seem to recoil or shrink from the light.
- **UV Blacklights:** Ultraviolet (UV) light can reveal stains, markings, and disturbances caused by Boogeymen. Some Boogeymen leave behind a faint residue—often a sticky, glowing substance known as "Boogie Goo." A UV blacklight can highlight these residues, marking the creature's trails and the areas it frequents. Use a handheld UV flashlight to scan surfaces in suspected hiding places, such as closet floors, under beds, and attic corners.
- **Motion-Activated Spotlights:** For long-term monitoring of areas where Boogeyman activity is suspected, install motion-activated spotlights. These lights flood the area with brightness the moment they detect movement, forcing a lurking Boogeyman to retreat. Position these spotlights in strategic locations, such as entryways to closets, basements, and attics, to illuminate darkened spaces and expose any intrusions.

2. Sound Traps: Turning Silence Into an Alarm

Boogeymen are adept at manipulating sound, often creating unsettling noises to provoke fear. However, sound can also be used **against them**. **Sound traps** are devices designed to detect and capture the subtle auditory disturbances Boogeymen produce, as well as disrupt their activities by flooding the environment with noise.

Key Sound Equipment:

- **Ultrasonic Motion Detectors:** These detectors emit high-frequency sound waves that bounce off objects and detect even the slightest movement. When a Boogeyman passes through the detector's field, it triggers an alarm, alerting you to its presence. Set up these detectors near likely hiding spots, such as the entrance to closets or the underside of beds, to catch a Boogeyman in motion. The sudden sound of the alarm can also serve to disorient the creature, giving you precious moments to prepare a response.
- **White-Noise Machines:** Boogeymen thrive in silence, using it as a canvas for their subtle noises—creaks, whispers, or scratching sounds. White-noise machines fill the room with a continuous stream of neutral sound, drowning out the Boogeyman's attempts to create an unsettling atmosphere. Use these machines in bedrooms, particularly at night, to block the creature's efforts to manipulate sound and invoke fear. Some white-noise machines come with remote controls, allowing you to adjust the volume or change the sound profile as needed.
- **Parabolic Microphones:** Capturing the faint noises a Boogeyman makes requires sensitive audio equipment. A parabolic microphone can pick up distant or quiet sounds, such as whispering, scratching, or the faint rustling of fabric. Use this microphone when monitoring suspected activity zones, pointing it towards closets, attics, or other hidden areas to listen for signs of a lurking Boogeyman. By recording these sounds, you can gather evidence of its presence and analyze its behavior patterns.
- **Portable Audio Disrupters:** These small devices emit bursts of sound across a range of frequencies, disrupting the Boogeyman's control over its environment. Use these disrupters when you suspect a Boogeyman is nearby, activating them to create a sonic barrier that disorients the creature. Some models include a "panic button" feature, allowing you to quickly trigger an audio burst if you encounter a Boogeyman directly.

3. Anti-Fear Amulets: Protecting the Mind and Spirit

Boogeymen are fear-feeders, drawing power from the anxiety and terror of those they target. Carrying **anti-fear amulets** can protect your emotional state, preventing the Boogeyman from exploiting your fear and using it against you.

Recommended Amulets and Talismans:

- **Obsidian Amulet:** Obsidian is known for its protective properties, particularly against negative energies and fear. Wearing an obsidian amulet helps to ground the wearer, providing a shield against the Boogeyman's psychic influence. Its dark, reflective surface is believed to absorb and deflect negative energies, making it harder for the Boogeyman to latch onto your fear.
- **Moonstone Talisman:** Moonstone is associated with emotional balance and the dispelling of irrational fears. Wearing a moonstone talisman or placing moonstone crystals around your bed can help stabilize emotions, preventing the Boogeyman from manipulating feelings of dread. Moonstones are especially effective during nighttime encounters, as their calming energy aligns with the moon's protective light.
- **Sigil-Inscribed Charms:** Craft a charm by inscribing protective sigils onto a small piece of wood, metal, or stone. These sigils act as **spiritual wards**, creating a barrier between you and the Boogeyman. Popular sigils include symbols of strength, courage, and light. Carry the charm in your pocket, wear it as a necklace, or place it in key locations around the house, such as under the bed or above the doorway, to create zones of protection.
- **Herbal Sachets:** Some herbs, like sage, rosemary, and lavender, are known for their protective qualities. Create a small sachet filled with these dried herbs and keep it on your person or place it near areas where Boogeyman activity has been suspected. The scent and properties of the herbs help to purify the environment, deterring the Boogeyman and reducing its ability to influence your emotions.

4. Capture Equipment: Containing the Boogeyman

Once a Boogeyman has been identified and confronted, the next step is to **contain it** safely. Traditional traps are ineffective against these ethereal creatures, so specialized tools are necessary for capture.

Key Capture Tools:

- **Shadow Nets:** Woven from fibers treated with a mixture of **salt, silver, and ash**, shadow nets are designed to capture and hold Boogeymen. These nets work by disrupting the Boogeyman's ability to dissolve into shadows, momentarily binding it in place. Shadow nets are lightweight and flexible, making them easy to carry and deploy. To use, cast the net towards the suspected location of the Boogeyman, ensuring it fully covers the area. The net's treated fibers will glow faintly if they come into contact with the Boogeyman's form, signaling a successful capture.
- **Mirror Traps:** Boogeymen can be lured into mirrors, which act as gateways to their dimension. A **mirror trap** is created by inscribing the back of a mirror with a binding sigil, usually in a circular pattern with symbols representing containment and reflection. Place the mirror in a location where the Boogeyman is likely to appear, such as near a closet or under the bed. Once the Boogeyman is reflected in the mirror, it becomes trapped within its own image. To seal the trap, cover the mirror with a cloth inscribed with protective symbols and store it in a secure, dark place.
- **Crystal Jars:** Clear quartz crystals are known for their ability to absorb and contain energies. **Crystal jars** are glass containers lined with clear quartz shards and sealed with a lid etched with binding runes. When a Boogeyman is sufficiently weakened or trapped using other methods, open the jar near its form. The jar's crystal-lined interior will draw in the Boogeyman, trapping it within. Seal the lid immediately and secure it with wax mixed with powdered silver for an additional layer of protection.

5. Protective Clothing: Ward Off Direct Contact

Boogeymen can physically interact with their environment, and direct contact with them can be unsettling or even dangerous. Wearing **protective clothing** can help prevent this interaction.

- **Salt-Lined Gloves:** Wear gloves with a lining made of salt crystals and iron filings to protect your hands from direct contact with a Boogeyman. Salt has long been used as a deterrent against dark entities, while iron disrupts their ability to manipulate energy. These gloves allow you to handle objects and touch surfaces where the Boogeyman may be lurking without risking physical or psychic harm.
- **Hooded Cloaks:** A cloak treated with protective herbs like sage and lavender, along with embroidered sigils on the inner lining, acts as a shield against the Boogeyman's touch. The hood helps cover the head, protecting the wearer from potential psychic attacks. The cloak's materials—preferably wool or heavy cotton—are chosen for their insulating properties, further hindering the Boogeyman's attempts to penetrate the wearer's defenses.

Conclusion: Preparing for the Boogie Safari

Equipping yourself with the right tools and gear is essential for successfully confronting and handling a Boogeyman. By using special lights, sound traps, anti-fear amulets, and capture equipment, you can navigate the darkened spaces where Boogeymen dwell and take control of the encounter. Remember, the Boogeyman thrives on fear and the unknown. Your gear not only serves as a means of detection and capture but also as a source of **confidence**—a critical asset in countering the Boogeyman's influence.

In the following chapters, we will delve into techniques for using this gear effectively during encounters with Boogeymen and explore strategies for cleansing spaces to prevent their return. With the right preparation and tools at hand, you can face the darkness and banish these creatures back to the shadows where they belong.

Chapter 9: The Temporalfudge Device: Time-Bending Safari Tech

The Boogeyman's nature is inherently tied to the fabric of space and time. It moves through shadows, bends light to obscure its presence, and slips in and out of our reality with ease. Traditional means of tracking and capturing a Boogeyman are often thwarted by its ability to manipulate time and space in its immediate surroundings, using these distortions to elude capture. To counter this, experts have developed a groundbreaking tool known as the **Temporalfudge Device**, an instrument that allows one to manipulate the flow of time within the Boogie World and, to a limited extent, within our reality.

The Temporalfudge Device is an intricate piece of safari technology designed to **slow down** the Boogeyman's movements, effectively creating a time bubble that grants the user a significant advantage during encounters. In this chapter, we will explore the **construction**, **function**, and **operation** of this device in detail, providing an in-depth understanding of how to wield time itself to capture and contain these elusive creatures.

Understanding the Boogie World's Time Distortion

To comprehend how the Temporalfudge Device works, one must first understand the **nature of time within the Boogie World**. Unlike our reality, where time flows in a linear and predictable fashion, the Boogie World is a dimension where time is **fluid** and can stretch, compress, or loop at will. This elasticity allows Boogeymen to move through spaces and moments at an altered pace, often appearing and disappearing in the blink of an eye.

Boogeymen exploit these temporal anomalies to their advantage. When they sense a threat, they can effectively "speed up" their movements relative to the environment around them, making them nearly impossible to capture through conventional means. The Temporalfudge Device was developed specifically to counteract this ability, leveling the playing field by **slowing down** the Boogeyman's movements within a localized area and buying the user crucial seconds to act.

The Temporalfudge Device: Construction and Components

The Temporalfudge Device is a marvel of **arcane engineering**, combining elements of both technology and metaphysical principles. Its construction requires precision and the use of rare materials that interact with the flow of time itself. Below is a breakdown of the device's key components:

1. **Temporal Quartz Core:** At the heart of the Temporalfudge Device is a **temporal quartz core**, a crystal known for its unique interaction with time. Temporal quartz is harvested from the deepest parts of caves, where the mineral has formed under conditions of intense pressure and energy over millennia. This quartz has the natural ability to absorb and emit temporal energy, making it the ideal material for manipulating time. It is carefully cut and treated with a mixture of **liquid mercury** and **moonlight essence**, which enhances its temporal properties.

2. **Gears of Iron and Silver:** Surrounding the temporal quartz core are finely crafted gears made of iron and silver, metals chosen for their symbolic and metaphysical properties. Iron is known to disrupt malevolent entities, while silver is associated with purity and reflection. These gears form the mechanical aspect of the device, allowing the user to calibrate the temporal field's size and strength. The gears interlock with remarkable precision, rotating in a specific pattern that channels the quartz core's energy outward.

3. **Runic Engravings:** The device's casing is inscribed with **ancient runes**, each representing different aspects of time, protection, and binding. These runes, etched into the metal with a mixture of **salt, powdered sapphire, and charcoal**, form a protective barrier that stabilizes the temporal field, preventing it from collapsing or spiraling out of control. The runes must be carved by hand, following precise geometric patterns that align with the flow of temporal energy.

4. **Energy Conduit Rods:** Four energy conduit rods extend outward from the device's main body, made of **obsidian** fused with thin veins of **gold**. These rods serve to direct and stabilize the temporal field around the user. When activated, the rods emit a faint glow, indicating the flow of temporal energy as it spreads out from the device to encompass the target area.

5. **Activation Dial:** The top of the device features a rotating **dial** marked with symbols representing different increments of time alteration. The user turns the dial to adjust the level of time manipulation, ranging from a slight slowing to near stasis. The dial is encased in a **crystal dome**, ensuring that the user can monitor its position even in low-light conditions.

6. **Temporal Charge Cells:** The device is powered by **temporal charge cells**, small vials containing distilled **moonlight essence** and **witch-hazel oil**. These cells provide the energy needed to fuel the time-manipulation process. A fully charged cell can maintain a temporal field for approximately 5 minutes, after which the cell must be replaced or recharged under the light of a full moon.

How the Temporalfudge Device Works: Creating a Time Bubble

When activated, the Temporalfudge Device generates a **temporal field**—a localized bubble of time distortion that expands outward from the device. This bubble affects everything within its radius, causing time to **slow down** significantly for anything caught inside it, including Boogeymen. The effect is not instantaneous; it requires a few seconds for the temporal field to stabilize and reach full strength.

The Mechanics of Operation:

1. **Calibrating the Device:** Before using the device, the user must calibrate the temporal field by turning the activation dial to the desired time distortion level. For capturing a Boogeyman, it is recommended to set the dial to a moderate level—slowing down time to approximately one-tenth of its normal flow. This setting provides enough time to react while minimizing the strain on the temporal quartz core.
2. **Activation Sequence:** To activate the Temporalfudge Device, the user presses a small button on the side of the casing, which triggers the rotation of the iron and silver gears. As the gears begin to turn, the temporal quartz core starts to glow faintly, emitting a soft hum. The energy conduit rods extend outward, channeling the quartz's energy into the surrounding space. Within moments, the temporal field begins to expand, indicated by a ripple effect that distorts the air around the user.
3. **Establishing the Temporal Field:** The field's expansion is subtle; objects within its radius may appear to shimmer slightly, as if viewed through a heat haze. As the field stabilizes, time within its boundary slows down. This slow-motion effect is most noticeable with fast-moving objects, such as a Boogeyman attempting to flee. Once the field is fully established, the Boogeyman's movements become sluggish, giving the user the upper hand in capture attempts.
4. **Maintaining Control:** While the field is active, the user must maintain a firm grip on the device, keeping it oriented towards the target area. Any sudden movements can disrupt the field, causing it to collapse prematurely. The device will hum at a steady pitch when functioning correctly; fluctuations in the pitch signal changes in the field's integrity, alerting the user to potential malfunctions.

Using the Temporalfudge Device During Boogie Safari
Effectively employing the Temporalfudge Device requires **timing, precision, and strategy**. Here are key guidelines for using the device during an encounter with a Boogeyman:

1. **Strategic Positioning:** Before activating the device, position yourself near the Boogeyman's suspected hiding place. Boogeymen often attempt to flee or use their shadow-manipulation abilities when confronted. Having the device ready at the entrance to a closet, under a bed, or near an attic door maximizes your chance of capturing the Boogeyman within the temporal field as it emerges.
2. **Initiate the Field Quickly:** The moment you spot the Boogeyman, activate the device without hesitation. The few seconds it takes for the field to stabilize are crucial. During this period, the Boogeyman may attempt to escape, but the expanding temporal bubble will gradually slow its movements, providing you with an opportunity to deploy capture tools, such as a shadow net or mirror trap.
3. **Monitor the Field's Integrity:** While the temporal field is active, watch for signs of fluctuation. If the air within the field starts to ripple erratically or the device's hum changes in pitch, it may indicate that the Boogeyman is attempting to disrupt the field. In such cases, focus on maintaining a steady grip on the device and adjust the activation dial if necessary to stabilize the time bubble.
4. **Capture and Contain:** Once the Boogeyman is slowed within the temporal field, use the opportunity to deploy your capture tools. Shadow nets work particularly well in tandem with the Temporalfudge Device, as the slowing effect prevents the Boogeyman from evading the net. Alternatively, position a mirror trap directly in front of the creature, allowing its reflection to be captured as the temporal field holds it in place.
5. **Deactivation:** After successfully capturing the Boogeyman, turn the activation dial to the "neutral" position to deactivate the device. The temporal field will collapse gradually, returning time to its normal flow. Keep the device aimed at the captured Boogeyman until the field fully dissipates to prevent any last-moment escape attempts.

Maintenance and Recharge of the Temporalfudge Device

To ensure the device remains functional for future use, it requires regular maintenance and recharging:

1. **Recharge Under Moonlight:** The temporal charge cells need to be recharged under the light of a full moon to restore their energy. Place the cells in a **moonlight bath**—a small, reflective dish filled with water and moonstone crystals—overnight to allow them to absorb lunar energy.
2. **Inspect for Wear:** Periodically inspect the gears and runic engravings for signs of wear or damage. Gears should turn smoothly without grinding, and runes should remain clear and unblemished. Use a soft cloth dipped in saltwater to clean the device, especially the temporal quartz core, to remove any residual energy from previous uses.
3. **Replace Components:** If the temporal quartz core develops cracks or the energy conduit rods lose their luster, replace them immediately. Faulty components can result in a malfunctioning field, posing a danger to the user by causing time distortions to backfire.

Limitations of the Temporalfudge Device

While the Temporalfudge Device is a powerful tool, it has its limitations. The temporal field has a finite range (approximately a 10-foot radius) and duration (5 minutes per charge cell). Additionally, using the device repeatedly within a short period can strain the quartz core, reducing its effectiveness. Therefore, it is recommended to use the device sparingly and in situations where it offers a strategic advantage.

Conclusion: Harnessing Time for the Boogie Safari

The Temporalfudge Device is a sophisticated and indispensable tool for anyone seeking to confront and capture a Boogeyman. By harnessing the power of time manipulation, it allows the user to level the playing field, slowing down these elusive entities and providing a critical window for action. However, mastery of the device requires a combination of **knowledge, skill, and caution**, as mishandling its power can lead to unintended consequences.

In the upcoming chapters, we will explore further techniques for using captured Boogeymen to understand their behaviors, as well as methods for safeguarding your home from future encounters. With the Temporalfudge Device in your arsenal, you are now equipped to navigate the complexities of the Boogie World and emerge victorious against the shadows.

Chapter 10: Boogie Goo Recipe: A Vital Tool for Containment

Capturing a Boogeyman is a daunting task, and even more challenging is **containing** it. These creatures are masters of evasion, capable of slipping through shadows and bending reality to escape. To counter this, experts have developed **Boogie Goo**—a sticky, viscous substance with unique properties designed to trap and contain Boogeymen. When applied, Boogie Goo adheres to the entity's shadowy form, rendering it immobile and preventing it from vanishing into thin air or slipping back into the Boogie World.

This chapter provides a comprehensive, step-by-step guide to creating **Boogie Goo**, detailing the required ingredients, preparation process, and application techniques for maximum effectiveness. Crafting Boogie Goo is a delicate process involving a mixture of **rare components**, alchemical principles, and a bit of arcane knowledge. By following these instructions precisely, you can produce a batch of Boogie Goo that will become an indispensable tool in your Boogeyman containment arsenal.

Ingredients for Boogie Goo: The Rare and the Arcane

Boogie Goo requires a combination of ingredients that possess **binding, purifying, and enhancing** properties. These components are carefully selected for their ability to interact with a Boogeyman's essence, making it nearly impossible for the creature to escape once ensnared. Some of these ingredients are common, while others are more exotic and difficult to procure.

Core Ingredients:

1. **Obsidian Powder (2 tablespoons):**
   Finely ground obsidian is essential for Boogie Goo due to its natural affinity for absorbing negative energy and disrupting supernatural entities. Its reflective properties also help contain the Boogeyman's essence within the goo. You can obtain obsidian powder from specialized occult shops or by grinding down small pieces of obsidian stone using a mortar and pestle.

2. **Salt (1/4 cup):**
   Salt is a traditional protective substance used in many cultures to ward off dark forces. Its purifying properties make it an effective component in Boogie Goo, enhancing the goo's ability to bind and neutralize the Boogeyman's shadowy form. **Sea salt** or **rock salt** is preferred over table salt due to its purity and unprocessed nature.

3. **Honey (1/2 cup):**
   Honey provides the base viscosity of the Boogie Goo, giving it a sticky consistency necessary for trapping. It also symbolizes the sweetness of light, acting as a counteragent to the darkness within which Boogeymen thrive. Use **raw, organic honey** to maintain its natural properties.

4. **Mandrake Root Extract (3 drops):**
   Mandrake root is known for its potent mystical properties, often used in spells of binding and control. The extract acts as a magical adhesive within the goo, enhancing its ability to cling to supernatural entities. You can find mandrake root extract in occult supply stores or make your own by steeping a piece of dried mandrake root in alcohol for several weeks.

5. **Activated Charcoal (1 tablespoon):**
   Activated charcoal is added to give the goo its dark color, allowing it to blend into the shadows where Boogeymen hide. More importantly, it has absorption properties that help neutralize the Boogeyman's ethereal energy, aiding in containment.

6. **Moonstone Dust (1 teaspoon):**
   Ground moonstone is a rare and vital component that lends the Boogie Goo its mystical properties. Moonstone is associated with the moon's protective energy and acts as a stabilizer within the goo, preventing the Boogeyman from phasing out of the physical plane. Moonstone dust can be purchased online or from specialty stores. If you choose to grind your own moonstone, be sure to use protective gear, as fine particles can be sharp.

7. **Silver Shavings (1/2 teaspoon):**
   Silver is known for its purifying and protective qualities, and a small amount of silver shavings enhances the binding strength of the Boogie Goo. Use a fine file to shave small pieces from a silver coin or piece of jewelry. The shavings should be fine enough to disperse evenly within the goo.

8. **Ash of Burned Sage (1 tablespoon):**
   Sage is traditionally used for cleansing spaces of negative energies. By adding the ash of burned sage, the Boogie Goo gains an extra layer of spiritual protection, creating an environment that the Boogeyman finds difficult to penetrate.

9. **Binding Oil (7 drops):**
   This oil is a blend of **frankincense**, **myrrh**, and **cedarwood** essential oils, each chosen for their binding and protective properties. Mix these oils together in equal parts to create a small vial of binding oil, which helps activate the magical properties of the Boogie Goo.

10. **Distilled Water (1 cup):**
    Distilled water is used to adjust the consistency of the Boogie Goo, making it easier to spread or pour. Avoid tap or mineral water, as impurities can weaken the goo's binding properties.

Preparation: Crafting Boogie Goo Step-by-Step

Creating Boogie Goo is an intricate process that must be performed with care and precision. Follow the instructions below to ensure the best results:

1. **Prepare Your Workspace:**
   Set up your workspace in a quiet, undisturbed area. Lay down a cloth or paper to protect surfaces, as some ingredients (like obsidian powder and charcoal) can stain. Gather all ingredients and tools, including a mixing bowl, wooden spoon, measuring spoons, and a small pot for heating.

2. **Mix the Dry Ingredients:**
   In a large mixing bowl, combine the **obsidian powder, salt, activated charcoal**, and **moonstone dust**. Stir these dry ingredients together using a wooden spoon (metal utensils can interfere with the goo's properties). Ensure that the powders are thoroughly blended into a homogeneous mixture.

3. **Prepare the Liquid Base:**
   In a small pot, combine the **honey** and **distilled water**. Place the pot over low heat and stir until the honey is fully dissolved in the water. Be careful not to let the mixture boil, as high heat can alter the honey's natural properties. Remove the pot from heat once the honey is fully incorporated into the water.

4. **Add the Mandrake Root Extract and Binding Oil:**
   To the warm honey-water mixture, add **3 drops of mandrake root extract** and **7 drops of binding oil**. Stir gently to incorporate these ingredients. The mandrake extract enhances the binding properties of the goo, while the binding oil activates its magical attributes. As you stir, focus your intention on creating a substance that will trap and neutralize the Boogeyman.

5. **Combine Dry and Liquid Mixtures:**
   Slowly pour the warm liquid mixture into the bowl of dry ingredients, stirring continuously with the wooden spoon. The mixture will start to thicken as the powders absorb the liquid. Continue stirring until the mixture becomes a smooth, viscous paste. It should have a dark, glossy appearance with a texture similar to molasses.

6. **Add Silver Shavings:**
   Sprinkle the **silver shavings** into the goo and stir thoroughly to distribute them evenly throughout the mixture. The silver shavings not only add to the goo's binding strength but also give it a faint shimmer, indicating its potency.

7. **Infuse with Ash of Burned Sage:**
   Finally, sprinkle the **ash of burned sage** into the goo while stirring slowly. This final step imbues the mixture with protective energy, ensuring that the Boogeyman will remain trapped once ensnared.

8. **Cool and Store:**
   Allow the Boogie Goo to cool at room temperature for about 30 minutes. Once cooled, transfer it into an airtight glass jar for storage. Avoid using plastic containers, as they can absorb the goo's properties over time, reducing its effectiveness. Store the jar in a dark, cool place, such as a cupboard, away from direct sunlight. Properly stored, Boogie Goo can retain its potency for up to six months.

Tips for Best Results

- **Moonlight Charging:** For an extra boost of power, place the sealed jar of Boogie Goo under **moonlight** (preferably during a full moon) for several hours. This infuses the goo with lunar energy, enhancing its binding capabilities.
- **Stirring the Goo:** Whenever you are preparing to use Boogie Goo, stir it thoroughly with a wooden or silver spoon to re-activate its binding properties. The ingredients may settle over time, so a good stir ensures the components are evenly distributed.
- **Adjusting Consistency:** If the Boogie Goo becomes too thick or dry over time, add a few drops of distilled water and stir to restore its original viscosity. If it is too runny, mix in a small amount of activated charcoal or salt to thicken it.

Application: How to Use Boogie Goo for Maximum Effectiveness

Once prepared, Boogie Goo can be used in various ways to trap and contain Boogeymen. Here are some application methods for best results:

1. **Spread Along Entrances:** Apply a thin layer of Boogie Goo along the **threshold of a closet**, **attic door**, or **under the bed**. These are common entrances for Boogeymen. The goo creates an invisible barrier that ensnares the creature as it attempts to cross, sticking to its form and preventing it from retreating.
2. **Direct Application:** If you spot a Boogeyman, use a **wooden spatula** or a **brush** to fling a small amount of goo directly at its shadowy form. The goo will adhere to its surface, solidifying as it comes into contact with the Boogeyman's essence. This method is particularly effective when used in tandem with tools like the Temporalfudge Device, which can slow down the Boogeyman's movements, giving you a window to apply the goo.
3. **Seal Containers:** For long-term containment, use Boogie Goo to seal the edges of a **mirror trap** or **crystal jar** after capturing a Boogeyman. The goo prevents the entity from slipping through cracks or exploiting weak points in the containment vessel.

Precautions and Storage

- **Avoid Contact with Skin:** Boogie Goo is highly adhesive and can cling to human skin, causing discomfort or minor irritation. Always wear **protective gloves** when handling it.
- **Storage:** Keep the jar of Boogie Goo **sealed** when not in use, as prolonged exposure to air can dry it out. If the goo loses its stickiness, it will become less effective at containing Boogeymen.

Conclusion: A Vital Tool for Every Boogey Safari

Boogie Goo is an essential tool for those venturing into the realm of Boogeyman capture and containment. Its unique blend of mystical and physical properties makes it a powerful ally in immobilizing these shadowy entities and ensuring they remain contained. By following this recipe and preparation process, you can create a batch of Boogie Goo that will serve you well in your encounters with the Boogeyman.

In the following chapters, we will delve into advanced techniques for trapping Boogeymen and maintaining long-term containment. With your newly crafted Boogie Goo in hand, you are one step closer to mastering the art of the Boogie Safari.

Part 4: *The Art of the Capture*

Chapter 11: How to Know When to Catch One

Timing is crucial when attempting to catch a Boogeyman. These elusive creatures are experts at blending into the shadows, utilizing their surroundings, and sensing fear in their prey. Successfully capturing a Boogeyman depends not only on the tools and traps you have at your disposal but also on your ability to recognize the **optimal moments** for initiating the capture. By paying close attention to both **environmental** and **emotional cues**, you can identify when a Boogeyman is most vulnerable and increase your chances of a successful capture.

This chapter delves into the specific conditions that make it easier to catch a Boogeyman, including fluctuations in **environmental factors** like time of day, moon phases, and weather, as well as **emotional states** that heighten its presence. Understanding these cues will allow you to be prepared and ready to act when the time is right.

The Importance of Timing in Boogeyman Capture

Boogeymen are creatures of habit; they follow patterns that align with the cycles of nature and the emotional state of their surroundings. By studying these patterns, you can anticipate when they are most likely to manifest and be vulnerable to capture. Attempting to trap a Boogeyman at the wrong time often results in failure, as they can easily evade capture or retaliate with fear-inducing tactics. Conversely, knowing when they are at their weakest—or when their activity peaks—gives you a strategic advantage.

Environmental Cues: The Right Time and Place

Boogeymen are deeply attuned to environmental changes, which affect their behavior and movements. Recognizing these changes can help you determine when a Boogeyman is most active and when it might be best to lay your trap.

1. Time of Day: Nighttime Ambushes

Nighttime is when Boogeymen are at their most active. Darkness provides them with the cover they need to move about undetected and instill fear. During the day, Boogeymen tend to retreat into hiding places like closets, under beds, attics, or basements. However, their energy is lower in daylight, and they are less likely to reveal themselves.

Optimal Capture Time: The **twilight hours** (just after sunset) and the **dead of night** (between 2 AM and 4 AM) are ideal for attempting a capture. Twilight marks the Boogeyman's transition from dormancy to activity, while the dead of night is when its influence peaks. Boogeymen caught during these times are usually at their fullest strength, which paradoxically makes them more tangible and thus easier to trap.

Preparation: Set up traps, such as shadow nets or mirror traps, just before sunset to ensure they are in place when nighttime activity begins. If you plan to use Boogie Goo or the Temporalfudge Device, keep them ready and within reach during these hours, as you may need to act quickly once the Boogeyman appears.

2. Moon Phases: The Influence of Lunar Energy

Boogeymen are significantly affected by the **lunar cycle**, as the moon's energy influences the flow of fear and the boundary between our world and the Boogie World. Certain phases of the moon make Boogeymen more active, while others can weaken their power, providing the ideal opportunity for capture.

- **New Moon:** The new moon is a period of darkness, during which Boogeymen are at their most elusive and stealthy. They are harder to catch during this time as they blend seamlessly into the shadows. Avoid attempting a capture during the new moon unless absolutely necessary, as the Boogeyman is more likely to evade your efforts.
- **Full Moon:** During the full moon, the Boogeyman's powers are at their peak due to the abundance of lunar energy. This energy can make them bolder and more aggressive, leading to increased activity. While this makes them more dangerous, it also makes them **easier to detect** and trap. Their overconfidence can cause them to reveal themselves more fully, making it the perfect time to strike.
- **Waxing and Waning Phases:** The **waxing crescent** and **waning gibbous** phases are transitional periods when the Boogeyman's power fluctuates. During the waxing phase, their strength is increasing, making them more visible. In the waning phase, they are starting to lose energy, making them slower and less evasive. These phases are ideal for setting up traps and conducting reconnaissance in preparation for a capture attempt during the full moon.

Optimal Capture Time: The best time to catch a Boogeyman is on the **night of the full moon** or the **days leading up to it** during the waxing gibbous phase. The Boogeyman will be more active and likely to show itself during these periods, giving you a clear target.

3. Weather Patterns: The Boogeyman's Reaction to Storms

Boogeymen are known to react strongly to certain weather conditions, particularly **thunderstorms** and **heavy rain**. The sound of thunder and the flicker of lightning create an atmosphere of fear and unease, which Boogeymen feed on. During storms, they become more confident and bold, often venturing out of their hiding places to sow fear.

Optimal Capture Time: During a **thunderstorm**, Boogeymen are at their most visible and active. The storm's intensity disrupts their usual caution, making them more likely to fall into traps or be caught with tools like the Temporalfudge Device. This is an excellent time to prepare your gear and keep a vigilant watch on areas where Boogeyman activity is suspected.

Preparation: If you anticipate a storm, set up **sound traps** and **motion-activated lights** in key areas. The sudden flashes of light and changes in noise during a storm can disorient the Boogeyman, allowing you to catch it off-guard.

Emotional Cues: The Power of Fear and Calm

The Boogeyman is intrinsically linked to human emotions, particularly fear. Its presence often heightens in response to the emotional states of those around it. Recognizing these emotional cues can be just as important as environmental signals in determining the right time to capture the creature.

1. Heightened Fear in the Household

Boogeymen feed on fear, growing stronger and more assertive when anxiety, dread, or terror are present. This is why they often target homes during periods of emotional turmoil, such as after a frightening event or during stressful life changes.

Optimal Capture Time: If you notice a **spike in fear** within the household—manifested through frequent nightmares, anxiety, or a pervasive sense of being watched—it indicates that the Boogeyman is drawing closer and is more likely to be caught. While this heightened fear makes the Boogeyman more powerful, it also makes it more reckless and prone to exposing itself.

Preparation: Create a **safe zone** in the house, such as a brightly lit room with protective symbols, where family members can retreat to while you prepare for the capture. This zone helps contain the fear and prevents the Boogeyman from exploiting it during the capture attempt.

2. Lulls in Activity: The Calm Before the Storm

Boogeymen often go through periods of **quiet** where they appear to retreat, causing a deceptive sense of calm. This is usually a sign that they are gathering strength or planning their next move. However, this lull also presents a window of opportunity.

Optimal Capture Time: Use these quiet periods to **set traps** and **prepare equipment** for when the Boogeyman makes its next appearance. The Boogeyman is less vigilant during these lulls, giving you the element of surprise when it resumes activity.

Preparation: During this calm, set up **mirror traps** in strategic locations, apply **Boogie Goo** barriers, and ensure that the **Temporalfudge Device** is ready for immediate use. By being proactive during the Boogeyman's downtime, you increase the likelihood of a successful capture when it re-emerges.

3. Children's Emotional States: Indicators of Imminent Activity

Children are particularly sensitive to the presence of Boogeymen, and their emotional states often serve as a barometer for the creature's activity. Sudden shifts in a child's mood—such as a joyful child becoming withdrawn, fearful, or exhibiting irrational anger—can signal that a Boogeyman is preparing to manifest.

Optimal Capture Time: If a child begins experiencing frequent **nightmares**, **night terrors**, or an intense fear of certain areas (like closets or under the bed), it indicates that the Boogeyman is nearby and active. This heightened state is the perfect time to lay your trap, as the Boogeyman will likely appear to capitalize on the child's fear.

Preparation: Use the child's fear as a lure by setting up **Boogie Goo** barriers and **sound traps** near their bedroom. Have protective measures in place, such as **anti-fear amulets**, to safeguard the child while you prepare for the Boogeyman's appearance.

Final Preparations: Combining Cues for a Successful Capture

When planning to capture a Boogeyman, **synchronize** environmental and emotional cues for the best results. For instance, capturing a Boogeyman during a full moon, at night, while a thunderstorm rages, and while fear in the household is high provides the ideal set of conditions. This combination ensures that the Boogeyman is active, visible, and overconfident, making it easier to trap.

Checklist for Preparation:

- **Gear Ready:** Have your **Temporalfudge Device**, **Boogie Goo**, **shadow nets**, and **mirror traps** prepared and within easy reach.
- **Traps Set:** Position traps in areas of suspected activity, such as closets, attics, and under beds, especially during the twilight hours.
- **Safe Zones:** Create a well-lit, protected area in the house where family members can stay during the capture attempt.
- **Emotional Readiness:** Carry **anti-fear amulets** and focus on maintaining a calm, confident demeanor to prevent the Boogeyman from exploiting your fear.

By recognizing the signs and timing your actions based on these environmental and emotional cues, you can significantly increase your chances of a successful Boogeyman capture. In the chapters to follow, we will explore advanced techniques for containing and studying captured Boogeymen, furthering your mastery of the Boogie Safari. With this knowledge, you are now equipped to act with precision and confidence when the moment arrives to confront the darkness.

Chapter 12: What to Do During a Full Moon

The **full moon** has long been associated with mystery, magic, and the supernatural. In the realm of Boogeymen, the full moon is a time of both **heightened power** and **increased vulnerability**. Its luminous presence disrupts the darkness they thrive in, but it also fuels their strength, granting them a boldness not usually displayed during other lunar phases. To the experienced Boogey Safari hunter, the full moon presents a unique window of opportunity to confront, trap, and study these creatures.

This chapter will delve into the effects of the full moon on Boogeymen, how it amplifies their abilities, and the vulnerabilities it exposes. You will also learn **strategies and preparations** for dealing with Boogeymen during this lunar phase, maximizing your chances of a successful encounter.

The Significance of the Full Moon for Boogeymen

Boogeymen are intimately connected to the cycles of the moon. Unlike the new moon, when they can move stealthily in the shadows, the full moon casts a bright light that illuminates their lurking places, challenging their ability to remain hidden. However, this same lunar energy that exposes them also **enhances their supernatural abilities**. Understanding this duality is key to successfully navigating a full moon encounter.

- **Amplification of Abilities:** During a full moon, the Boogeyman's powers are magnified. Its shadow manipulation becomes more fluid and dynamic, allowing it to distort reality in its immediate vicinity. It can create more vivid illusions, manipulate ambient sounds with greater complexity, and generate an atmosphere of heightened fear.
- **Increased Boldness:** The full moon emboldens the Boogeyman, pushing it to take greater risks in pursuit of its prey. It is more likely to venture out from its usual hiding spots, cross thresholds into new areas, and interact more directly with its environment. This increased activity makes the Boogeyman more visible and, consequently, more vulnerable.
- **Heightened Senses:** Boogeymen's senses, especially their ability to detect fear, are enhanced during a full moon. They become acutely aware of changes in their environment and the emotional states of those nearby. This heightened awareness can make them more difficult to approach and trap, requiring careful planning and control over one's emotions.

How the Full Moon Makes BoogeymenVulnerable

Despite their amplified abilities, Boogeymen are not invincible during a full moon. The moon's light has a **purifying quality** that disrupts the dark energies they rely on for concealment and mobility. This disruption forces them into more tangible forms, making it possible to detect and capture them with the right tools.

- **Visibility:** Under the full moon, a Boogeyman's shadowy form becomes more **distinct**. While it can still blend into dark corners, the contrast between light and shadow makes its movements easier to track. The bright, silvery light of the moon can outline its shape, allowing it to be spotted even when it attempts to cloak itself.

- **Slowed Movement:** The full moon's light exerts a **gravitational pull** on a Boogeyman's essence, subtly hindering its ability to phase in and out of reality. This makes it less agile and more susceptible to physical traps like shadow nets and mirror traps.
- **Altered Perception:** The heightened sensory awareness Boogeymen experience during a full moon can work against them. They may become overwhelmed by the intensity of their surroundings, leading them to make mistakes or expose themselves in ways they wouldn't otherwise.

Preparing for a Full Moon Encounter: Gathering Your Tools

A full moon encounter requires careful preparation and the right set of tools to take advantage of the Boogeyman's vulnerabilities while counteracting its enhanced abilities.

Essential Tools for a Full Moon Capture:

1. **Full-Spectrum Flashlights:** These lights are crucial during a full moon, as they can cut through the heightened shadows created by the Boogeyman. Full-spectrum flashlights expose its true form, preventing it from escaping into darkness.
2. **Boogie Goo:** The increased visibility of the Boogeyman makes this an ideal time to use **Boogie Goo**. Its sticky nature can trap the Boogeyman when it attempts to retreat to darker spaces. Apply the goo to the entrances of closets, the underside of beds, and around windows to create barriers the Boogeyman cannot cross.
3. **Temporalfudge Device:** With the Boogeyman's movements already slightly hindered by the full moon, the **Temporalfudge Device** becomes even more effective. The time-slowing effect can be used to further immobilize the Boogeyman, giving you a clear opportunity to deploy traps and containment methods.
4. **Mirror Traps:** Boogeymen are more likely to appear in reflections during a full moon. Use **mirror traps** strategically in rooms with direct moonlight to capture the Boogeyman's image. Inscribe the mirror's back with binding sigils to ensure the entity cannot break free once trapped.
5. **Anti-Fear Amulets:** Since the Boogeyman's ability to detect and exploit fear is heightened during a full moon, wearing **anti-fear amulets** is essential. Moonstone and obsidian amulets work particularly well during this phase, as they resonate with lunar energy to protect the wearer's mind from the Boogeyman's influence.

Strategies for Confronting a Boogeyman During a Full Moon

Timing and patience are key when confronting a Boogeyman under the full moon's influence. Here are some **strategies** to guide you through the encounter:

1. Lure It Into the Open: Using the Moon's Light as Bait

The full moon's light is both a beacon and a trap for Boogeymen. Use it to your advantage by positioning yourself near areas where moonlight streams in through windows or doorways. Boogeymen are drawn to shadows, but during a full moon, they will venture closer to the light to assess their surroundings.

How to Execute:

- Leave curtains slightly open in rooms where you suspect Boogeyman activity. The shafts of moonlight will force the creature to either expose itself or retreat further into confined spaces, limiting its options.
- Place traps, such as shadow nets, around the moonlit areas to capture the Boogeyman if it attempts to cross.

2. Exploit Its Overconfidence: Triggering Its Vulnerabilities

During a full moon, Boogeymen become bolder and more aggressive. This overconfidence can be exploited to lure them into traps. By appearing vulnerable or creating situations that suggest fear, you can provoke the Boogeyman into showing itself.

How to Execute:

- Simulate fear by using sound traps that mimic the noises of a frightened child or the creaking of an opening closet door. The Boogeyman, sensing an easy target, may rush to exploit the situation, falling into a trap you have laid in its path.
- Position Boogie Goo along the edges of potential hiding spots. When the Boogeyman moves to investigate the source of the sound, it may inadvertently come into contact with the goo, becoming ensnared.

3. Control the Shadows: Manipulating Light and Darkness

With the full moon altering the balance of light and shadow, you can manipulate these elements to corral the Boogeyman into a desired area. Using **full-spectrum flashlights** and strategically placed objects, create an environment that limits its ability to move freely.

How to Execute:

- Place mirrors and reflective surfaces around the room to bounce moonlight into dark corners. Boogeymen are reluctant to cross spaces filled with reflective light, as it disrupts their shadow manipulation.
- Use full-spectrum flashlights to illuminate the Boogeyman's form, driving it towards areas where you have prepared traps, such as a corner lined with Boogie Goo or a mirror trap.

4. Employ the Temporalfudge Device: Creating the Perfect Moment

The slight hindrance in the Boogeyman's movement during a full moon makes it more susceptible to the effects of the **Temporalfudge Device**. By slowing down time within a specific area, you create the perfect moment to capture and contain the creature.

How to Execute:

- Wait for the Boogeyman to manifest fully, either in the moonlight or shadows. Activate the Temporalfudge Device to slow its movements, allowing you to approach with shadow nets or a mirror trap.
- Once the Boogeyman is within the device's temporal field, apply Boogie Goo directly to its form or the ground around it, ensuring that it cannot escape.

5. Safeguard Yourself: Emotional Control and Anti-Fear Measures

The Boogeyman's ability to sense and exploit fear is at its peak during the full moon. Therefore, maintaining emotional control is paramount. Wear **anti-fear amulets** to shield your mind from the Boogeyman's influence, and keep a firm grip on your confidence.

How to Execute:

- Before beginning your full moon confrontation, meditate or perform a grounding ritual to center your emotions. Visualize a barrier of light surrounding you, reflecting the moon's purifying energy.
- Carry moonstone or obsidian amulets on your person, particularly around the chest or throat area, as these regions are sensitive to psychic influence. This will help you resist the Boogeyman's attempts to induce fear or panic during the encounter.

Post-Capture Protocol: Securing the Boogeyman

After successfully trapping the Boogeyman during a full moon, it is essential to follow a secure **post-capture protocol** to prevent its escape:

1. **Seal with Boogie Goo:** Apply a ring of Boogie Goo around the edges of the capture site, whether it's a mirror, crystal jar, or a physical space like a closet. This prevents the Boogeyman from phasing through gaps or using its shadow manipulation to slip away.
2. **Store in Moonlight-Protected Containers:** Transfer the captured Boogeyman into a **moonlight-protected container**, such as a crystal jar lined with moonstone and silver. The jar should be inscribed with binding runes and stored in a dark, secure location.
3. **Cleanse the Area:** Perform a **sage burning** or use a **sound cleansing ritual** with bells or chimes to purify the area where the capture took place. This removes any residual fear energy and disrupts the Boogeyman's influence on the space.

Conclusion: Embracing the Full Moon's Power

The full moon is a time of opportunity in the Boogie Safari world. While it grants the Boogeyman enhanced abilities, it also provides you with the chance to confront it at its most tangible. By understanding the interplay of light, shadow, and fear during the full moon, you can turn the creature's boldness against it and successfully trap and contain it.

In the chapters ahead, we will explore more advanced methods for studying Boogeymen once they have been captured and how to use this knowledge to further safeguard your environment. Armed with your tools and strategies, the full moon becomes not a time to fear, but a time to strike against the shadows lurking in your midst.

Chapter 13: The Perfect Trap: How to Lure a Boogeyman

Boogeymen are elusive and intelligent creatures that thrive on fear and darkness, making them challenging to capture. They are masters of stealth and deception, capable of evading most conventional means of detection and capture. However, with a strategic approach and the right **lures** and **traps**, you can draw a Boogeyman out of hiding and into your carefully prepared trap. This chapter provides a comprehensive guide to setting up the **perfect lure**—from creating convincing decoys to using fear-bait techniques that tempt the Boogeyman to reveal itself.

Understanding Boogeyman Behavior: The Key to a Successful Lure

Boogeymen are drawn to specific stimuli, particularly fear, darkness, and the perception of vulnerable prey. However, they are also cautious and will quickly retreat if they sense a threat. To lure a Boogeyman effectively, you must strike a balance between **attraction** and **deception**: the lure needs to be enticing enough to provoke the creature's curiosity while masking the danger of the trap itself. Understanding these motivations and weaknesses is the first step in setting up a successful lure.

Setting Up the Perfect Trap: Types of Lures and Baits

Different strategies work best depending on the type of Boogeyman you're dealing with, its hiding spot, and the environment in which you're setting the trap. Here are the most effective methods for luring Boogeymen into a trap:

1. Decoy Traps: Creating Illusions of Vulnerability

Boogeymen are particularly attracted to signs of life, movement, and the perception of vulnerability. **Decoy traps** are designed to exploit this attraction by creating an illusion that the Boogeyman cannot resist. These traps simulate the presence of a target—typically a child or animal—enticing the Boogeyman to come out of hiding.

Sound-Based Decoys

Boogeymen are highly sensitive to sound, especially those associated with fear, anxiety, or distress. **Sound-based decoys** use recorded noises to mimic the sounds that typically attract Boogeymen, such as a child crying, whispering, or the creaking of a door.

- **How to Set Up:** Position a small speaker in a concealed location near where you suspect the Boogeyman is hiding, such as under a bed, in a closet, or in the attic. Select sounds that resonate with common fears: soft sobbing, faint whispers, or footsteps pacing back and forth. Adjust the volume to be just audible enough to make the Boogeyman think it has found an ideal target.
- **Trap Mechanism:** Surround the speaker with a **circle of salt** mixed with **ground obsidian** to act as a containment field. Place **shadow nets** or **Boogie Goo** around the perimeter to ensnare the Boogeyman when it moves in to investigate the sound. The decoy noise will lure the creature into the trap, while the salt barrier and nets will keep it contained.

Movement-Based Decoys

Boogeymen are drawn to movement, especially when it appears unguarded or vulnerable. **Movement-based decoys** simulate natural, lifelike motions that suggest the presence of a potential victim.

- **How to Set Up:** Use **motorized dolls**, **stuffed animals**, or **puppets** that can twitch, sway, or move slightly. For example, a doll with a head that turns slowly or a toy animal that rocks back and forth creates the illusion of life. Set these decoys near common Boogeyman hiding spots, such as at the foot of a bed or by an open closet door.
- **Trap Mechanism:** Apply **Boogie Goo** directly around the base of the decoy, covering the area where the Boogeyman is likely to reach out to touch or interact with it. Additionally, place **motion-activated lights** nearby to flood the area with sudden brightness when movement is detected, startling the Boogeyman and trapping it in place.

2. Fear-Bait Traps: Exploiting the Boogeyman's Hunger for Fear

Boogeymen are drawn to fear like moths to a flame, feeding off the emotional energy of their surroundings. **Fear-bait traps** are designed to simulate an environment rich in fear, tempting the Boogeyman to approach in search of sustenance.

Emotional Decoys

Fear-bait traps work best when there is an actual emotional element involved, such as a person acting as an **emotional decoy**. This strategy requires careful control over the participant's emotions to avoid overwhelming them.

- **How to Set Up:** Choose a participant who can simulate fear convincingly. They should sit or lie in a vulnerable position—on a bed, in a chair, or on the floor near a closet. The participant should express signs of fear, such as trembling, soft sobbing, or muttering phrases like "I'm scared." The Boogeyman, sensing this outpouring of fear, will be lured out to investigate and feed on it.
- **Trap Mechanism:** Before beginning, surround the participant with a **protective ring** of **salt and moonstone** to keep them safe. Place **shadow nets** just beyond this ring and have **Boogie Goo** ready to deploy. As the Boogeyman moves toward the participant, trigger the nets to ensnare it while keeping the decoy protected within the salt barrier.

Artificial Fear

If using a live decoy is not an option, artificial fear-baiting can be just as effective. This method involves creating an environment that radiates fear without requiring an actual emotional state.

- **How to Set Up:** Use **sound decoys, strobe lights,** and **distorted mirrors** to create an unsettling atmosphere in the room. Strobe lights mimic the sporadic flashes of movement that Boogeymen find appealing, while distorted mirrors create visual disorientation. Set up sound decoys to emit random, eerie noises at irregular intervals.
- **Trap Mechanism:** Coat the floor near the mirrors and sound devices with a thin layer of **Boogie Goo**, ensuring it covers the space where the Boogeyman is most likely to step. Place **motion sensors** linked to **ultrasonic alarms** around the room to detect the creature's approach. When it steps into the goo, activate the alarm to further disorient it and seal its movement.

3. Environmental Traps: Manipulating Space and Light

Boogeymen are adept at using darkness and shadows to their advantage, but with the right techniques, you can **manipulate the environment** to turn these elements against them.

Shadow Corridors

Boogeymen often travel through shadows, moving between darkened spaces like a network of pathways. By creating **shadow corridors**, you can funnel the creature toward a trap.

- **How to Set Up:** Use **candles, lanterns,** and **mirrors** to create a path of alternating light and shadow in a room. Place candles in strategic locations to form narrow corridors of darkness leading to a focal point where you have set up the trap.
- **Trap Mechanism:** At the endpoint of the corridor, place a **mirror trap** inscribed with containment sigils. Apply **Boogie Goo** around the base of the mirror to prevent the Boogeyman from escaping once it approaches. As the creature moves through the shadow corridor, it will be funneled toward the mirror, lured by the illusion of a safe hiding place. When it steps into the goo, the mirror trap activates, capturing its reflection and containing it within the glass.

Light Bait

Boogeymen avoid direct light, but their curiosity can sometimes override their caution if the light source appears dim or unstable.

- **How to Set Up:** Use a **flickering flashlight** or a **dim lantern** as bait. Place the light in an area known for Boogeyman activity, such as the corner of a basement or the edge of a bed. The Boogeyman, intrigued by the unstable light source, will move closer to investigate.
- **Trap Mechanism:** Surround the light with **Boogie Goo** and **motion-activated nets**. When the Boogeyman steps into the light to investigate, the motion-activated nets will spring into place, ensnaring the creature while the goo binds its shadowy form to the ground.

4. Combining Traps for Maximum Effectiveness

The most effective way to lure and trap a Boogeyman is to **combine multiple lures and traps** into a single, cohesive strategy. For example, use sound decoys to draw the Boogeyman out, shadow corridors to guide it toward a specific location, and Boogie Goo to ensnare it once it reaches the endpoint. By layering these techniques, you reduce the creature's options for escape and increase the likelihood of a successful capture.

Final Tips for a Successful Lure

1. **Be Patient:** Boogeymen are cautious and will often circle around a lure multiple times before approaching. Stay patient and maintain the illusion of vulnerability without revealing the trap too early.
2. **Stay Calm:** Remember that Boogeymen can sense fear. If you are acting as a decoy or present during the lure, keep your emotions in check. Use **anti-fear amulets** to shield yourself from the creature's influence.
3. **Pre-Set Traps:** Ensure all traps, including shadow nets, mirror traps, and Boogie Goo, are in place before activating the lure. Once the Boogeyman starts to approach, you may not have time to set traps without alerting it to the danger.

Conclusion: Mastering the Art of the Lure

Luring a Boogeyman is an art that requires a combination of strategy, patience, and an understanding of the creature's psychology. By using **decoy traps, fear-bait**, and **environmental manipulation**, you can tempt the Boogeyman into revealing itself, providing the perfect opportunity for capture. In the following chapters, we will explore the next steps: how to contain a captured Boogeyman and what to do once it is securely trapped. With the knowledge gained in this chapter, you are now equipped to set the perfect lure and turn the tables on these shadowy entities.

Chapter 14: Containment Strategies: How to Keep One Under Control

Catching a Boogeyman is a significant accomplishment, but the real challenge lies in **containing** it. These shadowy entities are notorious for their ability to slip through cracks, escape from the most well-guarded traps, and return to their lurking, fear-inducing habits. To ensure a captured Boogeyman remains **secure**, you must employ a combination of physical, mystical, and psychological containment strategies tailored to its nature. This chapter provides an in-depth look at the various methods for keeping a Boogeyman under control, from **containment cubes** and **mystical seals** to **maintenance rituals** that ensure the trap remains effective over time.

Understanding the Nature of Containment

Boogeymen are inherently ethereal creatures that exist on the edge of our reality. Their essence is tied to shadows, darkness, and fear, giving them an uncanny ability to manipulate their environment. To contain a Boogeyman successfully, you must use methods that target its **shadowy form**, disrupt its **manipulative powers**, and **seal** it within a designated space where it cannot exert its influence.

When choosing a containment strategy, consider the **type of Boogeyman** and its behaviors. Some are stronger and more adept at escaping than others, so a more complex, layered approach may be necessary. Regardless of the method used, constant vigilance is crucial, as Boogeymen will seize any opportunity to escape their confines.

1. Physical Containment: Specialized Containment Cubes

Physical containment is the first line of defense against a captured Boogeyman. **Containment cubes** are specially designed containers that trap the Boogeyman's essence within a defined space, preventing it from slipping through shadows or phasing into alternate dimensions.

Building a Containment Cube

A containment cube is constructed using materials that inherently disrupt a Boogeyman's ability to manipulate shadows and escape. The process of building a cube requires precision and specific materials to create an unbreakable prison.

Materials Needed:

- **Obsidian Panels:** Four panels of obsidian to form the cube's walls. Obsidian absorbs negative energy and blocks ethereal forms from passing through. The panels should be cut to exact dimensions (at least 12x12 inches each) and polished to a reflective finish.
- **Silver Edging:** Silver is known for its purifying properties. Edge the corners and seams of the cube with **silver strips** to reinforce the containment and reflect the Boogeyman's energy back into the cube, preventing it from exerting its influence outward.

- **Lid and Base:** The lid and base of the cube should be crafted from **hardened glass** infused with moonstone dust. The glass allows for observation of the entity while the moonstone stabilizes the cube's energy, making it harder for the Boogeyman to disrupt.

Assembly:

1. **Carve Runes:** Before assembling the cube, carve **binding runes** into the obsidian panels using a silver-tipped engraving tool. The runes should represent concepts of containment, silence, and protection. This step infuses the cube with protective magic.
2. **Construct the Cube:** Assemble the panels, securing the edges with silver strips. Seal the base to the cube using a mixture of **Boogie Goo** and powdered iron. The Boogie Goo creates a sticky, impervious bond, while the iron disrupts the Boogeyman's attempts to phase through the seams.
3. **Attach the Lid:** The lid should be removable but snug. Coat its edges with Boogie Goo and silver powder before sealing it shut. This ensures that, once closed, the cube becomes an impenetrable barrier.

Using the Containment Cube

To transfer a captured Boogeyman into the cube, use **shadow nets** or a **mirror trap** to guide the creature toward the open lid. Once it is inside, close the lid immediately, sealing it with Boogie Goo along the edges. The reflective obsidian surfaces will contain its form, while the runes and silver reinforce the prison.

2. Mystical Seals: Binding the Boogeyman's Essence

Mystical containment is equally important, as it prevents the Boogeyman from using its ethereal powers to manipulate its surroundings or slip away. **Mystical seals** are inscribed symbols and barriers that reinforce the physical container, binding the creature's essence and blocking its escape.

Creating Mystical Seals

Mystical seals require careful inscription of ancient symbols that resonate with binding and protective energies. These seals act as a metaphysical lock, suppressing the Boogeyman's abilities and securing it within the containment cube.

Materials Needed:

- **Silver Ink:** A mixture of powdered silver, sage ash, and moonstone dust. Silver ink is used to draw the seals directly onto the surface of the containment cube or surrounding area.
- **Parchment Paper:** To inscribe supplementary seals that can be placed around the cube for added protection.
- **Binding Runes:** Use ancient symbols associated with containment, suppression, and stillness. Recommended runes include the Norse **Algiz** (protection) and **Isa** (stillness) to halt the Boogeyman's movements.

Application:

1. **Inscribe the Cube:** Use a brush dipped in silver ink to paint binding runes onto each side of the containment cube. Focus on the corners and edges, as these are the weak points through which the Boogeyman might attempt to escape.
2. **Set Up a Protective Circle:** If possible, place the containment cube within a **protective circle** inscribed on the floor. Use chalk mixed with powdered moonstone to draw a circle around the cube. Add additional runes around the perimeter to reinforce the barrier.
3. **Seal the Cube:** Once the Boogeyman is inside the cube, use a drop of **binding oil** (a blend of frankincense, myrrh, and cedarwood) on each of the four corners of the lid. This final step locks the mystical seals into place, ensuring that the Boogeyman cannot disrupt the containment.

Recharging Mystical Seals

Mystical seals gradually weaken over time as the Boogeyman exerts pressure against them. To maintain their effectiveness, you must **recharge** the seals regularly:

- **Full Moon Rituals:** Every full moon, place the containment cube under direct moonlight. This recharges the moonstone-infused glass and enhances the power of the runes.
- **Smoke Cleansing:** Burn sage or frankincense near the cube to cleanse the area and reinforce the protective energy of the seals. Direct the smoke toward the seals to purify and strengthen them.

3. Environmental Controls: Setting Up a Containment Space

In addition to physical and mystical containment, you must also control the **environment** surrounding the Boogeyman's prison to prevent escape. The containment space should be designed to isolate the creature and disrupt its natural abilities.

Choosing the Containment Space

- **Location:** Choose a secluded area, such as a **basement**, **attic**, or a **warded room** with limited access. The room should be free of windows or large mirrors, as these can serve as portals through which the Boogeyman might attempt to escape.
- **Lighting:** Maintain **dim, consistent lighting** within the containment space. Avoid complete darkness, as Boogeymen gain strength and mobility in total shadow. The light should not be too bright, however, as the Boogeyman may become agitated and attempt to break free.
- **Salt Barriers:** Create **salt barriers** around the perimeter of the room and the base of the containment cube. Salt purifies and neutralizes the Boogeyman's energy, preventing it from manipulating its surroundings.

Monitoring the Containment Space

- **Sound Traps:** Set up **sound traps** near the containment cube to alert you of any attempts at escape. These traps emit ultrasonic pulses that resonate with the cube's walls, creating a reverberating hum when the Boogeyman tries to breach its prison.
- **Temperature Sensors:** Install **temperature sensors** in the room. Sudden drops in temperature often indicate that the Boogeyman is gathering energy to escape. If this occurs, reinforce the mystical seals and ensure all physical containment measures are intact.

4. Maintenance Rituals: Keeping the Boogeyman Secure

Boogeymen are relentless in their attempts to escape. To keep one under control, you must perform regular maintenance rituals to strengthen the containment and address any signs of weakening.

Weekly Binding Rituals

- **Smudging:** Use a smudging stick made of **sage, cedar, and lavender** to cleanse the containment space and the cube itself. This removes residual negative energy that the Boogeyman may have accumulated.
- **Rune Repainting:** Examine the cube's runes weekly. If any appear faded or disrupted, repaint them using the silver ink mixture. This ensures that the mystical barriers remain strong and active.

Monthly Full Moon Recharging

- **Moonlight Bath:** Place the cube in a **moonlight bath** (a circle of moonstone crystals) under direct moonlight for several hours. This recharges the moonstone dust and silver seals, reinforcing the Boogeyman's prison.
- **Incantation:** Recite an **incantation** while the cube is in the moonlight bath to renew the binding. A simple yet effective incantation is:
  "By moon's bright light and runes' old might, I bind thee still, 'neath silver's will."
  Repeat this three times while focusing on reinforcing the containment.

Conclusion: Securing the Shadows

Containing a Boogeyman requires a comprehensive strategy that addresses both its physical and ethereal nature. By employing **containment cubes, mystical seals, environmental controls**, and **maintenance rituals**, you create a multi-layered prison that keeps the Boogeyman securely trapped. Vigilance is key; regularly inspect and reinforce the containment measures to prevent escape. In the following chapters, we will explore how to study a captured Boogeyman safely and how to use this knowledge to further protect your environment from future incursions. With these containment strategies mastered, you are now ready to keep even the most cunning Boogeyman under control.

Chapter 15: Boogeyman Containment Units: How They Work

Capturing a Boogeyman is only half the battle; keeping it securely contained is where the real skill of a Boogey Hunter shines. While traditional methods like containment cubes and mystical seals are effective, expert hunters often rely on more advanced and sophisticated **containment units** tailored to the specific traits of Boogeymen. These units range from **enchanted boxes** to **pocket dimensions**, each designed to create an environment that neutralizes the Boogeyman's abilities and keeps it imprisoned indefinitely.

In this chapter, we will delve into the various types of containment units used by professional Boogey Hunters. We will explore their construction, functionality, and the unique properties that make them effective against different kinds of Boogeymen. By understanding these specialized units, you can select the best method for long-term containment based on your needs and the nature of the Boogeyman you've captured.

Understanding Containment Units: Controlling the Uncontrollable

Boogeymen are supernatural entities with the ability to **phase through shadows**, **manipulate space**, and **draw strength from fear**. These abilities make simple containment methods, like traditional boxes or cages, insufficient for long-term imprisonment. Specialized containment units are crafted using a blend of **arcane knowledge**, **alchemical materials**, and **dimensional magic** to create barriers that Boogeymen cannot penetrate. The essence of these units lies in their capacity to not only physically contain the creature but also **disrupt its connection** to the elements it relies on for escape.

1. Enchanted Boxes: Traditional Yet Effective

Enchanted boxes are a classic form of Boogeyman containment used by hunters for centuries. While simple in appearance, these boxes are constructed using **ritualistic processes** that imbue them with potent magical properties. Enchanted boxes function by creating a **spiritual and physical lock** that prevents the Boogeyman from manipulating shadows or crossing into other dimensions.

Design and Construction of Enchanted Boxes

To build an enchanted box, a hunter must adhere to specific guidelines to ensure the box can withstand the Boogeyman's attempts to break free.

Materials Needed:

- **Ebony Wood:** Known for its density and spiritual protection properties, ebony wood forms the body of the box. The wood must be cut and shaped during a **new moon** to enhance its absorptive qualities.
- **Silver Lining:** The interior of the box is lined with **silver sheets** inscribed with binding runes. Silver's purifying properties weaken the Boogeyman's strength and prevent it from exerting its will on the box's structure.

- **Mirror Inlay:** Incorporate small **mirror shards** on the inner walls of the box. Boogeymen are trapped by reflections, and these mirror shards create a fragmented reality within the box that confuses and disorients the creature.
- **Runic Inscriptions:** The exterior of the box is carved with ancient **binding runes** using a silver-tipped stylus. These runes form a magical barrier, preventing the Boogeyman from phasing through the wood.

Construction Process:

1. **Prepare the Wood:** Cut and sand the ebony wood panels to form a cube with an airtight lid. Before assembly, soak the wood in a **saltwater bath** mixed with powdered moonstone to infuse it with protective properties.
2. **Line the Interior:** Affix the silver sheets to the inner walls of the box. In the center of each sheet, place a small mirror shard, facing inward. These shards reflect the Boogeyman's image, trapping it in a maze of reflections.
3. **Carve the Runes:** Using the silver-tipped stylus, carve runes around the exterior. Focus on symbols representing **containment**, **silence**, and **binding**. To complete the enchantment, coat the runes with a mixture of **boogie oil** (frankincense, cedarwood, and myrrh) to seal in the magic.
4. **Inscription Ritual:** Once the box is assembled, perform a ritual under the light of a **full moon**, invoking protective spirits and sealing the box's energy. Place a drop of **blood** (yours or another consenting party) on the lid to form a life-bond, ensuring the Boogeyman cannot break the enchantment without harming itself.

How Enchanted Boxes Work

Enchanted boxes function by creating a **multi-layered barrier** that isolates the Boogeyman from the elements it relies on:

- The **ebony wood** absorbs and contains its energy, making it difficult for the Boogeyman to sense the outside world.
- The **silver lining** disrupts its ability to phase through shadows, as silver reflects light and repels dark energy.
- The **mirror inlay** confuses the creature, trapping it in a fragmented reflection of itself, making it unable to focus its power for an escape.
- The **runic inscriptions** act as a metaphysical lock, binding the Boogeyman's essence to the box and preventing it from utilizing its dimensional abilities.

Maintenance: Enchanted boxes require regular **recharging**. Every full moon, place the box in a **circle of salt** and recite a binding incantation to strengthen its hold. This keeps the magical properties active and prevents the runes from weakening.

2. Pocket Dimensions: The Ultimate Containment Unit

For particularly powerful Boogeymen or those that have proven adept at escaping physical containment, **pocket dimensions** offer the most secure form of imprisonment. A pocket dimension is a small, self-contained realm created using **advanced magical rituals** and **dimensional manipulation**. Once a Boogeyman is placed inside, it is isolated from both our reality and the Boogie World, effectively trapping it in a timeless, empty space.

Creating a Pocket Dimension

Crafting a pocket dimension is a complex process that requires extensive knowledge of **dimensional magic** and **arcane geometry**. The entry point to the pocket dimension is usually housed within a **dimensional box** or orb.

Materials Needed:

- **Crystal Orb or Gem:** A **clear quartz crystal orb** serves as the focal point for the pocket dimension. It must be flawlessly cut, as any imperfections could create weak points in the dimensional boundary.
- **Dimensional Fabric Weave:** A specially enchanted cloth woven with **moon silk** and **ether thread**. This fabric forms the outer shell of the pocket dimension, reinforcing its structure.
- **Binding Runes:** Inscribe binding runes on the crystal using **liquid silver** mixed with **dragon's blood resin** to anchor the dimensional energy.
- **Dimensional Key:** A **small, inscribed key** crafted from **meteorite iron**. This key is used to open and close the pocket dimension, allowing access only when necessary.

Creation Process:

1. **Prepare the Orb:** Cleanse the quartz orb with a **moonlight bath** to purify it and clear it of any residual energy. Then, inscribe the surface with **binding runes** using a fine brush dipped in the silver and resin mixture.
2. **Weave the Fabric:** Enchant the **dimensional fabric weave** by sewing it with incantations under the light of a waxing crescent moon. This process binds the fabric to the concept of dimensional stability, preventing the pocket dimension from collapsing or shifting.
3. **Ritual of Creation:** In a secluded, warded space, lay out the dimensional fabric in a circle. Place the orb in the center and perform the **Ritual of Creation**—a series of incantations and sigil drawings that will open the doorway to the pocket dimension within the orb. Visualize a space that is dark, silent, and endless, where the Boogeyman will be unable to interact with any external energy.
4. **Sealing the Orb:** Once the ritual is complete, seal the orb using the **dimensional key**. This key becomes the only means of opening the pocket dimension, ensuring that the Boogeyman remains trapped within its confines.

How Pocket Dimensions Work

A pocket dimension functions by **isolating** the Boogeyman from all external influences:

- Inside the pocket dimension, **time and space are suspended**, leaving the Boogeyman in a state of perpetual limbo. This prevents it from drawing strength from fear or darkness, rendering it powerless.
- The **dimensional fabric** forms an impenetrable boundary that the Boogeyman cannot cross. Any attempt to escape will be absorbed by the fabric and redirected into the infinite void.
- The **crystal orb** acts as a conduit, anchoring the pocket dimension to our reality while keeping it separate. The runes on the orb lock the Boogeyman inside, and only the **dimensional key** can release it.

Maintenance: Pocket dimensions require minimal maintenance. However, inspect the **crystal orb** periodically for cracks or blemishes, as these can weaken the dimensional boundary. Reapply the silver and resin mixture to the runes if they begin to fade.

3. Portable Containment: Enchanted Pouches and Jars

For temporary containment or transport, hunters often use **enchanted pouches** or **sealed jars**. These units are not intended for long-term imprisonment but can securely hold a Boogeyman during the transfer to a more permanent containment unit.

Enchanted Pouches

An **enchanted pouch** is a small bag made from **shadow silk**—a rare fabric that absorbs dark energy and nullifies shadow-based powers. The pouch is lined with **salt crystals** and **iron dust**, creating a barrier that the Boogeyman cannot phase through.

- **How It Works:** The pouch's material absorbs the Boogeyman's ethereal energy, while the salt and iron disrupt its ability to manipulate shadows. Drawstrings, embroidered with binding runes, seal the pouch shut, trapping the Boogeyman inside.
- **Usage:** Enchanted pouches are ideal for short-term containment when transferring the Boogeyman between different locations or units.

Sealed Jars

Sealed jars made of **obsidian glass** serve as temporary containment units for particularly small or weakened Boogeymen. The jars are sealed with a **lid inscribed with protective runes** and coated with **Boogie Goo** to prevent the creature from slipping through cracks.

- **How It Works:** The obsidian glass absorbs negative energy, while the sealed lid traps the Boogeyman's form. The internal darkness of the jar creates a space where the creature remains disoriented and unable to focus its power for escape.

Conclusion: The Art of Imprisonment

Containment units are the cornerstone of effective Boogeyman capture and control. Whether using a **classic enchanted box**, a **pocket dimension**, or a **portable enchanted pouch**, each unit is designed to address the Boogeyman's unique traits and abilities. By mastering these containment strategies, you ensure that once a Boogeyman is captured, it stays securely imprisoned, unable to continue its haunting activities. The following chapters will explore how to study a contained Boogeyman and use this knowledge to fortify your defenses against future encounters. With these advanced containment methods in your arsenal, you are well-equipped to keep even the most cunning Boogeyman under control.

Part 5: *Navigating the Boogie World*

Chapter 16: Crossing Over: Entering the Boogie Dimension

To truly understand the Boogeymen and their nature, sometimes a hunter must take the ultimate risk: **crossing over into the Boogie World** itself. This shadowy realm exists on a different plane of reality, an ever-shifting labyrinth of darkness, fear, and the distorted essence of nightmares. Navigating this dimension is fraught with dangers, as it is not only home to Boogeymen but is also a place where the laws of reality bend and break. Entering the Boogie World requires careful preparation, protective rituals, and knowledge of how to return safely to our realm.

In this chapter, you will learn the step-by-step process for **crossing over into the Boogie World**, including the **rituals** required to open a gateway, the **spells** to protect you while inside, and the methods for finding your way back. These instructions should not be undertaken lightly; even the most experienced hunters face great peril when venturing into this dark dimension.

Understanding the Boogie World: The Realm of Shadows

The **Boogie World** is a **dimensional plane** that exists parallel to our reality. It is a place where shadows dominate, and time and space are fluid. In this world, fear becomes tangible, taking on forms that can trap or even consume the unprepared. The Boogie World is not bound by the physical laws of our universe; distances can stretch infinitely, and paths often loop back on themselves. To navigate this realm, you must rely not on your senses but on your intuition, instincts, and the protective spells that keep you anchored to reality.

Entering the Boogie World is dangerous, as the moment you step into it, you become a target for the creatures that inhabit it. Therefore, every hunter must arm themselves with **rituals**, **spells**, and **protective gear** to survive and return unscathed.

1. Preparing for the Journey: Tools and Gear

Before attempting to cross into the Boogie World, you must gather specific items to aid you in your journey and protect you from the dangers within.

Essential Items for Crossing Over:

- **Mirror Portal:** A **full-length mirror** is required to serve as the portal between our world and the Boogie World. It must be cleansed with moonwater and sage smoke before use. The mirror's frame should be adorned with protective runes carved into its surface using a silver stylus.
- **Moonstone Amulet:** Wear a **moonstone amulet** around your neck to keep your essence anchored to our world. Moonstone resonates with the lunar energy that bridges dimensions, helping you maintain a sense of direction and reality within the Boogie World.
- **Salt and Iron Powder:** A **pouch of salt mixed with powdered iron** serves as both a protective ward and a way to create temporary barriers in the Boogie World. This mixture disrupts the energy of Boogeymen and can provide you with a few moments of safety if surrounded.
- **Binding Oil:** A vial of **binding oil** (a blend of frankincense, cedarwood, and myrrh) can be used to anoint objects or draw protective sigils on the ground.

- **Ritual Dagger:** A **ritual dagger** made of silver is essential for carving runes and symbols into surfaces in the Boogie World to create protective zones or to initiate the return ritual.
- **Protective Cloak:** A **cloak woven from shadow silk** is crucial. Shadow silk repels the dark energies of the Boogie World, providing you with a buffer against direct attacks from Boogeymen.

2. The Crossing Ritual: Opening the Portal

The Boogie World cannot be accessed through physical means alone. To cross over, you must perform a **ritual** that opens a gateway in a **mirror**, which serves as the entry point to the dimension. This ritual requires concentration, focus, and the right incantations.

Steps to Perform the Crossing Ritual:

1. **Prepare the Mirror:** Begin by placing the mirror in a darkened room. Use sage smoke to cleanse the mirror, removing any residual energy that might interfere with the portal's formation. Carve protective runes along the mirror's frame using the silver stylus. The recommended runes include **Algiz** (protection) and **Ehwaz** (journey) to guard against danger and ensure a safe crossing.
2. **Create the Protection Circle:** Surround the mirror with a **circle of salt and iron powder**. This circle acts as a barrier, keeping the energies of the Boogie World contained and preventing them from spilling into our reality. Stand inside the circle with the mirror.
3. **Anoint the Mirror:** Using the binding oil, anoint the four corners of the mirror. This anointing marks the mirror as a threshold between worlds, activating its latent properties as a dimensional bridge.
4. **Recite the Incantation:** Hold your moonstone amulet and face the mirror. Recite the following incantation to open the portal:
   "By shadow's edge and moon's bright grace,
   Open the path to the darkened place.
   Mirror's veil, thin as night,
   Show the way, grant me sight."
   As you speak these words, focus on your reflection, visualizing it becoming a doorway into darkness.
5. **Enter the Mirror:** If performed correctly, the surface of the mirror will ripple like water, signaling the opening of the portal. Step forward with one hand outstretched. The mirror will yield, and you will feel a cold sensation as you pass through the barrier into the Boogie World.

3. Navigating the Boogie World: Survival and Protection Spells

Once inside the Boogie World, you must remain vigilant. The environment will be disorienting, with paths that twist and turn, shadows that move on their own, and echoes of fear that try to cloud your mind. The following spells and techniques are essential for survival:

Protective Spells

- **Light of the Moon Spell:** The darkness in the Boogie World is oppressive and seeks to consume all light. To counter this, cast the **Light of the Moon Spell** to create a small aura of light around you. Hold your moonstone amulet and chant:
  "By moon's soft glow, by silver's gleam,
  Keep the darkness from my dream."
  This spell creates a protective bubble of light that repels shadows, providing you with a clear space to move and think.
- **Binding Barrier:** If a Boogeyman approaches, create a **binding barrier** using the salt and iron powder. Draw a circle on the ground around you while reciting:
  "Iron binds, salt repels,
  In this space, darkness dwells.
  Hold the line, firm and clear,
  No shadow may cross, nor come near."
  This barrier provides a temporary sanctuary, giving you time to plan your next move or prepare an escape.

Navigational Techniques

- **Follow the Echoes:** Sound behaves strangely in the Boogie World, often echoing from places that do not correspond to physical locations. Follow **echoes** that resonate with a low, steady hum; these typically lead to areas where the dimensional fabric is thinner and more stable, allowing for clearer navigation.
- **Avoid the Reflections:** The Boogie World is filled with reflective surfaces that can trap your essence if you look into them. Avoid staring into pools of liquid darkness or mirrored walls. Instead, use your moonstone amulet to sense the direction of safe passage.

4. The Return Ritual: Finding Your Way Back

Returning from the Boogie World is just as perilous as entering it. The longer you stay, the harder it becomes to find the portal and reestablish the connection to your reality.

Steps to Perform the Return Ritual:

1. **Find a Stable Location:** Locate an area where the shadows are less dense and the echoes are clearer. This indicates a point where the dimensional boundary is more permeable.
2. **Draw the Rune of Passage:** Use your ritual dagger to carve the **Rune of Passage** (Dagaz) into the ground or a nearby surface. This rune symbolizes the transition between states of being and will guide you back to the mirror portal.
3. **Recite the Incantation:** Stand within the carved rune and hold your moonstone amulet. Close your eyes and visualize the mirror you used as the portal. Recite the incantation:
   "By rune's edge and moonstone's light,
   Guide me back through shadowed night.
   Mirror's veil, take me home,
   From this world, no more to roam."
   Focus your mind on the image of the mirror until you feel a pull at your core.
4. **Cross Through:** Open your eyes. The mirror portal should appear before you, rippling like water. Step forward and pass through, back into your room. The sensation of coldness will fade as you re-enter our reality.
5. **Close the Portal:** Immediately upon returning, anoint the mirror with binding oil and use salt to draw a sealing rune (Isa) across its surface. This closes the gateway and prevents any lingering energy from crossing over.

5. Aftercare: Cleansing and Restoring Energy

Crossing into the Boogie World is taxing both physically and mentally. After your return, follow these steps to cleanse and restore your energy:

- **Sage Cleansing:** Burn sage to cleanse your aura and the area around the mirror. Walk through the smoke, allowing it to remove any residual negativity or darkness that may have followed you back.
- **Moonstone Recharging:** Place your moonstone amulet in a bowl of water mixed with salt and moonstone dust. Leave it overnight under the moonlight to recharge its protective properties.
- **Rest:** Rest for at least 24 hours after crossing over. The experience of the Boogie World drains energy and mental fortitude, making recovery essential.

Conclusion: Venturing Into the Unknown

Crossing into the Boogie World is a journey not to be undertaken lightly. It requires meticulous preparation, a deep understanding of protective spells, and the courage to navigate a realm where fear takes on physical form. By following the rituals and using the protective items described in this chapter, you can safely venture into the Boogie World and return with valuable knowledge about its inhabitants. The chapters that follow will explore the insights gained from such journeys and how they can aid in fortifying defenses against Boogeymen in our world. Armed with these skills, you now possess the means to confront the darkness on its own terms.

Chapter 17: A Map of the Boogie World

The **Boogie World** is a realm of shadows, fear, and illusion, where the usual rules of space and time twist into something dark and unpredictable. This ever-shifting dimension is vast, and its geography reflects the nightmares and anxieties of our reality. While entering the Boogie World is a dangerous endeavor, knowing the **lay of the land** can significantly increase a hunter's chances of survival and successful navigation. This chapter serves as an **illustrated guide** to the various regions of the Boogie World, providing detailed descriptions of each area—from the **Closet Caves** to the **Underbed Abyss**—along with tips for traversing these terrains.

Mapping the Boogie World: An Overview

The Boogie World is divided into several **regions**, each with its unique characteristics and dangers. The boundaries between these regions are fluid, often changing based on the fears and emotions that fuel the Boogeymen. Nonetheless, certain landmarks remain relatively constant, serving as navigational beacons for those who dare to cross into this realm. Each region correlates with common areas where Boogeymen dwell in our reality, such as closets, under beds, and attics.

While there is no single definitive map of the Boogie World, hunters and explorers have pieced together a rough outline based on their experiences. Visualizing these regions can help you orient yourself within the realm and avoid the most perilous areas.

1. The Closet Caves

Description: The **Closet Caves** are a labyrinth of dark, twisting tunnels lined with jagged shadows that seem to breathe and move. This region corresponds with closets in the human world, where Boogeymen frequently lurk. The walls of the caves are covered in reflective surfaces that capture and amplify the fear energy emitted by those who pass through. The air here is thick, carrying whispers of past fears, which disorient and confuse intruders.

Features:

- **Echoing Chambers:** Large caverns within the Closet Caves resonate with echoes, making it difficult to discern the source of sounds. These chambers can trap explorers in loops of sound, leading them in circles.
- **Shadow Stalactites:** Long, dripping shadows hang from the ceilings, known as shadow stalactites. If touched, they drain energy and can cause vivid hallucinations.

Travel Tips:

- **Avoid Reflections:** The reflective surfaces on the cave walls can trap your image, creating distorted versions of yourself that may attack. Use a **moonstone amulet** to repel the reflections and disrupt their hold on your mind.
- **Sound Navigation:** Follow the sound of **steady, rhythmic drips**, as these often lead to exits. Avoid erratic noises, as they are usually traps designed to confuse.

2. The Underbed Abyss

Description: The **Underbed Abyss** is a vast, seemingly endless expanse of darkness that stretches out beneath a blanket of shadowy mist. This region represents the under-bed spaces in the human world, where Boogeymen hide and feed on the fears of those lying above. The ground here is soft and unstable, shifting with each step, threatening to pull travelers into its depths. The Abyss is also home to creatures known as **Fear Leeches**, which burrow into the darkness and latch onto those who show fear.

Features:

- **Mist Pools:** Pools of thick, black mist dot the landscape, exuding a cold that numbs the senses. These pools serve as portals that Boogeymen use to travel between the Boogie World and our reality.
- **Fear Leeches:** Small, slug-like creatures that sense fear and attach to travelers, sapping their strength and willpower. They are nearly invisible, detectable only by the faint trails of slime they leave behind.

Travel Tips:

- **Stay Moving:** The ground of the Abyss becomes more treacherous the longer you remain in one spot. Keep moving steadily to avoid being swallowed by the shifting darkness.
- **Use Salt:** Scatter **salt** in a circle around yourself if you need to stop. The salt will repel the Fear Leeches and temporarily solidify the ground beneath you.

3. The Attic Eyrie

Description: High above the Closet Caves and Underbed Abyss lies the **Attic Eyrie**, a region of the Boogie World that is cluttered with the spectral remnants of forgotten memories and discarded hopes. The atmosphere here is dense with nostalgia and the echoes of childhood fears. This area is reminiscent of the attics in old houses, filled with broken toys, cobwebs, and relics of the past. Light filters in through cracks, creating stark contrasts between blinding brightness and deep shadow.

Features:

- **Memory Shards:** Shattered pieces of forgotten memories litter the floor. When touched, these shards play out scenes from the past, distracting and ensnaring those who linger too long.
- **Cobweb Mazes:** Thick, sticky cobwebs stretch between ancient beams and rafters, forming mazes that trap the unwary. These webs can sense movement and tighten around those who struggle, making escape difficult.

Travel Tips:

- **Avoid the Light:** While the beams of light may seem like safe zones, they can burn and blind, leaving you vulnerable to attack. Instead, use **shadow silk cloth** to shield your eyes and navigate through the dimmer areas.
- **Ignore the Voices:** The Attic Eyrie is filled with the murmurs of forgotten dreams. These voices will attempt to lure you into dark corners or distract you from your path. Focus on your **moonstone amulet** to keep your mind clear.

4. The Mirror Halls

Description: The **Mirror Halls** are an unsettling maze of corridors lined with mirrors of various shapes and sizes. The mirrors do not reflect reality as we know it but instead show twisted, distorted images designed to evoke fear and uncertainty. This region serves as a hub of sorts, connecting to multiple other areas in the Boogie World. Boogeymen often use the mirrors as portals, stepping in and out to navigate the realm.

Features:

- **False Reflections:** Mirrors in this region display false images, often showing your worst fears or alternate versions of yourself. Some mirrors act as traps, imprisoning your reflection and preventing you from leaving.
- **Portal Mirrors:** Certain mirrors serve as doorways to other parts of the Boogie World or even back to our reality. Identifying these mirrors requires intuition and careful observation.

Travel Tips:

- **Mark Your Path:** Use **chalk mixed with moonstone dust** to mark the mirrors you pass. This helps avoid becoming lost in the maze and prevents you from stepping into a reflection trap.
- **Identify Portals:** Look for mirrors with a faint **silver glow**—these are often portal mirrors. Stand in front of them and hold your moonstone amulet to activate the gateway.

5. The Fear Fields

Description: The **Fear Fields** are open, desolate plains where fear itself grows like tall grass. This region emanates a constant hum of anxiety, and the air is thick with an unsettling tension. Every step through the fields heightens the sense of dread, making it harder to think clearly or move with purpose. This is where Boogeymen often come to harvest fear, cultivating it like crops.

Features:

- **Fear Stalks:** Tall, dark stalks rise from the ground, swaying in an invisible wind. When touched, they release a cloud of fear spores that induce hallucinations and panic.
- **Fear Harvesters:** Shadowy figures known as Fear Harvesters roam the fields, collecting fear to sustain the Boogeymen. These entities do not attack directly but can amplify your fears, making you vulnerable.

Travel Tips:

- **Stay Low:** Move through the Fear Fields in a crouched position to avoid disturbing the fear stalks. Use **binding oil** to anoint your feet, leaving a trail that repels the Fear Harvesters.
- **Mental Shields:** Constantly focus on positive, empowering thoughts. The Fear Fields feed on doubt and anxiety, so maintaining mental fortitude is key to passing through safely.

6. The Edge of the Void

Description: The **Edge of the Void** is the outermost boundary of the Boogie World, a region where darkness gives way to a swirling, infinite abyss. This area is in constant flux, with reality fraying at the edges. Strange lights dance in the distance, and the ground is unstable, breaking off into nothingness. It is said that the Edge of the Void is where the Boogeymen draw their power, tapping into the primordial fear of the unknown.

Features:

- **Rifts:** Cracks in the ground reveal glimpses of the Void below. Gazing into these rifts can pull at your consciousness, causing a sensation of falling into emptiness.
- **Whispering Winds:** The winds here carry whispers that seem to come from all directions, sowing seeds of doubt and fear.

Travel Tips:

- **Avoid the Rifts:** Do not approach or look directly into the rifts. Use **binding oil** to draw a circle around yourself if you need to rest, anchoring your presence to the spot.
- **Listen Closely:** The winds may carry clues to safe passage. Ignore the whispers of fear and listen for **steady, rhythmic tones**, which often indicate stable ground.

Conclusion: Navigating the Shadows

The Boogie World is a place of nightmares and shifting realities, where the geography itself seems to feed on fear and uncertainty. By familiarizing yourself with its regions—the Closet Caves, Underbed Abyss, Attic Eyrie, Mirror Halls, Fear Fields, and Edge of the Void—you equip yourself with the knowledge needed to navigate its treacherous terrain. Each area presents unique challenges, but with the right tools, spells, and mental fortitude, you can explore this dark realm and return to our world with invaluable insights. As you prepare for your next venture into the Boogie World, remember that the shadows are not your allies, but they can be understood and, ultimately, outmaneuvered.

THE SPOOKY JOURNEY BEGINS – | 85 |

Map of the Boogie World.

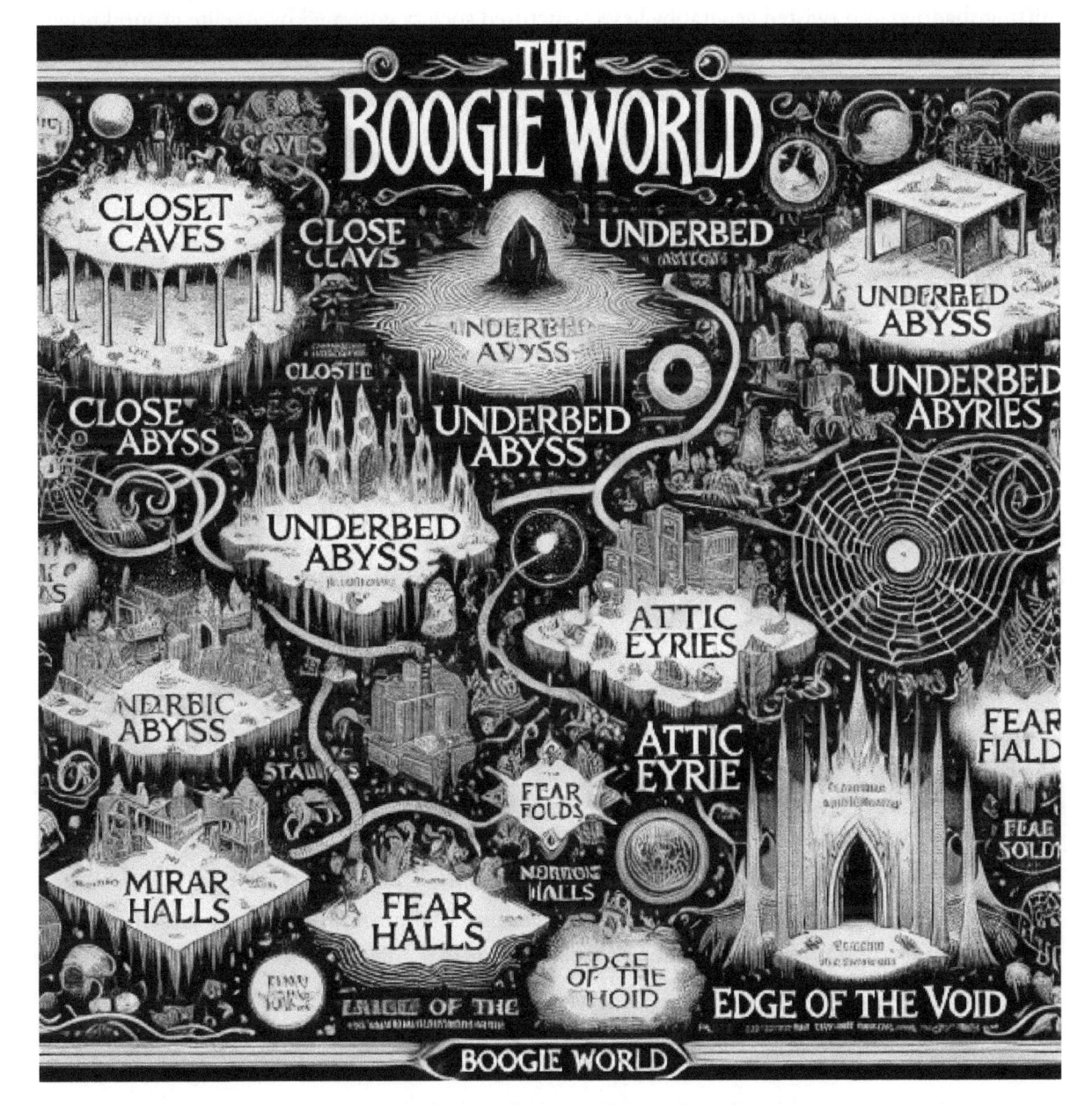

Chapter 18: The Council of Fear: Ruling Entities of the Boogie World

The **Boogie World** is not a chaotic, lawless realm as it might appear to outsiders. Beneath its shifting shadows and twisted geography lies a structured society governed by an elite group known as the **Council of Fear**. This council comprises the most powerful and ancient of the Boogeymen, entities that wield immense influence over different regions of the Boogie World. They maintain a fragile balance within this dimension, enforcing rules, overseeing the distribution of fear energy, and controlling the movements of lesser Boogeymen.

This chapter provides an in-depth guide to these ruling entities, their domains, abilities, and how they shape the landscape of the Boogie World. Understanding the **Council of Fear** is essential for any hunter daring to explore the Boogie World, as their presence often dictates the behavior of other Boogeymen and the shifting nature of the realm.

The Nature of the Council of Fear

The Council of Fear is a **loose alliance** of Boogeymen who have attained a level of power and knowledge far beyond that of typical entities. Each member of the council governs a specific **domain** within the Boogie World, their influence shaping the environment and the behavior of other Boogeymen within it. Despite their cooperation on the council, these ruling entities do not always work harmoniously; they are as prone to scheming and power struggles as any mortal rulers. However, they adhere to a set of ancient laws that keep the balance of the Boogie World intact.

Roles of the Council:

1. **Maintain Order:** The council ensures that lesser Boogeymen respect the boundaries between the Boogie World and the mortal realm, intervening when breaches threaten the stability of their dimension.
2. **Harvest and Distribute Fear:** They oversee the collection of **fear energy**, which sustains both the Boogie World and its inhabitants. This energy is channeled to maintain their territories, creating the eerie landscapes within their domains.
3. **Enforce Laws:** The Council of Fear enforces rules that govern the behavior of all Boogeymen, including prohibitions against revealing their true forms in the human world and the regulation of how they feed on fear.

Each member of the council has unique powers and attributes, reflective of the regions they control. Here, we explore the **five most prominent council members**, their domains, and the characteristics that make them formidable.

1. **Lord Grimsnare: Warden of the Closet Caves**

Description: Lord Grimsnare is the oldest member of the council and the ruler of the **Closet Caves**. He manifests as a gaunt, elongated figure draped in a cloak made of tattered darkness. His eyes glow with an eerie, pale light that pierces the gloom of his domain. Known for his keen intellect and merciless demeanor, Grimsnare embodies the fear of the unknown, hiding within dark closets, waiting to strike when least expected.

Abilities:

- **Shadow Melding:** Grimsnare can seamlessly meld into the shadows of the Closet Caves, becoming indistinguishable from the darkness around him. This makes him nearly impossible to detect until he chooses to reveal himself.
- **Fear Echoes:** He can manipulate the echoes within the caves, projecting the sound of footsteps, whispers, or laughter to confuse and disorient intruders. The echoes feed on fear, amplifying his power and allowing him to alter the cave's layout at will.

Influence: Grimsnare maintains strict control over the Closet Caves, overseeing the movements of lesser Boogeymen and ensuring the caves remain an endless, shifting labyrinth. His presence commands respect, and his decisions often dictate the actions of other council members.

Weakness: Despite his power, Grimsnare is vulnerable to **bright, direct light**, which can disrupt his shadow melding and force him into a physical form. Using **full-spectrum flashlights** or light-based incantations can weaken his hold over the Closet Caves.

2. Lady Umbragloom: Mistress of the Underbed Abyss

Description: **Lady Umbragloom** is the enigmatic ruler of the **Underbed Abyss**. Her form is amorphous, constantly shifting between a mass of writhing tendrils and a shadowy, ethereal silhouette. Her presence exudes a chilling coldness, and her voice echoes with the cries of countless nightmares. Lady Umbragloom represents the terror that hides beneath the safety of the bed, waiting to engulf those who dare to peer into the abyss.

Abilities:

- **Fear Leeches:** Lady Umbragloom commands the **Fear Leeches** of the Underbed Abyss, using them to siphon off the fear of those who venture too close. She can summon these creatures to overwhelm intruders, draining their willpower and energy.
- **Shifting Ground:** She controls the ground of the Abyss, making it undulate and shift beneath trespassers, throwing them off balance and dragging them deeper into the darkness.

Influence: Within the Underbed Abyss, Lady Umbragloom governs with an air of haunting mystery. She allows lesser Boogeymen to roam freely, provided they respect her domain and offer a portion of their harvested fear. Her influence extends to all under-bed spaces in the human world, marking them as portals to her domain.

Weakness: Lady Umbragloom's powers are disrupted by **purifying herbs**, such as sage and lavender. Carrying these herbs can repel her Fear Leeches and stabilize the shifting ground, providing a safe path through her territory.

3. The Shattered One: Overlord of the Mirror Halls

Description: The Shattered One is a fragmented entity, appearing as a collection of broken, reflective surfaces floating in a vaguely humanoid shape. His voice echoes from every direction within the **Mirror Halls**, often overlapping and creating a cacophony of whispers and laughter. He represents the fear of self-reflection and distorted reality, exploiting the insecurities of those who gaze into his mirrors.

Abilities:

- **Mirror Portals:** The Shattered One can open portals within any mirror, allowing him to traverse his domain instantly and appear wherever his influence is present.
- **False Reflections:** He can create **false reflections** of those who enter the Mirror Halls, manifesting their worst fears and insecurities. These reflections act independently, attacking the intruder both physically and psychologically.

Influence: The Shattered One controls all mirrors in the Boogie World, using them as gateways to the other regions. His power allows him to spy on intruders and council members alike, making him one of the most informed and manipulative members of the council.

Weakness: His fragmented nature makes him vulnerable to **sound-based disruptions**. Using **tuning forks** or harmonic chants can shatter his hold over the mirrors, forcing his reflections to dissipate temporarily.

4. Sir Noxus: Lord of the Attic Eyrie

Description: **Sir Noxus** takes on the appearance of an armored knight, cloaked in cobwebs and shadows, with eyes that glow like embers in the darkness. He carries an aura of authority and commands the **Attic Eyrie** as a place of forgotten fears and lingering memories. Sir Noxus embodies the dread of childhood relics and the forgotten traumas stored away in the corners of the mind.

Abilities:

- **Memory Shards:** Sir Noxus can manipulate the **Memory Shards** scattered throughout the Attic Eyrie, summoning them to play out scenes from an intruder's past. These shards can trap individuals in loops of nostalgia or fear.
- **Web Wards:** He can conjure webs to create barriers or ensnare those who attempt to navigate his domain. These webs sense emotions and tighten around those who struggle or show fear.

Influence: Sir Noxus commands respect among the lesser Boogeymen, particularly those who haunt attics and forgotten spaces. His domain is a place of secrets, and his knowledge of the past grants him leverage over other council members.

Weakness: The webs and memory traps of the Attic Eyrie can be cut using **silver blades** anointed with binding oil. Breaking free from these traps weakens Sir Noxus's control over his domain.

5. Wraithen: Guardian of the Edge of the Void

Description: **Wraithen** is the most elusive and terrifying of the council members. His form is indistinct, a constantly shifting mass of shadow and light with an ever-changing face. He guards the **Edge of the Void**, where reality frays, and the Boogie World meets the abyss of nothingness. Wraithen embodies the fear of the unknown and the existential dread that haunts all sentient beings.

Abilities:

- **Rift Manipulation:** Wraithen can open and close the rifts at the Edge of the Void, creating passages that lead to other regions or into the abyss itself. He uses these rifts to control the movement of other entities within the Boogie World.
- **Whispering Winds:** He commands the winds that blow across the Edge of the Void, using them to sow fear and doubt in the minds of intruders, pushing them toward the abyss.

Influence: Wraithen's authority extends to the boundaries of the Boogie World. He serves as the final gatekeeper, ensuring that only those who truly belong in the realm remain. His control over the rifts gives him leverage over the other council members, who rely on him to maintain the integrity of the Boogie World's boundaries.

Weakness: Wraithen is sensitive to **symbols of hope and light**, such as drawn runes representing the sun or life. Inscribing these symbols on the ground can repel him and force the rifts to close, securing a path away from the Edge of the Void.

Conclusion: The Council's Influence on the Boogie World

The **Council of Fear** shapes the Boogie World, dictating the flow of fear energy and the behavior of its inhabitants. By understanding these ruling entities—Lord Grimsnare, Lady Umbragloom, The Shattered One, Sir Noxus, and Wraithen—you gain crucial insights into the forces at work within this shadowy dimension. Knowledge of their abilities, domains, and weaknesses is vital for any hunter who ventures into the Boogie World. However, one must always proceed with caution; the council members are as cunning as they are powerful, and they will not hesitate to exploit the fears of those who challenge their dominion. In the chapters that follow, we will explore strategies for evading the council's gaze and navigating their territories without drawing their ire.

Chapter 19: Boogeymen Psychology: What They Fear

While Boogeymen are the embodiment of fear in the human world, they are not **fearless** themselves. In fact, their very existence within the **Boogie World** and their insidious activities in our realm are driven by deep-seated fears of their own. Understanding these fears is crucial for hunters seeking to exploit the weaknesses of Boogeymen during a hunt.

This chapter delves into the **psychology of Boogeymen**, exploring the fears that drive their actions, shape their behaviors, and, most importantly, reveal their vulnerabilities. By knowing what Boogeymen fear, hunters can turn the tables on these entities, using their own terror as a weapon to trap or repel them. We will discuss the most common fears shared by all Boogeymen, as well as the unique fears of specific types, providing techniques to exploit these weaknesses during encounters.

The Nature of Boogeyman Fear

Boogeymen, despite their fearsome nature, are **creatures of darkness** that have developed a variety of fears over centuries of existence. Their fear is not the primal, instinctual terror experienced by humans; instead, it is a deep-rooted **existential dread** tied to their identities, roles, and the fragile balance they maintain between the Boogie World and our reality.

Boogeymen draw power from fear but simultaneously despise the idea of losing their dominance and control over it. They exist in a state of **paradox**: they are both the hunters and the hunted within the intricate tapestry of fears they weave. Knowing and understanding this paradox provides a critical advantage when confronting them.

1. Common Fears of Boogeymen

All Boogeymen, regardless of their specific form or domain, share several fundamental fears. These fears are connected to the aspects of reality that threaten their very nature and existence. By identifying these fears, hunters can devise tactics to repel or trap Boogeymen during a hunt.

1.1 The Fear of Light and Revelation

Boogeymen thrive in darkness and shadows, hiding from direct scrutiny. They fear **light** because it reveals their true forms, stripping away the illusion and mystery that give them power. Light not only weakens their abilities but also confronts them with their own **insubstantial existence**. The brighter the light, the more exposed and vulnerable they become.

How to Exploit This Fear:

- **Full-Spectrum Flashlights:** During a hunt, use **full-spectrum flashlights** to flood the area with light. This forces the Boogeyman into a physical form, making it easier to track and trap. Aim the beam directly at its shadowy body to weaken its defenses.
- **Magnesium Flares:** Carry **magnesium flares** as a last-resort tool. When ignited, these flares produce an intense, blinding light that can momentarily paralyze a Boogeyman, allowing you to set up traps or retreat.
- **Mirror Traps:** Set up **mirror traps** around areas known for Boogeyman activity. Mirrors reflect light in unpredictable ways, confusing and disorienting the creature. This disorientation can be exploited to herd the Boogeyman toward containment areas.

1.2 The Fear of Purity and Symbols of Hope

Boogeymen are inherently drawn to negativity, chaos, and despair. They abhor symbols of **hope**, **purity**, and **order**, which represent forces that threaten to dissolve the fear energy they feed on. Objects and symbols that emanate positive energy disrupt the dark aura of Boogeymen, making them uneasy and diminishing their power.

How to Exploit This Fear:

- **Sigils of Hope:** Draw **sigils of hope** and **light** using chalk or silver ink on surfaces around your home. These symbols create a protective barrier, preventing Boogeymen from entering. The most effective sigils include runes such as **Sowilo** (representing the sun) and **Wunjo** (representing joy).
- **Holy Water:** Boogeymen react strongly to **holy water** or other blessed substances. Sprinkle holy water at entry points such as closets, under beds, and dark corners. The purifying effect acts like a repellant, forcing the Boogeyman to retreat.
- **Positive Affirmations:** Chant positive affirmations aloud during a hunt. The sound waves produced by positive thoughts disrupt the energy field of the Boogeyman, creating an environment it finds intolerable.

1.3 The Fear of Being Bound

Boogeymen fear **binding** because it strips them of their freedom and power. As entities that rely on movement through shadows and dimensions, the idea of being confined is antithetical to their existence. Binding magic, rituals, and physical restraints such as **shadow nets** or **enchanted boxes** tap into this fear.

How to Exploit This Fear:

- **Binding Spells:** Use **binding spells** during confrontations. Recite incantations that focus on the concept of immobilization, such as:
  "By shadow's thread, by binding's might,
  I fix you now, halt your flight."
  These words resonate with the fear of containment, temporarily restricting the Boogeyman's movements.
- **Salt Circles:** Lay down **salt circles** around the target area. Salt has purifying properties that repel darkness and prevent Boogeymen from crossing the boundary. Encircle the creature to restrict its movements and force it into a confined space.
- **Boogie Goo:** Deploy **Boogie Goo** along known paths the Boogeyman frequents. This sticky substance traps shadows, anchoring the Boogeyman and exploiting its fear of being pinned in place.

2. Unique Fears of Specific Types of Boogeymen

While all Boogeymen share common fears, each type possesses unique anxieties related to its role and domain within the Boogie World. Understanding these specific fears provides hunters with targeted strategies for subduing different kinds of Boogeymen.

2.1 Closet Boogeymen: The Fear of Exposure

Closet Boogeymen, like **Lord Grimsnare**, thrive in secrecy. Their greatest fear is **exposure**—having their hidden domain thrown open to light and scrutiny. They rely on the darkness of closed spaces to maintain their influence and dread the act of being dragged into the open.

How to Exploit This Fear:

- **Open Closet Doors:** During a hunt, leave **closet doors wide open** and shine light into the space. This act symbolizes the removal of their protective darkness, creating an environment that forces them into the open.
- **Reflective Lining:** Line the interior of closets with **aluminum foil** or other reflective materials. This disrupts the darkness, making it difficult for the Boogeyman to blend in and creating a sense of vulnerability.

2.2 Underbed Boogeymen: The Fear of Sudden Movement

Underbed Boogeymen, governed by entities like **Lady Umbragloom**, rely on the stillness and safety of the bed above. They fear **sudden movement** and disturbances, which threaten their hiding spots and disrupt their feeding cycle.

How to Exploit This Fear:

- **Frequent Bed Shifts:** If you suspect an Underbed Boogeyman, **move the bed regularly**. Lift it, shake it, or flip the mattress. These actions send vibrations through the space, unsettling the creature and making it retreat to the Boogie World.
- **Stomp Ritual:** Perform a **stomp ritual** at the edge of the bed, where you stomp your feet in a rhythmic pattern. The vibrations create an unstable environment under the bed, exploiting the Boogeyman's fear of disruption.

2.3 Mirror Boogeymen: The Fear of Shattering

Mirror Boogeymen, like **The Shattered One**, are inherently tied to reflections. Their greatest fear is **shattering**, which not only represents their physical destruction but also symbolizes the loss of control over the distorted realities they create.

How to Exploit This Fear:

- **Tuning Forks:** Carry a **tuning fork** tuned to a high frequency. When struck and placed against a mirror, the vibrations can disrupt the mirror's surface, creating fractures. The sound waves exploit the Boogeyman's fear of being shattered, forcing it to withdraw.

- **Shatter Mirrors:** In extreme cases, breaking a **mirror trap** containing a Boogeyman can force it back into the Boogie World. However, be cautious, as this may release chaotic energy. Ensure that the area is protected with a **circle of salt** before attempting this tactic.

2.4 Attic Boogeymen: The Fear of Decluttering

Attic Boogeymen, such as **Sir Noxus**, thrive on the chaos of clutter and forgotten relics. They fear **organization** and **decluttering**, which represent the removal of their hiding places and the memories they use to manipulate their environment.

How to Exploit This Fear:

- **Organize the Space:** Clean and organize attics, removing old items and reducing the available shadows. Decluttering forces the Boogeyman into fewer hiding spots, making it easier to trap.
- **Dusting Ritual:** Perform a **dusting ritual** using sage or lavender. As you dust the area, chant:

  *"By broom's sweep and herb's clean scent,
  I banish thee from where you're pent."*

  This action represents clearing away not only physical dust but also the Boogeyman's presence.

Conclusion: Turning Fear into a Weapon

Boogeymen may wield fear as their greatest weapon, but they are not invulnerable. By understanding their psychology and identifying their fears—light, purity, binding, and others—you can craft strategies to turn their own dread against them. Exploiting these weaknesses requires a blend of **knowledge**, **courage**, and **tactical thinking**, allowing hunters to trap, repel, or banish these creatures effectively. In the chapters that follow, we will explore advanced techniques for confronting Boogeymen using these insights, delving into the rituals and tools necessary to transform fear into a potent weapon. Armed with this understanding, you are now equipped to confront the shadows with confidence.

Part 6: *Boogeyman Case Studies*

Chapter 20: Case Study: The Closet Stalker

Closet Boogeymen, often referred to as **Closet Stalkers**, are among the most notorious of their kind. Their presence is felt in darkened closets where they wait, feeding on the unease and fear of those who sense something lurking just beyond the door. They are masters of the enclosed space, using the darkness to their advantage and employing a range of psychological tactics to unsettle their targets.

This chapter presents a **real-life account** of the capture of a particularly elusive Closet Stalker, offering insight into its behaviors, the signs of its presence, and the strategies used to successfully capture and contain it. This case study serves as a guide for other hunters facing similar encounters, outlining effective tactics and the tools needed to confront these shadowy entities.

The Setting: A Suburban Household Encounter

The case occurred in a typical suburban household—a two-story home with three bedrooms, each equipped with a standard closet. The family, consisting of two parents and a young child, had reported strange occurrences over several months. The child often awoke in the middle of the night, pointing fearfully toward the closet, convinced that something was hiding inside. Over time, the parents also began to notice unsettling events: the closet door would be ajar in the morning despite being firmly shut the night before, clothes would occasionally be strewn on the floor, and faint whispers could be heard emanating from the closet in the dead of night.

Recognizing the classic symptoms of a **Closet Stalker**, the family contacted a local Boogey Hunter for assistance. The hunter arrived equipped with tools and a carefully planned strategy for dealing with the entity.

Initial Investigation: Confirming the Boogeyman's Presence

The first step in dealing with a potential Closet Stalker is to confirm its presence. Closet Boogeymen are skilled at concealing themselves, making it difficult to detect them directly. The hunter began with a preliminary investigation to identify telltale signs of the Boogeyman's activity.

Signs Observed:

1. **Temperature Drops:** Upon entering the child's bedroom, the hunter noted a significant drop in temperature near the closet. Boogeymen often draw in warmth to feed their energy, leaving a cold, unnatural chill around their hiding place.
2. **Unsettling Whispers:** With the room in complete silence, faint whispering noises emanated from the closet, indicating that the Boogeyman was trying to instill fear in its surroundings.
3. **Shadow Movements:** When the hunter shined a flashlight inside the closet, subtle movements could be seen in the corners of the room, shadows that shifted as if trying to avoid the light.

Detection Tools Used:

- **Thermal Sensor:** The hunter used a thermal sensor to confirm cold spots within the closet. The sensor displayed irregular patterns of cold, forming a vaguely humanoid shape in the corner.
- **Sound Recorder:** A sound recorder captured the faint whispers. Upon playback, the whispers seemed to echo the child's fears, indicating that the Boogeyman had been feeding on the child's anxieties.

These signs confirmed the presence of a Closet Stalker. With identification established, the hunter moved on to the planning and execution of the capture.

Capture Planning: Tools and Tactics

Closet Stalkers are cunning and can quickly retreat into the Boogie World if threatened, so the hunter devised a plan to **lure**, **trap**, and **contain** the entity. The following tools were assembled to facilitate the capture:

Tools and Materials:

- **Full-Spectrum Flashlight:** Used to flood the closet with light, revealing the Boogeyman's form and forcing it out of hiding.
- **Mirror Trap:** A specially prepared mirror inscribed with containment runes to trap the Boogeyman's reflection.
- **Salt and Iron Powder:** To create a barrier around the closet, preventing the Boogeyman from escaping once it was lured out.
- **Boogie Goo:** Applied to the floor within the closet to ensnare the Boogeyman's shadowy form.
- **Enchanted Box:** A containment unit crafted from ebony wood, silver-lined on the inside, and carved with binding runes, designed to imprison the entity once captured.

Luring the Boogeyman:

The hunter employed a **fear-baiting tactic** using an emotional decoy. The child's room was darkened, and the hunter played a recording of the child's voice expressing fear, along with soft sobbing noises. This sound decoy simulated the child's fear, attracting the Boogeyman's attention.

Preparation:

- **Salt Barrier:** A circle of **salt and iron powder** was placed around the closet door to prevent the Boogeyman from fleeing once it emerged.
- **Mirror Trap Positioning:** The mirror trap was placed directly opposite the closet, ready to capture the Boogeyman's reflection when it appeared.
- **Boogie Goo Application:** The floor inside the closet was coated with a thin layer of Boogie Goo to ensnare the Boogeyman if it attempted to move.

Execution: The Confrontation and Capture

As the sound decoy played, the whispers within the closet grew louder, indicating the Boogeyman's increasing agitation. The hunter approached the closet door, full-spectrum flashlight in hand, prepared to flood the interior with light. Timing was crucial; the Boogeyman needed to be forced out into the open without giving it a chance to slip away.

Step-by-Step Capture Process:

1. **Illumination:** The hunter swung the closet door open and immediately shined the **full-spectrum flashlight** into the dark interior. The sudden burst of light caused a shadowy figure to writhe and recoil, becoming partially visible. The Boogeyman, caught off guard, was forced to the front of the closet, unable to retreat into the shadows.
2. **Mirror Trap Activation:** As the Boogeyman emerged from the darkness, the hunter directed it toward the **mirror trap**. The reflective surface captured the entity's form, holding its reflection in a fragmented, distorted state. The Boogeyman howled as its power diminished, thrashing against the confines of the mirror's containment runes.
3. **Binding with Boogie Goo:** With the Boogeyman momentarily trapped by the mirror's enchantment, the hunter moved quickly to apply **Boogie Goo** around the entity. The goo adhered to the creature's shadowy body, restricting its movements and binding it to the spot.
4. **Final Containment:** The hunter then retrieved the **enchanted box** and positioned it in front of the mirror. Using a silver stylus, they traced a rune of passage on the mirror's surface, opening a channel between the mirror and the box. The Boogeyman, now partially subdued by the mirror and the goo, was drawn into the box. As it entered, the hunter sealed the lid, locking it shut with a binding incantation.

Post-Capture Containment

With the Boogeyman successfully trapped inside the enchanted box, the hunter moved on to the containment phase. Ensuring the entity remained imprisoned required specific rituals and maintenance.

Containment Protocols:

1. **Runic Reinforcement:** The hunter inscribed additional binding runes onto the box's surface using silver ink to reinforce the initial containment spells.
2. **Full Moon Charging:** The box was placed in a **moonlight bath** during the next full moon to recharge its enchantments, ensuring the Boogeyman could not break free.
3. **Placement in a Protected Area:** The box was stored in a **warded room** lined with salt and iron powder to provide an extra layer of security.

Lessons Learned: Key Takeaways from the Capture

This encounter with the Closet Stalker provided valuable insights into the tactics and weaknesses of Closet Boogeymen. Here are some key takeaways for hunters facing similar entities:

1. **Exposure Is Key:** Closet Boogeymen rely heavily on the safety of darkness. Shining a full-spectrum light into their hiding place forces them out into the open, where they are vulnerable to traps.
2. **Reflection as a Weapon:** Mirror traps are highly effective against Closet Stalkers, as they use the Boogeyman's own nature against it, trapping it in its reflection.
3. **Control the Space:** Creating a **salt barrier** around the closet restricts the Boogeyman's movements, ensuring it cannot escape once lured out.
4. **Rapid Containment:** The Boogeyman must be contained quickly once exposed. The use of **Boogie Goo** to immobilize the entity and an **enchanted box** for long-term imprisonment is crucial for successful containment.

Conclusion: The Importance of Understanding Your Quarry

The capture of the Closet Stalker in this case study illustrates the importance of **preparation**, **knowledge**, and **strategic use of tools** in confronting a Boogeyman. By understanding its behaviors, fears, and weaknesses, the hunter was able to exploit the entity's reliance on darkness and entrap it using light and reflection. The successful containment of this Boogeyman not only secured the household but also added valuable experience to the hunter's arsenal for future encounters.

In the chapters to come, we will explore further case studies and advanced techniques for dealing with other types of Boogeymen, expanding on the strategies required to face the diverse and fearsome inhabitants of the Boogie World.

Chapter 21: Case Study: The Underbed Creeper

Underbed Creepers are some of the most unsettling and persistent types of Boogeymen. They make their homes in the dark, confined spaces under beds, feeding on the latent fears of those who sleep above. Unlike their Closet Stalker counterparts, Underbed Creepers are known for their stealth and patience. They thrive in silence, waiting for the moment when the room is completely still and quiet to manifest their influence.

This chapter provides a chilling **case study** of an encounter with a particularly cunning Underbed Creeper, offering a detailed look into its behavior, the signs that led to its discovery, and the strategies used to outsmart and ultimately trap it. Through this real-life account, we explore the best techniques and tools for handling these elusive Boogeymen, turning their own methods of fear against them.

The Case: A Nighttime Terror

The case began in a modest family home, where a series of **nighttime disturbances** had left the household in a state of anxiety and unrest. The primary victim was a teenage girl who reported a recurring sensation of being watched while she lay in bed. More disturbingly, she occasionally felt the unmistakable pressure of something crawling underneath her mattress. Her sleep was frequently interrupted by whispers and scratching sounds emanating from the floor beneath her bed.

The family had attempted to alleviate these disturbances by placing objects under the bed, keeping the lights on, and even rearranging the room's furniture. However, the noises persisted, and the girl's sleep grew increasingly troubled. Recognizing the classic symptoms of an Underbed Creeper, the family contacted a Boogey Hunter to address the situation.

Initial Investigation: Gathering Clues

Upon arrival, the hunter conducted a **thorough inspection** of the bedroom and its surroundings. Underbed Creepers are notoriously difficult to detect, as they blend seamlessly with the shadows and avoid exposure. However, the hunter looked for specific signs that indicated the presence of the entity.

Signs Observed:

1. **Cold Pockets:** The hunter discovered areas of intense cold directly beneath the bed. Using a thermal sensor, the temperature under the bed was found to be several degrees lower than the rest of the room, forming a circular pattern indicative of the Creeper's influence.
2. **Scratch Marks:** Faint scratch marks were found on the wooden floorboards under the bed, arranged in irregular patterns. The scratches resembled claw marks, suggesting that the entity had been **clawing** at the underside of the bed to manifest its presence.
3. **Stagnant Fear:** When the hunter examined the bed's surroundings using a **fear gauge**, the readings indicated high levels of residual fear energy. Underbed Creepers are known to create an atmosphere of dread in their hiding spots, which can be measured by tools that detect emotional energy.

Detection Tools Used:

- **Thermal Sensor:** Detected cold pockets indicative of the Creeper's presence.
- **Fear Gauge:** Measured the emotional energy in the room, confirming the build-up of fear around the bed.
- **Sound Recorder:** Placed under the bed for several hours, it captured faint, rhythmic scratching noises that coincided with the girl's descriptions.

With the presence of an Underbed Creeper confirmed, the hunter prepared to confront and capture the entity, using techniques tailored to exploit the Creeper's unique weaknesses.

Capture Planning: Tools and Techniques

Underbed Creepers are notoriously difficult to lure out into the open due to their inherent caution and tendency to retreat into the **Underbed Abyss** when threatened. The hunter needed to employ a strategy that would **force** the Creeper into an exposed position while simultaneously preventing its escape.

Tools and Materials:

- **Salt and Iron Powder:** To create a boundary around the bed, restricting the Creeper's movement and preventing it from retreating.
- **Binding Oil:** Used to anoint the bedframe, making it difficult for the Creeper to hide within the shadows.
- **Motion-Activated Lanterns:** Positioned around the room to flood the space under the bed with light the moment the Creeper attempted to move.
- **Mirror Trap:** Placed under the bed, its surface coated with a layer of moonstone dust to enhance its reflective properties.
- **Shadow Nets:** Deployed in the corners of the room to catch the Creeper if it tried to flee.

Luring the Creeper:

The hunter opted to use a **sound decoy** and an **emotional baiting tactic**. Creepers are attracted to the fear of their victims, so the hunter used recordings of the girl's fearful murmurs during sleep, played softly beneath the bed. To amplify the lure, the hunter also placed a **stuffed toy** on the bed, which had been infused with the girl's scent, creating the illusion that she was present and vulnerable.

Preparation:

- **Salt Boundary:** A thick line of **salt mixed with iron powder** was laid out in a circle around the bed. This barrier would prevent the Creeper from slipping back into the darkness beneath the bed once lured out.
- **Lantern Placement: Motion-activated lanterns** were strategically placed around the bed's perimeter, ready to light up the area once the Creeper moved.
- **Mirror Trap Setup:** The mirror trap was carefully positioned under the bed at an angle, so any movement from the Creeper would be reflected into the mirror's surface.

Execution: Outwitting the Underbed Creeper

After setting up the traps and preparing the decoy, the hunter dimmed the lights in the room, leaving only a faint glow from the motion-activated lanterns. The room was filled with an eerie silence, broken only by the soft playback of the recorded whispers.

Step-by-Step Capture Process:

1. **Initial Lure:** The sound decoy began to work almost immediately. From beneath the bed, the hunter detected a subtle shift in the air as the Creeper stirred in response to the noises. Its natural instinct to approach the source of fear had overridden its caution.
2. **Forced Movement:** As the Creeper crawled toward the edge of the bed, the hunter triggered the **motion-activated lanterns**, flooding the area with light. The sudden brightness caused the Creeper to recoil, revealing a twisted, shadowy figure with elongated limbs clawing at the air in an attempt to retreat.
3. **Mirror Trap Activation:** With the Creeper now exposed, the hunter directed it toward the **mirror trap** under the bed. The Creeper, disoriented by the light and the salt barrier, moved directly into the trap's line of sight. The mirror's surface rippled as it absorbed the Creeper's reflection, holding it in place.
4. **Binding with Shadow Nets:** As the Creeper struggled within the mirror's influence, the hunter quickly cast **shadow nets** over the bed's perimeter, further immobilizing the entity. The nets shimmered with a faint, silver glow, signifying that they had latched onto the Creeper's form.
5. **Final Containment:** The hunter then retrieved a **binding vial** filled with moonstone-infused oil and poured it onto the bedframe, creating a **binding rune** with silver ink. This finalized the containment process, sealing the Creeper's essence to the mirror trap.

Post-Capture Containment

With the Creeper successfully captured, the next step was to ensure it remained securely imprisoned. Underbed Creepers are notorious for their attempts to break free, requiring constant vigilance and maintenance of the containment measures.

Containment Protocols:

1. **Mirror Trap Sealing:** The mirror trap was placed inside an **enchanted box** lined with silver and inscribed with containment runes. The hunter closed the box and locked it with a silver clasp anointed with binding oil, ensuring that the Creeper could not phase through the container.
2. **Periodic Reinforcement:** Every **full moon**, the box would be placed under moonlight to recharge the binding runes. The mirror trap itself was cleansed with sage smoke to prevent the Creeper from gathering strength within its prison.
3. **Ward Placement:** The room where the box was stored was lined with protective wards, including **salt lines** and **iron powder**, to create a barrier against any residual influence the Creeper might attempt to project.

Lessons Learned: Key Strategies for Dealing with Underbed Creepers

This case study highlights several effective strategies for confronting and capturing an Underbed Creeper. Here are the key takeaways:

1. **Manipulate Fear:** Underbed Creepers are drawn to the fear of their targets. By using **sound decoys** and emotional baiting, hunters can lure the Creeper out of its hiding place, forcing it into an exposed position.
2. **Control the Light:** Motion-activated lanterns are a powerful tool against Creepers. The sudden introduction of light disrupts their shadowy movements, leaving them vulnerable to capture.
3. **Use Mirrors Wisely:** Mirror traps are especially effective against Underbed Creepers, as they rely heavily on reflections to manipulate their environment. Positioning a mirror beneath the bed creates a reflective barrier that exploits the Creeper's inherent weaknesses.
4. **Barrier and Binding:** Encircle the bed with **salt and iron powder** to prevent the Creeper from retreating once it emerges. Seal the room with **binding oil** to reinforce the traps and ensure that the entity remains contained after capture.

Conclusion: Mastering the Art of the Hunt

The capture of the Underbed Creeper in this case study illustrates the importance of understanding the psychology and behaviors of these elusive Boogeymen. By employing a combination of **lures, light manipulation, barriers,** and **mirror traps**, the hunter successfully outsmarted and contained the Creeper. This encounter serves as a testament to the effectiveness of preparation, knowledge, and the strategic use of specialized tools in confronting the most insidious inhabitants of the Boogie World.

In the following chapters, we will continue to explore advanced techniques for dealing with other types of Boogeymen, providing you with a comprehensive toolkit for navigating the shadows and facing these creatures head-on.

Chapter 22: Case Study: The Night Terror Wraith

Among the myriad forms of Boogeymen, the **Night Terror Wraith** is one of the most terrifying and dangerous. Unlike other Boogeymen that lurk in closets or under beds, the Night Terror Wraith attacks at the most vulnerable time: during sleep. Known for inducing **sleep paralysis** and feeding on **nightmares**, these entities create an overwhelming sense of dread and helplessness in their victims.

This chapter provides a comprehensive **case study** of an encounter with a particularly powerful Night Terror Wraith. It details the signs that indicated its presence, the strategies used to lure it out, and the methods employed to neutralize and contain it. By understanding the nature of these fearsome Boogeymen, hunters can better prepare for future encounters with these sleep-haunting entities.

The Case: A Family's Descent into Nightmare

The encounter took place in a quiet, suburban neighborhood where an entire family had been experiencing **recurring nightmares** and episodes of sleep paralysis. The primary victim was the family's teenage son, who reported seeing a dark, shadowy figure looming over him during bouts of paralysis. He described a suffocating pressure on his chest and an intense sense of malevolence during these episodes. Other family members also experienced nightmares filled with the sensation of being watched, chased, or trapped, leading to growing anxiety and insomnia.

Recognizing the hallmarks of a **Night Terror Wraith**, the family contacted a seasoned Boogey Hunter. The hunter arrived, well-prepared to deal with an entity known to manipulate sleep and instill paralyzing fear.

Initial Investigation: Identifying the Wraith

Night Terror Wraiths are elusive, often leaving minimal physical evidence of their presence since they operate primarily in the realm of sleep. However, the hunter knew to look for certain signs that could confirm the Wraith's presence and its feeding habits.

Signs Observed:

1. **Sleep Paralysis Episodes:** The hunter interviewed each family member, confirming frequent incidents of sleep paralysis accompanied by the sensation of an ominous presence. The teenage son's detailed descriptions—particularly of the shadowy figure sitting on his chest—indicated a classic Night Terror Wraith encounter.
2. **Nightmare Residue:** Using a **nightmare detector** (a device attuned to emotional energy), the hunter identified traces of residual fear in the son's bedroom, particularly around the bed. The detector emitted a low, rhythmic hum when pointed at the headboard, signifying the presence of lingering nightmare energy.

3. **Cold Spots:** The hunter observed unnatural cold spots in the room, concentrated near the head of the bed. Night Terror Wraiths are known to draw warmth from their surroundings to manifest and induce sleep paralysis.

Detection Tools Used:

- **Nightmare Detector:** A small, handheld device that senses residual emotional energy, specifically fear and anxiety left behind by nightmares.
- **Thermal Imaging Camera:** Used to identify the cold spots, revealing an irregular pattern of chilling emanations near the bed.
- **Audio Recorder:** Placed by the bed overnight, it captured faint, eerie whispers that coincided with the family's reports of hearing ominous noises during their nightmares.

Formulating a Plan: Tools and Techniques

Neutralizing a Night Terror Wraith is particularly challenging because it operates within the **realm of sleep**. To confront the Wraith, the hunter needed to employ a strategy that would draw the entity into the physical world, where it could be trapped and contained. The hunter also had to ensure the safety of the family during the process, as direct contact with a Wraith could result in psychological harm.

Tools and Materials:

- **Dreamcatcher Wards:** Created using a blend of **moonstone beads**, **sage**, and **woven silver thread**, these wards were designed to capture nightmare energy and disrupt the Wraith's influence over dreams.
- **Nightmare Oil:** An infusion of **lavender**, **mugwort**, and **frankincense**, used to anoint the headboard and frame of the bed, creating a barrier against the Wraith's entry into the dream realm.
- **Binding Candles:** Black candles inscribed with **binding runes** and coated with silver dust, used to lure the Wraith into a containment circle.
- **Mirror Trap:** A large, round mirror coated with **moonstone dust** and inscribed with runes to capture the Wraith's reflection, immobilizing it.
- **Boogie Goo:** Applied around the bed to restrict the Wraith's movements once it was drawn into the physical world.

Luring the Wraith:

The hunter chose to use a combination of **dream manipulation** and **reflective surfaces** to lure the Wraith out of the dream realm. By creating an environment that appeared vulnerable yet protected, the Wraith would be compelled to reveal itself, seeking to dominate the situation.

Preparation:

- **Dreamcatcher Wards:** The hunter placed dreamcatcher wards around the room, focusing on the headboard of the bed. These wards would not only trap residual nightmare energy but also disrupt the Wraith's ability to induce sleep paralysis.
- **Anointing with Nightmare Oil:** The bedframe was anointed with nightmare oil, forming a protective barrier that would make it more difficult for the Wraith to directly interact with the sleeper.
- **Mirror Trap Positioning:** The mirror trap was positioned on the floor at the foot of the bed, angled to reflect the space above the sleeper's chest. This placement was crucial, as the Wraith would likely approach the victim from above.
- **Boogie Goo Application:** A circle of Boogie Goo was applied around the bed's perimeter to act as a secondary containment measure, preventing the Wraith from slipping away once it was drawn out.

The Confrontation: Drawing Out the Night Terror Wraith

With the preparations complete, the hunter had the family remain outside the room while the teenage son volunteered to lie in the bed as bait. Armed with knowledge of the Wraith's habits and the protective measures in place, the hunter initiated the process.

Step-by-Step Confrontation:

1. **Creating Vulnerability:** The son lay in bed, feigning sleep while the hunter chanted a **dream manipulation incantation** designed to draw the Wraith's attention. The dreamcatcher wards shimmered faintly, signaling that they had begun to trap the residual nightmare energy, which the Wraith would sense.
2. **Inducing Manifestation:** As the room darkened and the temperature dropped, indicating the Wraith's approach, the hunter lit the **binding candles** around the bed. The flames flickered unnaturally, casting long shadows across the room. The Wraith, sensing its prey, moved in.
3. **Revealing the Wraith:** The moment the Wraith attempted to mount the victim's chest, the hunter activated the **mirror trap** by tilting it slightly. The Wraith's shadowy form became visible in the mirror's surface—a grotesque figure with elongated limbs and hollow, piercing eyes. It froze momentarily, disoriented by the reflection.
4. **Binding the Wraith:** With the Wraith exposed, the hunter recited a **binding incantation**, raising the nightmare oil-anointed dagger. The Wraith thrashed, a guttural wail filling the room as the binding runes inscribed on the candles began to glow. The hunter moved swiftly,

pouring **Boogie Goo** onto the mirror's surface. The goo expanded, flowing over the Wraith's reflected form, immobilizing it.

5. **Final Containment:** The hunter then carefully lifted the mirror trap, placing it inside an **enchanted box** lined with silver and carved with binding runes. The box's lid was closed and sealed with a mixture of Boogie Goo and powdered iron, securing the Wraith within.

Post-Capture Containment

Containing a Night Terror Wraith requires continuous maintenance, as these entities possess a relentless desire to escape and resume their feeding on fear.

Containment Protocols:

1. **Mirror Trap Cleansing:** The mirror inside the enchanted box must be **cleansed weekly** with sage smoke to prevent the Wraith from gathering energy within its confines.
2. **Runic Reinforcement:** The box is stored in a **warded room** lined with runes of binding and symbols of hope, further weakening the Wraith's power. These runes are repainted monthly using a mixture of silver ink and binding oil.
3. **Nightmare Purification:** During every **full moon**, the box is placed in a circle of **moonstone crystals** to purify any residual nightmare energy that may seep out, ensuring that the Wraith remains subdued.

Lessons Learned: Effective Tactics for Night Terror Wraiths

This case study reveals several key strategies for dealing with Night Terror Wraiths:

1. **Dream Disruption:** Night Terror Wraiths rely on their ability to manipulate sleep and induce paralysis. Using **dreamcatcher wards** disrupts their influence, making it more difficult for them to control the victim's sleep.
2. **Reflective Traps:** Mirrors, particularly those coated with moonstone dust, can capture and immobilize Wraiths by reflecting their grotesque forms. Positioning the mirror to face the victim's chest exploits the Wraith's tendency to approach its target from above.
3. **Light and Binding:** Candlelight, particularly from candles inscribed with binding runes, weakens the Wraith and creates a boundary that forces it into a specific area where it can be trapped.
4. **Anointed Barriers:** Anointing the bedframe and the room's perimeter with **nightmare oil** creates a barrier that the Wraith finds difficult to penetrate, preventing it from directly influencing the dreamer.

Conclusion: Conquering the Sleep Invader

The capture of the Night Terror Wraith in this case study highlights the complexities and dangers involved in confronting these sleep-invading Boogeymen. By understanding the Wraith's behavior, weaknesses, and feeding habits, the hunter was able to devise a plan that disrupted its influence, lured it into the physical realm, and trapped it using reflective surfaces and binding magic. This encounter serves as a guide for other hunters facing similar threats, demonstrating the power of preparation, the strategic use of tools, and the importance of maintaining vigilance in the realm of sleep.

In the next chapters, we will delve deeper into advanced techniques and additional case studies, further expanding on the knowledge and strategies needed to confront the most formidable inhabitants of the Boogie World.

Part 7: *Global Boogeymen: A Worldwide Perspective*

Chapter 23: Boogeymen Around the World

The concept of the **Boogeyman** is a near-universal presence across human cultures. While the **form, nature, and characteristics** of these entities differ from one culture to another, they all share a common thread: the embodiment of fear, particularly that of the unknown, lurking in the shadows. In each society, stories of creatures that feed on fear and thrive in darkness serve as cautionary tales for children and adults alike, reflecting deep-rooted anxieties and beliefs.

This chapter explores the **worldwide spectrum of Boogeymen**, introducing various cultural interpretations of these fearsome beings. From the European Krampus to the Japanese Namahage, the Boogeymen and their equivalents in different cultures offer a rich tapestry of myth and folklore. Understanding these diverse representations provides a broader perspective on how the **Boogeyman archetype** is both a personal and cultural manifestation of fear.

1. European Boogeymen: Shadows of the Old World

Europe's long history and diverse traditions have given rise to some of the most well-known and varied forms of Boogeymen. These entities often represent the fears and superstitions of their respective regions, serving as both a moral reminder and a source of fright.

1.1 Krampus (Austria, Germany)

Description: Krampus is one of the most iconic and fearsome Boogeyman figures in European folklore. Depicted as a demonic creature with horns, cloven hooves, and a long, lolling tongue, Krampus carries chains and a bundle of birch sticks to punish naughty children. The legend states that Krampus accompanies Saint Nicholas during the Christmas season, doling out punishment to those who have misbehaved.

Cultural Context: In Austrian and German traditions, Krampus represents the duality of reward and punishment, serving as a counterpart to the benevolent Saint Nicholas. His presence embodies the fear of consequences and the darkness that follows disobedience.

Hunting Insight: Krampus is a classic example of a **punishing Boogeyman**, one who emerges to enforce moral standards. While modern hunters do not typically encounter Krampus himself, understanding his legend helps in dealing with Boogeymen who feed on guilt and fear of retribution.

1.2 Babau (Italy)

Description: The Babau is a formless, shadowy creature that hides in dark places, waiting to snatch up disobedient children. Often described as a black, amorphous entity, the Babau has no definitive shape or features, making it a terrifying figure of imagination.

Cultural Context: In Italy, parents invoke the Babau to scare children into behaving, emphasizing the unknown and the mysterious nature of danger. The Babau symbolizes the fear of what cannot be seen or understood, a pervasive theme in many Boogeyman legends.

Hunting Insight: Boogeymen that align with the Babau archetype thrive on **vague, formless fear**. They often inhabit shadows and corners, avoiding direct confrontation. To trap such entities, hunters must create defined boundaries of light and focus on using reflective surfaces to force these shadowy forms into the open.

1.3 Butzemann (Germany)

Description: The Butzemann, or "Boo Man," is a mischievous and often malevolent spirit that roams rural areas. It is said to take on various forms, appearing as a shadowy figure or a scarecrow-like being. The Butzemann is known for its ability to shapeshift and cause disturbances, especially during the night.

Cultural Context: The Butzemann represents the chaotic and unpredictable nature of the wilderness and the dangers lurking outside the safety of home. German folklore uses this figure to caution against wandering too far into the unknown.

Hunting Insight: Shape-shifting Boogeymen like the Butzemann require **traps** that can adapt to different forms. Hunters use multi-layered binding runes and enchantments that respond to changes in shape, making it harder for such entities to escape confinement.

2. Asian Boogeymen: Spirits of Fear and Punishment

In many Asian cultures, Boogeymen often take the form of **spirits** or **demons** that are tied to moral conduct, household harmony, and spiritual beliefs. They act as enforcers of cultural norms and punishers of bad behavior, feeding on fear, guilt, and chaos.

2.1 Namahage (Japan)

Description: The Namahage are ogre-like creatures from Japanese folklore, traditionally associated with New Year's Eve. They are depicted as tall, masked figures with wild hair, wearing straw garments and carrying large knives. Namahage roam villages, knocking on doors to seek out lazy or misbehaving children, threatening to take them away if they do not reform.

Cultural Context: In Japanese tradition, Namahage serve as a reminder to maintain discipline and hard work. Their visits during New Year celebrations symbolize the driving out of bad luck and negative behavior, reinforcing social and cultural values.

Hunting Insight: Namahage-like Boogeymen embody **disciplinary fear**. Hunters confronting such entities often find that **rituals** of purification and order, such as rearranging rooms or reciting incantations of discipline, can weaken their influence and drive them back.

2.2 Pishacha (India)

Description: Pishacha are flesh-eating demons from Hindu mythology. They are described as dark, shadowy figures with distorted faces and glowing red eyes. Known to haunt cremation grounds and abandoned places, Pishacha are said to possess people, driving them mad with fear and hallucinations.

Cultural Context: In Indian folklore, Pishacha represent the chaotic forces of darkness and the consequences of indulging in negative emotions such as anger, jealousy, and hatred. They embody the fear of losing control over one's mind and spirit.

Hunting Insight: Pishacha-like Boogeymen exploit **mental vulnerabilities**. Hunters use protective charms, mantras, and herbal wards (such as tulsi and neem) to purify the environment and prevent possession. Direct confrontation involves binding rituals that target the Boogeyman's grip on the victim's psyche.

2.3 Phi Am (Thailand)

Description: The Phi Am is a spirit in Thai folklore known to visit people during their sleep. It manifests as a heavy, shadowy figure that sits on the sleeper's chest, causing **sleep paralysis** and inducing terrifying dreams. Victims awake feeling suffocated and disoriented, believing that they have been attacked by a malevolent spirit.

Cultural Context: The Phi Am represents the fear of the unknown in the dark hours of the night. It also acts as a warning to maintain spiritual and physical health, as those who are vulnerable or weakened are said to be more susceptible to its attacks.

Hunting Insight: Boogeymen like the Phi Am often use **sleep and paralysis** to overpower their victims. Hunters combat these entities with **dreamcatcher wards**, moonstone charms, and rituals that cleanse the sleeping area, disrupting the entity's ability to induce nightmares and paralysis.

3. African Boogeymen: Guardians of Tradition and Morality

African folklore features a wide variety of Boogeyman-like figures, often rooted in **tribal myths** and **ancestral beliefs**. These entities are frequently seen as guardians that punish those who stray from cultural norms or challenge the natural order.

3.1 Tokoloshe (Southern Africa)

Description: The Tokoloshe is a small, dwarf-like creature in Zulu mythology, often depicted as a mischievous and malevolent spirit that can become invisible at will. It is said to climb onto sleeping people's chests, causing **nightmares** or even illness. Tokoloshes are believed to be summoned by sorcerers to harm others.

Cultural Context: The Tokoloshe represents the fear of witchcraft, the supernatural, and the power of curses. It is also seen as a cautionary figure, reminding individuals to remain spiritually vigilant and to respect the boundaries of the spiritual world.

Hunting Insight: Tokoloshe-like Boogeymen require **spiritual defenses**, such as protective talismans and herbs like **African wormwood**. Elevating beds on bricks is a traditional method to prevent these creatures from climbing up, while hunters employ charms and rituals to reveal the invisible entity and trap it.

3.2 Adze (Ghana, Togo)

Description: The Adze is a vampiric spirit in Ewe folklore that can transform into a firefly or other small creature to enter homes. In its natural form, it is a shadowy, ethereal being that feeds on the life force of sleeping individuals, particularly children.

Cultural Context: The Adze symbolizes the fear of malicious spirits that prey on the vulnerable. It also serves as a reminder to maintain spiritual health and protect one's home from supernatural threats.

Hunting Insight: Boogeymen resembling the Adze exploit **weak points** in household defenses. Hunters use **protective wards** around windows and doorways to prevent entry. In cases where the Adze has already entered a home, they employ light-based traps and iron implements to capture and contain the entity.

4. The Americas: Spirits of Fear and Chaos

Across the Americas, Boogeymen take on forms that reflect the cultural beliefs, natural environments, and societal norms of various regions. They are often seen as spirits of chaos and fear that enforce moral behavior or guard the boundaries between the human world and the supernatural.

4.1 El Coco (Spain, Latin America)

Description: El Coco (also known as El Cucuy) is a shape-shifting entity that can appear as a shadowy monster, an old man, or even a hideous creature with a pumpkin-like head. It is known to hide in closets or under beds, waiting to snatch misbehaving children. The mere mention of its name can evoke fear in those who have grown up with stories of its nighttime prowling.

Cultural Context: In Latin American culture, El Coco serves as a cautionary figure used by parents to warn children against misbehavior. It embodies the fear of the unknown and the consequence of stepping outside the bounds of safety and societal norms.

Hunting Insight: Entities similar to El Coco thrive on **anxiety and guilt**. Hunters can counter these Boogeymen using **incantations of absolution** and by sealing entry points (such as closets) with salt and blessed water to strip the creature of its power.

4.2 La Llorona (Mexico)

Description: La Llorona, or "The Weeping Woman," is a ghostly figure known for wandering rivers and lakes, wailing for her lost children. Legend has it that she kidnaps children who wander too close to the water's edge, mistaking them for her own. Her presence is often marked by an eerie, mournful cry.

Cultural Context: La Llorona is a cautionary figure, warning children to stay away from dangerous waters. Her story reflects themes of loss, guilt, and the consequences of wrongdoings.

Hunting Insight: While La Llorona is more of a **spectral figure** than a traditional Boogeyman, entities resembling her operate through emotional manipulation. Hunters use **sound dampening wards** to mute her wails, breaking her hold on the area. They also use symbols of maternal protection, such as blessed cloth, to repel her influence.

Conclusion: The Global Face of Fear

The **Boogeyman** is not a single entity but rather a **universal archetype** that reflects humanity's fears, morals, and beliefs. By examining how different cultures perceive these entities—whether as punishing spirits, moral enforcers, or shadows of the unknown—we gain a deeper understanding of their power and the methods needed to confront them.

Each culture's version of the Boogeyman carries unique characteristics and weaknesses that hunters can exploit. From the shape-shifting Butzemann of Germany to the night-haunting Phi Am of Thailand, the diversity of Boogeymen around the world reveals that fear, in all its forms, is both **personal** and **cultural**. In the next chapters, we will delve into advanced techniques for tracking and capturing Boogeymen, drawing on the lessons learned from these global myths and legends. Armed with this knowledge, hunters can face the shadows with a broader, more informed perspective.

Chapter 24: 200 Mythical Boogeyman-Like Creatures Across the Globe

The Boogeyman archetype has manifested in countless forms across different cultures, evolving into various creatures that embody fear, punishment, and the mysteries of the unknown. From mischievous spirits to fearsome monsters, these **mythical Boogeyman-like entities** serve as cautionary figures, enforcers of moral conduct, and guardians of the boundaries between the human world and the supernatural. This chapter presents an extensive compilation of 200 such creatures from around the globe, providing a glimpse into the diverse ways societies understand and express fear through myth and legend.

1. Europe: Guardians of Tradition and Nightmares

Europe's Boogeymen often come from folklore and mythology, representing deep-seated fears rooted in cultural norms, morality, and the dark, untamed wilderness.

1. **Baba Yaga (Slavic):** A fearsome witch who lives in a hut on chicken legs. She is known to fly in a mortar and wield a pestle, often kidnapping children or testing those who seek her help. Represents the fear of the unknown and the chaotic forces of nature.
2. **Krampus (Austria, Germany):** A demonic figure with horns and cloven hooves, who punishes naughty children during the Christmas season. Symbolizes the fear of moral consequences.
3. **Butzemann (Germany):** A shape-shifting spirit known to haunt the countryside. Takes on forms like scarecrows or shadows, instilling fear in those who stray into its territory.
4. **Babau (Italy):** An amorphous creature lurking in dark places. Parents invoke the Babau to scare children into good behavior, representing the fear of the unseen and unknown.
5. **Boeman (Netherlands):** A shadowy figure that hides in dark corners and closets, used to keep children from misbehaving. Thought to symbolize the fear of disobedience.
6. **Bicho Papão (Portugal):** A monster hiding under beds, closets, and dark places to scare misbehaving children. Descriptions vary, but it often takes on a formless or shadowy appearance.
7. **Zwarte Piet (Netherlands):** While now a controversial figure, historically seen as a companion to Saint Nicholas who punishes naughty children. His role as a punitive figure connects him to the Boogeyman archetype.
8. **Lutin (France):** Mischievous spirits that can be benevolent or malevolent, depending on how they are treated. Often appear as little men causing trouble in homes, representing the fear of mischief and chaos.
9. **Aulë (Iceland):** A boogeyman-like giant who kidnaps children who venture too far from home during the dark winter months. Represents nature's dangers in harsh climates.
10. **The Sandman (Germany, Scandinavian Countries):** While known for putting children to sleep, some versions portray the Sandman as a menacing figure who punishes those who refuse to sleep by sprinkling sand in their eyes, blinding them.
11. **Tomte (Sweden, Norway):** A household spirit that punishes families who do not maintain cleanliness and order in their homes. Known for its temper if disrespected.

12. **Bodach (Scotland):** A shadowy figure that climbs down chimneys to frighten children. It embodies the fear of the dark and the unknown.
13. **Le Croque-Mitaine (France):** A creature that hides in closets or under beds, ready to devour children who misbehave. Its name translates to "the hand-cruncher."
14. **Gloson (Sweden):** A spectral pig said to roam dark forests at night, frightening those who wander off the path. Represents the dangers of the unknown in natural settings.
15. **Schrat (Germany):** A forest spirit known to lead travelers astray, causing them to become hopelessly lost. Often connected with tales of punishment for disturbing the natural world.
16. **La Bête du Gévaudan (France):** A mythical wolf-like beast said to have terrorized the French countryside in the 18th century. Represents the fear of the wild and the unknown dangers lurking in the wilderness.
17. **Böggelmann (Germany):** A goblin-like creature that hides in dark corners, often used to scare children into behaving. Represents the fear of mischief and chaos.
18. **Ankou (Brittany, France):** A skeletal figure believed to be a harbinger of death. It travels the countryside at night, collecting the souls of the dead.
19. **Tenebris (Italy):** An entity that takes the form of a dense, dark fog, seeping into homes to feed on the fear of the inhabitants. Represents the fear of being enveloped by darkness.
20. **Die Nachtkrapp (Austria):** A large, black bird that swoops down at night to take away children who misbehave. Its shadowy form and fearsome screech instill a fear of nighttime dangers.

2. Asia: Spirits and Guardians of Order

Asian cultures often depict Boogeyman-like figures as spirits or demons that enforce social norms, punish the wicked, and maintain balance between the spiritual and physical worlds.

1. **Namahage (Japan):** Demonic ogres who visit homes on New Year's Eve, threatening to carry off lazy or misbehaving children. They serve as enforcers of discipline and social norms.
2. **Pishacha (India):** Flesh-eating demons that haunt cremation grounds and abandoned places, preying on the vulnerable and weak. Symbolize the fear of death and decay.
3. **Jinmenken (Japan):** Dogs with human faces that appear at night, usually along deserted streets. Said to be harbingers of misfortune or reminders of moral transgressions.
4. **Phi Am (Thailand):** A spirit that sits on a sleeper's chest, inducing sleep paralysis and nightmares. Represents the fear of the unseen during the vulnerable state of sleep.
5. **Toyol (Malaysia, Indonesia):** The ghost of a child invoked by sorcerers to steal valuables. Represents the fear of theft, especially by the supernatural.
6. **Mara (Buddhist Tradition):** A demon that represents inner turmoil, temptation, and fear. Not strictly a Boogeyman but embodies the psychological struggles that can terrify and paralyze.
7. **Pontianak (Malaysia, Indonesia):** The vengeful spirit of a woman who died during childbirth. It is said to appear as a beautiful woman to lure its victims before transforming into a terrifying figure.

8. **Gaki (Japan):** Hungry ghosts driven by insatiable greed and desire. They wander in search of satisfaction, embodying fears of excess and unfulfilled cravings.
9. **Rakshasa (India):** Demonic beings that shape-shift into terrifying forms to instill fear. Often dwell in dark forests or isolated places, embodying the dangers of the wilderness.
10. **Hantu Kum-Kum (Malaysia):** A vampiric spirit that preys on young women, especially those who defy social customs. Symbolizes the fear of stepping outside societal norms.
11. **Bakhtak (Persia/Iran):** A sleep paralysis demon that sits on a person's chest, choking them and instilling fear. Represents the suffocating nature of dread.
12. **Aswang (Philippines):** A shape-shifting monster that preys on pregnant women and children. Embodies fears surrounding motherhood, birth, and the vulnerability of children.
13. **Jiangshi (China):** The reanimated corpse of a deceased person that feeds on the life force of the living. Often appears at night, hopping toward its victims.
14. **Mae Nak (Thailand):** The vengeful spirit of a woman who died during childbirth. Her story is often used to caution people against disturbing the dead.
15. **Manananggal (Philippines):** A vampire-like creature that can separate its upper body to fly through the night. It preys on pregnant women and infants, instilling fear of the dark and unknown.
16. **Krasue (Thailand):** A floating female head with internal organs trailing below. Known to feed on blood and fear during the night.
17. **Churel (India, Pakistan):** A vengeful spirit of a woman who died during childbirth or because of mistreatment. Known to lure men to their doom, representing societal fears of feminine wrath.
18. **Rokurokubi (Japan):** A spirit that appears as an ordinary woman during the day but whose neck stretches to an unnatural length at night, searching for victims.
19. **Yanari (Japan):** House-dwelling spirits that cause mysterious noises and disturbances. They are known to haunt homes with negative energy.
20. **Hannya (Japan):** The vengeful spirit of a woman consumed by jealousy. Often depicted with a demonic, twisted face, representing the fear of overwhelming negative emotions.

3. Africa: Spirits of Fear, Chaos, and the Unknown

In African folklore, Boogeyman-like figures often symbolize the dangers of natural forces, spiritual imbalance, and moral transgressions.

1. **Tokoloshe (Southern Africa):** A small, dwarf-like creature that can become invisible and climb onto sleepers to cause nightmares or illness. Often associated with witchcraft.
2. **Adze (Ghana, Togo):** A vampiric spirit that takes the form of a firefly to enter homes and drain the life force of sleeping individuals.
3. **Kishi (Angola):** A two-faced demon with a handsome human face and a hyena's face at the back of its head. Lures in victims with its charm before attacking.
4. **Popobawa (Zanzibar):** A bat-like demon known to attack during the night, causing physical and psychological torment.

5. **Mami Wata (West Africa):** A water spirit associated with beauty, seduction, and fear. Known to lure individuals to the water's depths if they offend her.
6. **Inkanyamba (South Africa):** A gigantic, serpent-like creature dwelling in deep lakes. Its presence is linked to natural disasters like storms and floods.
7. **Jengu (Cameroon):** Water spirits that can be both benevolent and malevolent. Their wrath is feared if they are disrespected or neglected.
8. **Ogbanje (Nigeria):** Mischievous spirits believed to be born into children, causing them to die young and be reborn repeatedly to torment their families.
9. **Ninki Nanka (Gambia):** A dragon-like creature that lives in swamps and rivers. Seeing it is said to bring certain death.
10. **Eloko (Congo):** Forest spirits that guard hidden treasures. They are known to lure humans into the woods with hypnotic music.

3. Africa (Continued): Spirits of Fear, Chaos, and the Unknown

1. **Sasabonsam (Ghana):** A forest-dwelling monster with hooked feet and bat-like wings. Sasabonsam is known to snatch unwary travelers, embodying the fear of the untamed wilderness.
2. **Impundulu (Southern Africa):** Also known as the "Lightning Bird," this creature serves as a familiar to witches. It appears as a black and white bird that can transform into a man, causing illness and death at its master's bidding.
3. **Grootslang (South Africa):** A serpent-elephant hybrid believed to live in deep caves. It is said to lure people with treasures, then devours them, representing greed and the dangers of the unknown.
4. **Anansi (West Africa):** While primarily a trickster god, Anansi can sometimes take on a more malevolent role, using his wits to create fear and chaos among humans.
5. **Mbwiri (Central Africa):** A spirit associated with rivers and forests. It causes illness and misfortune if it feels neglected or disrespected.
6. **Mamlambo (South Africa):** A water-dwelling entity resembling a snake with a horse-like head. It lures its victims into rivers, representing the dangers of venturing into unknown waters.

4. The Americas: Guardians of Morality and Spirits of Chaos

The Americas host a plethora of Boogeyman-like creatures derived from Indigenous myths, colonial legends, and post-colonial folklore, often highlighting fears related to nature, morality, and the supernatural.

1. **El Coco (Spain, Latin America):** A shape-shifting entity that can appear as a monster, shadow, or old man, used to scare children into obedience. Symbolizes the fear of the unknown and consequences of misbehavior.

2. **La Llorona (Mexico):** The ghost of a woman who haunts bodies of water, searching for her drowned children. She kidnaps wandering children, embodying fears of loss and danger.
3. **Chupacabra (Latin America):** A creature that preys on livestock, draining their blood. It represents fears of agricultural loss and the mysteries of rural life.
4. **Pishtaco (Peru, Bolivia):** A vampire-like figure in Andean folklore, said to kill people for their fat. Reflects historical fears of colonial exploitation and violation of body and soul.
5. **El Sombrerón (Guatemala):** A short man with a big hat, who braids the hair of young women and horses. Haunts his victims with music, embodying the fear of obsession and supernatural possession.
6. **La Luz Mala (Argentina, Uruguay):** Ghostly lights appearing at night, said to lead travelers astray or signal death. Represents fear of the unknown and dangerous journeys.
7. **Duende (Latin America):** Small, mischievous spirits that dwell in forests or homes, causing trouble and fear among those who encounter them.
8. **El Silbón (Venezuela):** The ghost of a man who killed his father, cursed to wander with a sack of bones, emitting a haunting whistle. Hearing his whistle is said to bring death or misfortune.
9. **Lobisón (Argentina, Paraguay):** The seventh son in a family, cursed to become a werewolf every full moon. Reflects fears around family curses and the dark side of human nature.
10. **Cadejo (Central America):** A supernatural dog that appears on dark roads. There are two types: the white Cadejo, which protects travelers, and the black Cadejo, which brings misfortune.
11. **La Tunda (Colombia):** A shape-shifting woman who lures victims into the forest, feeding off their fear and vitality. Symbolizes the dangers of the unknown wilds and deceit.
12. **Wendigo (Native American, Northern US, Canada):** A cannibalistic spirit representing greed and excess. Believed to inhabit forests and winter landscapes, feeding on those who succumb to despair.
13. **Ciguapa (Dominican Republic):** A female spirit with backward-facing feet, who lives in the mountains. She lures men with her beauty, then causes them to lose their way.
14. **Boto Encantado (Brazil):** A river dolphin spirit that transforms into a handsome man, seducing and impregnating women, embodying the fear of water spirits and deception.
15. **Mohan (Colombia):** A forest-dwelling spirit that lures gold miners into the jungle, trapping them with his enchanting music. Symbolizes nature's wrath and the perils of greed.
16. **Tlanchana (Mexico):** A mermaid-like creature who lives in rivers and lakes, known for her beauty and her ability to ensnare travelers, representing the fear of water's hidden dangers.
17. **Yara-ma-yha-who (Australian Indigenous):** A small, red-skinned creature with suckers on its fingers. It waits in trees to drop on passing travelers, feeding on their blood.
18. **Curupira (Brazil):** A forest spirit with backward feet, who protects animals and punishes those who harm the forest. It confuses hunters by leading them astray.
19. **Mapinguari (Brazil):** A giant, sloth-like creature with a mouth on its stomach. It is said to inhabit rainforests and has a foul smell that induces fear in those who encounter it.

5. Oceania: Nature Spirits and Guardians of Tradition

Oceania's Boogeymen are often tied to nature, representing its dangers, mysteries, and the importance of respecting spiritual traditions.

1. **Taniwha (New Zealand Māori):** A water spirit that guards rivers, lakes, and the sea. Can be a protector or a punisher, depending on how it is treated.
2. **Yara-ma-yha-who (Australia):** A vampire-like creature living in fig trees. Known to drop onto passing travelers and drain their blood, embodying the fear of unseen dangers in the wild.
3. **Papinijuwari (Australian Aboriginal):** A giant, cyclopean creature known to roam the night, spreading sickness and feeding on the life force of those who encounter it.
4. **Manu Tūrangarere (New Zealand Māori):** A bird-like spirit known to protect forests and punish those who cause harm. Represents the guardian spirits of nature.
5. **Adaro (Solomon Islands):** A malevolent sea spirit that attacks fishermen and sailors. Represents the perils of the sea and the supernatural forces believed to reside there.
6. **Wahwee (Papua New Guinea):** A small, hairy creature that lives in forests, causing travelers to become disoriented and lost. Symbolizes nature's mystique and the fear of getting lost in the wild.

6. Middle East: Spirits of Night, Shadows, and Vengeance

Boogeyman-like creatures in Middle Eastern folklore often serve as moral enforcers, punishing the wicked and guarding sacred places.

1. **Ghoul (Arabian Folklore):** A shape-shifting demon that preys on travelers in the desert, often appearing as an animal to lure its victims. It embodies the fear of the unknown and danger lurking in desolate places.
2. **Jinn (Islamic Folklore):** Supernatural beings that can be benevolent or malevolent. They dwell in remote places like deserts and abandoned ruins, representing the unpredictable nature of the spiritual world.
3. **Ifrit (Islamic Folklore):** A powerful and malevolent form of Jinn, associated with the underworld and fiery wrath. Often invoked as a punisher of wicked deeds.
4. **Nasnas (Arabian Folklore):** A half-bodied creature that haunts isolated places, known for its ability to leap great distances to catch prey. Symbolizes fear of deformity and isolation.
5. **Al Basti (Turkish Folklore):** A female spirit that sits on sleepers' chests, causing nightmares and paralysis. Represents the fear of the night and the vulnerability of sleep.
6. **Karakondžula (Balkans):** A vampiric spirit that emerges during the twelve days of Christmas, causing mischief and fear in the homes it visits.
7. **Qutrub (Arabic):** A ghoul that haunts graveyards, preying on the corpses and the fear of death. It is believed to be repelled by salt and fire.
8. **Yeti (Himalayan Folklore):** A large, ape-like creature said to dwell in the snow-covered mountains. Represents the fear of the unknown dangers in harsh natural environments.

6. Middle East (Continued): Spirits of Night, Shadows, and Vengeance

1. **Um Al Duwais (Arabian Gulf):** A female jinn with alluring beauty who seduces men before revealing her hideous form to punish them. Represents fear of temptation and the unknown dangers of giving in to desire.
2. **Al Naddaha (Egypt):** A siren-like figure known to call out to travelers near the Nile River at night, luring them to a watery grave. Embodies the dangers of unexplained calls and wandering too far from safety.
3. **Karkadann (Persian Folklore):** A mythical beast similar to a rhinoceros, known for its ferocity and association with untamed wilderness. Represents the fear of natural forces beyond human control.
4. **Gul (Persian Folklore):** Similar to Arabian ghouls, these creatures haunt deserts and graveyards, feeding on the flesh of the dead. Symbolize the fear of death, decay, and the macabre.
5. **Al-Mi'raj (Islamic Folklore):** A small, horned rabbit believed to inhabit enchanted islands. Despite its size, it is incredibly deadly and feared for its ability to kill anything it touches, embodying fears of deceptively small dangers.

7. Southeast Asia: Haunting Spirits and Nightmarish Beings

1. **Pontianak (Malaysia, Indonesia):** The vengeful spirit of a woman who died during childbirth, appearing as a beautiful woman who transforms into a blood-sucking fiend. Symbolizes fears of death in childbirth and maternal loss.
2. **Manananggal (Philippines):** A vampiric creature that separates its upper body from its lower half to fly at night, preying on the unborn. Embodies fears around pregnancy and childbirth.
3. **Leyak (Bali, Indonesia):** A witch-like figure that can transform into various animals or detach its head, trailing organs, to seek out victims. Represents the fear of dark magic and those who practice it.
4. **Orang Minyak (Malaysia):** A supernatural entity covered in oil that attacks and abducts women. Symbolizes the fear of assault and invasion of personal safety.
5. **Kuntilanak (Indonesia):** A female ghost known to haunt specific locations, especially near banana trees, targeting men and infants. Represents the dangers associated with grief and loss.
6. **Hantu Tetek (Malaysia):** A large, busty spirit that smothers its victims, usually children, in its embrace. Reflects the fear of suffocation and claustrophobic environments.
7. **Hantu Kopek (Malaysia):** Similar to Hantu Tetek, this spirit lures children with sweets before attacking them, embodying the dangers of stranger interaction.
8. **Nang Tani (Thailand):** A ghost that inhabits banana trees and appears as a beautiful woman in a green dress. She helps or harms humans depending on their actions, symbolizing the dual nature of spirits.
9. **Kapre (Philippines):** A tree-dwelling giant who smokes cigars and frightens passersby. Represents the fear of forest spirits and the dangers of disturbing nature.

10. **Aswang (Philippines):** A shape-shifting creature that blends into society during the day and preys on humans at night, particularly the sick and weak. Symbolizes fears of deceit and hidden dangers.
11. **Pocong (Indonesia):** A ghost wrapped in a burial shroud, said to hop after people. It embodies the fear of the restless dead and improperly performed burial rites.
12. **Tiyanak (Philippines):** The spirit of a child who died before being baptized, taking on the form of a baby to lure travelers before transforming into a monster.
13. **Chao Phom (Thailand):** A malevolent spirit that inhabits homes and forests, often punishing those who disturb sacred places. Symbolizes fear of disrespecting spiritual boundaries.
14. **Rakshasa (India):** Demonic beings with shape-shifting abilities, known for devouring humans and causing chaos. Represent the darker side of human nature and inner demons.

8. Pacific Islands: Nature Spirits and Guardians of the Wild

1. **Taotaomo'na (Guam):** Spirits of ancient ancestors residing in the jungles and banyan trees. Known to protect nature fiercely, punishing those who disrespect the land.
2. **Menehune (Hawaii):** Small, elusive beings believed to live in deep forests and valleys. Often seen as mischievous but can turn malevolent if provoked.
3. **Kaang (Papua New Guinea):** A spirit of the rainforest that can take on the form of different animals to confuse and trap travelers, representing the dangers of the wild.
4. **Vaitara (Tahiti):** A spirit who lingers in coastal areas, pulling swimmers underwater. Symbolizes the fear of deep water and drowning.
5. **Tupua (Samoa):** Ancient spirits associated with specific locations such as mountains and forests. They demand respect and offerings, representing the sacredness of nature.
6. **Wairua (Maori, New Zealand):** Spirits that can be both protectors and tricksters, often seen around rivers, caves, and sacred groves. Reflects the dual nature of spirits in the Maori belief system.
7. **Pele (Hawaii):** The goddess of volcanoes who can appear as an old woman, testing those she meets. Her fiery temper represents the untamed power of nature.
8. **Teine Sa (Samoa):** Sacred fire spirits who punish those who disobey cultural taboos. Represent the fear of breaking traditional norms.

9. Central Asia: Mountain Spirits and Desert Phantoms

1. **Alma (Mongolia):** Also known as the "Almas," these creatures are similar to Bigfoot and believed to roam the mountains. Symbolize the untamed wilds and humanity's fascination with the unknown.
2. **Dev (Persian Folklore):** Giant, demonic beings that haunt deserts and mountains, often trapping those who wander into their domain.
3. **Karakurt (Turkmenistan):** A shape-shifting creature resembling a black widow spider. It is said to be able to take human form to lure its victims.

4. **Zheleznyi Pyos (Russia):** A mythical metal dog that guards treasure and sacred sites. Represents the fear of trespassing and the dangers of greed.
5. **Hyt (Kazakhstan):** A malevolent desert spirit known to create mirages to confuse and lead travelers astray. Reflects the dangers of the desert and the illusions it creates.

10. Eastern Europe: Witches, Forest Spirits, and Night Stalkers

1. **Strigoi (Romania):** The restless spirits of the dead who rise from their graves to haunt the living. They represent fears of death and the supernatural.
2. **Baba Roga (Balkans):** A witch-like figure who preys on disobedient children. Symbolizes the fear of dark, foreboding places and the consequences of misbehavior.
3. **Koschei (Russia):** An immortal, skeletal figure who hides his soul in a needle, inside an egg, within a duck, representing the elusive nature of death and the lengths one goes to avoid it.
4. **Moroi (Romania):** Spirits of the dead that return to drain the life force of the living. Symbolize the fear of those who refuse to stay dead.
5. **Mavka (Ukraine):** Forest spirits who appear as beautiful women to lure men into the forest, representing the danger of nature's allure.
6. **Leshy (Russia):** A forest guardian who can shape-shift to confuse travelers, symbolizing the protective yet fearsome aspect of nature.
7. **Rusalka (Slavic):** Water nymphs that haunt lakes and rivers, luring men to their watery doom. Reflect the dangers of water bodies and the spirits believed to inhabit them.
8. **Bannik (Slavic):** The bathhouse spirit who punishes those who disrespect the bathhouse customs, embodying fears of breaking social and spiritual taboos.
9. **Domovoi (Russia):** A household spirit that can become malevolent if the household is not maintained or respected.
10. **Vodyanoy (Slavic):** A male water spirit who drags people into rivers or lakes. Reflects the fear of water's mysterious dangers.

11. The Caribbean: Spirits, Legends, and Curses

The Caribbean folklore is rich with spirits and supernatural beings that often symbolize the fear of nature's fury, curses, and the consequences of straying from cultural norms.

1. **La Diablesse (Caribbean Islands):** A woman with one cloven hoof who lures men into the forest, where they become lost forever. Represents the dangers of temptation and wandering into unknown territory.
2. **Duppy (Jamaica):** Ghostly spirits of the dead, known to haunt people and bring misfortune. Can be warded off with salt, symbolizing the fear of restless spirits and the need for spiritual protection.
3. **Soucouyant (Trinidad and Tobago):** An old witch who sheds her skin at night, transforming into a ball of fire to enter homes and drink the blood of the sleeping. Embodies the fear of malevolent forces that hide in plain sight.

4. **Jumbie (Caribbean):** Mischievous spirits that haunt the night and cause trouble. The belief in Jumbies reflects the fear of the unknown forces at play in everyday life.
5. **Rolling Calf (Jamaica):** A monstrous spirit with blazing eyes and a rattling chain, known to roam rural paths and frighten travelers. Symbolizes the consequences of bad deeds, particularly theft.
6. **Zandoli (Haiti):** A creature resembling a large, shadowy lizard that creeps into homes to steal the breath of children. Reflects fears surrounding child safety and the dangers of neglect.
7. **Papa Bois (Trinidad and Tobago):** A forest spirit, half-man and half-goat, who protects animals and punishes hunters who overstep nature's boundaries. Represents nature's guardianship and the consequences of greed.
8. **Lajablesse (Dominica):** Similar to La Diablesse, she has a beautiful appearance but hides a dark secret, enticing those who stray from moral paths.
9. **Lougarou (Haiti):** A witch who can transform into animals, often seen as a threat to children and livestock. Reflects fears of witchcraft and the disruption of community harmony.
10. **Moko Jumbie (Virgin Islands):** Tall stilt-walking spirits that guard against evil. They can be benevolent protectors or vengeful spirits if angered.
11. **El Tiburón (Cuba):** A mythical shark-like creature that haunts the seas, representing the fear of deep waters and the unknown dangers of the ocean.
12. **Bacoo (Guyana):** A small, mischievous spirit that brings both luck and trouble. It can be captured in a bottle but becomes vengeful if mistreated.

12. North America: Indigenous Spirits, Urban Legends, and Nightmares

In North American folklore, both Indigenous myths and more recent urban legends have given rise to an array of supernatural beings that reflect fears of nature, isolation, and societal change.

1. **Skinwalker (Navajo):** A witch that can transform into animals, using its powers to terrorize and manipulate. Represents the fear of betrayal, dark magic, and loss of identity.
2. **Slender Man (Urban Legend, USA):** A tall, faceless figure with elongated limbs that preys on children. Though modern, it embodies the fear of the unknown and the faceless threats lurking in society.
3. **Wendigo (Algonquin Myth):** A spirit of cannibalism and insatiable hunger that possesses those who commit heinous acts. Symbolizes greed, consumption, and the dangers of losing one's humanity.
4. **La Lechuza (Mexico, Southwestern USA):** A witch that transforms into an owl to spy on people and bring misfortune. Represents the fear of gossip, envy, and supernatural retribution.
5. **Bogeyman (North America):** A general term for the monster that lives under the bed or in the closet, taking on many forms. Represents the fear of darkness and childhood anxieties.
6. **Chindi (Navajo):** The spirit left behind after a person dies, carrying all of their negative traits. It brings misfortune to those who encounter it, symbolizing the fear of unresolved grudges and curses.

7. **Pukwudgie (Wampanoag Myth):** Small, troll-like creatures with the ability to shape-shift and disappear. Known to lead people astray in the forest, embodying the fear of the wilderness and isolation.
8. **Jack-O'-Lantern (European Folklore, USA):** Originally from Irish myth, the carved pumpkin with a candle inside was believed to ward off spirits, symbolizing the thin veil between the living and the supernatural during Halloween.
9. **Hodag (Wisconsin, USA):** A fearsome creature said to inhabit forests, with the ability to smell the blood of its victims. Represents the fear of untamed wilderness and the unknown dangers within.
10. **Black-Eyed Children (Urban Legend, USA):** Children with pitch-black eyes who appear at doorsteps at night, seeking to be let inside. Embodies the fear of the uncanny and potential dangers disguised as innocence.
11. **Knocker (Appalachian Folklore):** Spirits that inhabit mines, causing noises and collapses. Known both as protectors and omens of disaster, reflecting the dangers of mining life.
12. **Momo (Missouri Monster, USA):** A hairy, Bigfoot-like creature known to stalk the forests and scare those who encounter it. Represents the fear of isolation and the unknown in rural areas.

13. South America: Spirits of Nature, Vengeance, and Supernatural Justice

South American myths often feature spirits that protect nature and enforce moral conduct, reflecting the region's deep connection with the environment.

1. **El Tunchi (Peru):** A forest spirit that whistles to lure travelers off their path. If they respond, it leads them to their doom, symbolizing the dangers of the unknown in the wild.
2. **La Cegua (Costa Rica):** A beautiful woman with a horse's skull for a head, who preys on unfaithful men. Represents the consequences of deceit and moral transgression.
3. **La Sayona (Venezuela):** A vengeful spirit of a woman who punishes unfaithful men, appearing as a beautiful woman before revealing her monstrous form.
4. **Yacuruna (Amazonian Tribes):** Water spirits that live in rivers, known for abducting those who disrespect the water. Symbolize the power and mystery of rivers.
5. **Jasy Jatere (Guarani Myth, Paraguay):** A forest guardian who protects the secrets of the wilderness and can enchant children who wander too far.
6. **Curupira (Brazil):** A nature spirit with backward feet, leading hunters astray to protect the forest. Embodies the protective yet vengeful side of nature.
7. **Lobisomem (Brazil):** A werewolf legend adapted from European myths, believed to transform on a full moon. Represents the fear of losing control to base instincts.
8. **El Cadejo (Guatemala, El Salvador):** A supernatural dog that can be either benevolent (white Cadejo) or malevolent (black Cadejo), guiding or misleading travelers.
9. **Ciguapa (Dominican Republic):** A forest spirit with backward-facing feet, who lures men into the wilderness, where they become lost. Embodies fears of entrapment and the dangers of natural allure.

10. **Floripondio (Peru):** A ghostly being that lives in flower fields, luring those who wander too far. Reflects the danger of straying from known paths and being seduced by beauty.

14. Oceania (Continued): Mythical Creatures and Enigmatic Spirits

The myths of Oceania often feature spirits that represent the untamed aspects of nature, as well as moral enforcers who protect sacred spaces.

1. **Kakamora (Solomon Islands):** Small, forest-dwelling spirits who live in caves and use blowpipes to shoot intruders. Embody the dangers of venturing into forbidden or sacred areas.
2. **Bunyip (Australian Aboriginal):** A water spirit that inhabits billabongs, swamps, and rivers, preying on those who approach its territory. Symbolizes the hidden dangers of water.
3. **Tupua (New Zealand Maori):** Sacred ancestors or nature spirits that guard certain places, punishing those who disturb them.
4. **Kaiaiwaro (New Guinea):** A river spirit that drags people underwater, representing the mysterious and often dangerous nature of river currents.
5. **Tamate Ma'i (Micronesia):** A supernatural being that appears to those who are near death or lost, symbolizing the transitional state between life and the spirit world.
6. **Kanaloa (Hawaiian Mythology):** A sea god associated with ocean depths, storms, and the dangers of the deep sea.

15. Central Asia (Continued): Spirits of Deserts, Mountains, and Isolation

Central Asian myths often feature beings that embody the harshness of the environment, the power of nature, and the consequences of moral failings.

1. **Albasti (Turkic Folklore):** A female demon that attacks people during sleep, causing sleep paralysis. Represents the fear of nocturnal forces and the vulnerability of sleep.
2. **Khyrkhyz (Kyrgyzstan):** A creature resembling a giant bird that lives in the mountains, known to swoop down on livestock and travelers.
3. **Mongolian Death Worm (Mongolia):** A legendary creature said to inhabit the Gobi Desert, capable of killing with a single touch. Represents the fear of the unknown dangers in harsh terrains.
4. **Chotgor (Mongolia):** Restless spirits of those who died violently, known to haunt the places of their demise. Embodies the fear of untimely death and unresolved spirits.
5. **Azhdaha (Persian Mythology):** A dragon-like creature known to inhabit underground rivers and caves, blocking access to water sources. Symbolizes drought, scarcity, and the fear of hidden dangers lurking beneath the surface.
6. **Alp (Turkic Mythology):** A nightmare demon that sits on the chest of sleepers, causing sleep paralysis. Often appears in the form of a shadowy figure or animal, reflecting fears of helplessness and the unknown during sleep.
7. **Dev (Uzbekistan, Tajikistan):** Giants with supernatural strength who reside in the mountains and forests, often guarding treasures. They represent the challenges and perils of unexplored territories.
8. **Mangai (Kazakhstan):** A female demon that haunts desolate places, especially in times of drought, punishing those who fail to respect nature's forces.
9. **Yelman (Kyrgyzstan):** A spirit of the mountains, known for its vengeful nature, causing landslides or avalanches when disturbed. Represents the wrath of nature and the importance of respecting sacred lands.

16. Eastern Europe (Continued): Witches, Forest Spirits, and Night Stalkers

Eastern European folklore is rich with entities that serve as moral enforcers, guardians of nature, and symbols of existential fears.

1. **Baba Roga (Balkan Folklore):** A witch-like creature known to kidnap and eat children who misbehave. Often depicted as an old woman with supernatural powers, embodying fears of dark, mysterious forces lurking in rural areas.
2. **Baba Yaga's Hut (Slavic):** The house of Baba Yaga, which stands on chicken legs, can act as a boogeyman-like entity itself, guarding secrets and intimidating those who approach it without proper respect.
3. **Poludnica (Slavic Mythology):** Known as the "Lady Midday," this spirit appears in fields during the hottest part of the day, causing illness or madness to those who work too long under the sun. Represents the dangers of nature and the need for balance.
4. **Likho (Slavic Folklore):** A one-eyed, skeletal figure embodying bad luck and misfortune. It represents the inevitability of hardship and the human desire to avoid misfortune.
5. **Zmora (Polish Folklore):** A spirit that sits on the chest of sleepers, causing nightmares and sleep paralysis. Symbolizes anxieties and fears manifesting during vulnerable moments of rest.
6. **Leshy (Russia):** A forest spirit that protects wildlife and punishes those who exploit the forest. Known to lead travelers astray, representing the wilderness's untamed and sometimes vengeful nature.
7. **Drekavac (Serbian Mythology):** A creature born from the soul of a deceased child, with a blood-curdling scream that brings bad omens. Reflects fears of death, the unknown, and supernatural retribution.
8. **Mara (Slavic Folklore):** A female spirit or demon that causes nightmares by sitting on people's chests while they sleep. Symbolizes the fears of oppression and loss of control.
9. **Rodzanice (Poland):** Spirits of fate that appear during childbirth to predict the future. While generally benevolent, angering them can bring curses and misfortune, representing the fear of unknown destinies.
10. **Mamuna (Poland):** A water demon known to kidnap children and leave changelings in their place. Reflects the fear of loss and the dangers of water bodies.

17. The Arctic and Northern Territories: Ice Spirits, Mysteries, and Nature's Wrath

The harsh climates of the Arctic and northern regions have given rise to spirits that embody the environment's dangers, isolation, and unforgiving nature.

1. **Qalupalik (Inuit Mythology):** A sea creature that lures children to the icy waters with its humming. It represents the perils of wandering too close to dangerous, unpredictable waters.
2. **Akkorokamui (Ainu, Japan):** A giant octopus-like sea spirit that dwells in the waters off the coast of Hokkaido. Known for its ability to cause storms and drown sailors, reflecting the fear of maritime dangers.
3. **Tornit (Inuit Mythology):** Giant, hairy beings who live in remote mountains and tundras. Known for their aggression if disturbed, they represent the harshness of the natural world and the consequences of disrespecting it.
4. **Wendigo (Algonquin Mythology):** A spirit embodying greed and cannibalism, often associated with winter, starvation, and isolation. Reflects fears of losing one's humanity to primal urges.
5. **Atshen (Inuit Mythology):** An evil spirit that haunts the forest, preying on those who get lost in the winter woods. Symbolizes the dangers of harsh climates and the unknown threats lurking within them.

18. Global Urban Legends: Modern Boogeymen

Modern urban legends have created a new breed of boogeyman-like entities that reflect contemporary fears in urbanized societies.

1. **Slender Man (Internet Urban Legend):** A tall, faceless figure with unnaturally long limbs, known to stalk children and appear in photographs. Symbolizes the fear of the faceless, ubiquitous dangers lurking in modern society.
2. **The Rake (Internet Urban Legend):** A humanoid creature with pale skin and hollow eyes, known for its disturbing presence in dark corners. Reflects the fear of the unknown and hidden dangers within the familiar.
3. **Black-Eyed Children (North America, Modern Folklore):** Children with entirely black eyes who appear on doorsteps, asking to be let inside. Embodies the fear of the uncanny and the potential for danger hidden in innocence.
4. **Bloody Mary (Western Folklore):** A vengeful spirit summoned by chanting her name into a mirror in a darkened room. Represents the fear of self-reflection, the unknown, and the supernatural consequences of tempting fate.
5. **Momo (Internet Hoax):** A disturbing figure with an elongated face and bulging eyes, associated with a modern scare involving messages encouraging harmful behavior. Reflects fears of technological dangers and the perils of internet culture.

Conclusion: The Worldwide Manifestations of Fear

These final entries complete our list of **200 boogeyman-like entities**, spanning a vast range of cultures, mythologies, and modern folklore. Each creature, whether ancient or newly conceived, represents a unique aspect of human fear—be it the unpredictability of nature, the dangers of moral transgressions, or the shadows of our subconscious. By exploring these varied beings, we see how deeply the archetype of the Boogeyman is embedded in the human psyche.

For hunters and scholars of the supernatural, this knowledge serves as both a guide and a caution. The tales and characteristics of these creatures are a testament to humanity's eternal struggle to understand and confront fear in all its forms. As we venture further into the study and practice of **Boogeyman containment**, we carry with us the wisdom and warnings of cultures worldwide, preparing to face whatever lurks in the shadows.

Chapter 25: Cultural Myths and Boogeymen: How Legends Shape Fear

Throughout human history, **folklore and mythology** have been the primary vessels for conveying cultural values, taboos, and shared anxieties. Embedded within these narratives is the archetype of the **Boogeyman**—a being that encapsulates the fears of a community, often used to enforce societal norms, teach moral lessons, or explain the inexplicable aspects of human experience. As societies have evolved, so too has the concept of the Boogeyman, shifting from ancient legends and myths to modern interpretations that reflect contemporary concerns.

This chapter explores how **cultural myths** have shaped the modern understanding of Boogeymen, delving into how these entities have evolved across different cultures and eras. By examining the origins, symbols, and functions of Boogeymen in folklore, we gain insight into their role in human psychology, morality, and the subconscious mind.

1. Origins of the Boogeyman Archetype: Universal Fears

The Boogeyman appears in nearly every culture, often representing universal fears such as darkness, the unknown, and the dangers of the natural world. The earliest Boogeymen were tied closely to the environments and social structures in which they were created, embodying both the **physical dangers** (like wild animals, natural disasters) and **social dangers** (such as moral transgressions or breaking taboos) of their respective cultures.

1.1 Fear of the Unknown: Darkness and Isolation

One of the oldest fears encoded in the Boogeyman mythos is the **fear of the dark** and the **unknown**. Ancient societies often associated nighttime with danger, as it was when predators roamed, and vision was limited. Myths like the **Qalupalik** of Inuit lore, who drags children into the icy waters, and the **Baba Yaga** of Slavic mythology, a witch hiding in the depths of the forest, underscore this primal fear of what lurks just beyond the campfire's light.

In these early stories, Boogeymen served as warnings to children and adults alike: stay close to the safety of the community, avoid venturing into the wilderness, and respect the rhythms of nature. The Boogeyman, therefore, became a **guardian of boundaries**, defining the line between safety and danger, known and unknown.

1.2 Moral and Social Control: Enforcing Norms through Fear

Many Boogeyman legends serve a **moral function**, acting as enforcers of social norms and customs. In **Western Europe**, the **Krampus** punished naughty children during the Christmas season, reinforcing the moral lesson that good behavior was rewarded, while misbehavior led to dire consequences. Similarly, the **Namahage** of Japan visits homes on New Year's Eve, scaring those who have been lazy or dishonest, embodying societal values of hard work, discipline, and integrity.

By creating figures that punish wrongdoers, societies used Boogeymen to **instill fear** in the populace, ensuring compliance with cultural values and taboos. These myths often targeted vulnerable groups—children, young women, or those who strayed from social expectations—reflecting the cultural anxieties and power dynamics of their times.

1.3 The Wilderness and Nature: Guardians of Sacred Spaces

In many cultures, the Boogeyman is closely linked to the **natural world**, embodying the dangers and mysteries of untamed environments. Forest spirits like the **Leshy** in Slavic mythology or the **Curupira** in Brazilian folklore act as protectors of nature, punishing those who harm the forest or take more than they need. These legends reflect a deep respect for nature's power and the fear of disrupting its delicate balance.

Such myths served to **regulate human interaction** with the environment, warning of the consequences of overexploitation, greed, or disrespecting sacred places. The Boogeyman, in this context, acted as a **spiritual enforcer**, maintaining harmony between humans and the natural world.

2. The Evolution of Boogeyman Myths: Adapting to Changing Societies

As cultures evolved, so did their myths, with the Boogeyman adapting to reflect new fears and social dynamics. The industrial revolution, urbanization, and technological advancements brought about new anxieties, leading to the creation of modern Boogeymen that embody the challenges of contemporary life.

2.1 From Wilderness to Urban Legends: The Rise of Modern Boogeymen

In the transition from rural to urban societies, the Boogeyman moved from forests, mountains, and caves to the **urban jungle** of cities. The **Slender Man**, a product of internet folklore, illustrates how the Boogeyman myth has evolved to fit the anxieties of the digital age. With his faceless appearance, Slender Man represents the **faceless dangers** lurking in the vast, anonymous expanse of the internet and modern society.

Similarly, the **Black-Eyed Children** of North American urban legends embody the fear of strangers and the uncanny, preying on the discomfort of encountering things that look familiar yet are disturbingly different. These modern myths reflect a shift in cultural anxieties, from the fear of nature and isolation to the **fear of technology**, loss of privacy, and the erosion of personal boundaries.

2.2 Nightmares and Psychology: Internalizing the Boogeyman

As psychological understanding advanced, the Boogeyman began to take on a more **internalized role**, embodying the fears and traumas of the human psyche. Legends like the **Night Terror Wraith** reflect the experience of sleep paralysis, giving a supernatural face to the terrifying sensation of waking up unable to move, with a shadowy presence looming overhead.

In many cultures, the Boogeyman became a symbol of **unconscious fears**—guilt, repressed emotions, or societal pressures. The **Mara** of Slavic folklore, for instance, is a spirit that causes nightmares by sitting on a sleeper's chest, representing the weight of anxiety and unresolved issues. This internalization of the Boogeyman aligns with the human tendency to project psychological conflicts onto external entities, transforming abstract fears into tangible forms.

3. Modern Media and the Commercialization of Boogeymen

In recent decades, the Boogeyman has also been shaped by **popular media**, with movies, books, and video games introducing new forms of these creatures into the collective consciousness. Films like **"Halloween"** and **"A Nightmare on Elm Street"** brought forth iconic modern Boogeymen, turning fears of crime, societal breakdown, and inner demons into marketable horror symbols.

The **commercialization** of the Boogeyman has both expanded its reach and diluted its original cultural significance. While ancient myths used the Boogeyman as a tool for social cohesion and moral instruction, modern representations often focus on shock and entertainment, playing on the **universal appeal of fear** without necessarily conveying the deeper cultural messages of traditional legends.

4. Cross-Cultural Influences: The Globalization of the Boogeyman

With globalization, Boogeyman myths have transcended cultural boundaries, leading to a **fusion** of legends and the birth of new hybrid forms. The **Soucouyant** of the Caribbean, a vampire-witch who sheds her skin to feed on the blood of her victims, shares similarities with Southeast Asian legends like the **Manananggal** and **Krasue**—vampiric creatures that detach their heads or torsos to prey on the living.

This cross-cultural blending reflects the **shared human experience** of fear, as well as the adaptability of the Boogeyman archetype to different contexts. As cultures interact and exchange stories, they continue to shape and reshape the Boogeyman, creating new forms that resonate with diverse audiences.

5. The Role of Boogeymen in Modern Society: Confronting and Understanding Fear

Today, Boogeymen continue to serve as mirrors of societal fears, from the **internet-age monsters** that embody our anxieties about technology, to the **traditional spirits** that remind us of the power of nature and the consequences of straying from moral paths. By examining the evolution of Boogeyman myths, we gain insight into the cultural values, taboos, and psychological struggles of both past and present societies.

The modern Boogeyman has become not only a figure of **fear** but also a **tool for introspection**. It forces us to confront the sources of our anxieties—whether they stem from guilt, the fear of the unknown, or the challenges of navigating a rapidly changing world. In understanding these myths, we can better grasp how fear shapes human behavior and society.

Conclusion: The Timeless Nature of the Boogeyman

From ancient myths guarding the boundaries of the village to modern urban legends haunting the vast expanse of the internet, the Boogeyman has been a **constant companion** to human civilization. Its form, nature, and purpose may change, but its underlying function remains the same: to personify the fears and dangers that lie in the shadows of our consciousness.

As we continue to explore and adapt these myths, we keep the **archetype of the Boogeyman** alive, allowing it to evolve alongside us. By studying the cultural origins and transformations of these legends, hunters and scholars can gain a deeper understanding of the **power of fear**—both as a destructive force and as a tool for guiding human behavior. In the chapters that follow, this knowledge will be crucial in unraveling the methods for detecting, confronting, and containing the ever-adaptable Boogeyman.

Part 8: *Advanced Tactics for Seasoned Boogey Hunters*

Chapter 26: Dealing with Multiple Boogeymen at Once

While encountering a single Boogeyman is a formidable challenge in itself, there are situations where **multiple Boogeymen** manifest simultaneously. This scenario is exceedingly dangerous, as Boogeymen can feed off each other's fear-inducing energies, creating an environment of intensified dread. Handling such encounters requires **strategic planning**, **team coordination**, and the use of advanced containment techniques. This chapter provides an extensive guide to managing situations where multiple Boogeymen are present, offering tactical approaches, equipment recommendations, and advice for developing a specialized **Boogey-hunting team**.

1. Understanding the Dynamics of Multiple Boogeymen

When two or more Boogeymen manifest in the same location, their presence often leads to a **compound effect** of fear and supernatural activity. Unlike solitary Boogeymen, which typically operate within specific territories or conditions, multiple entities can create **interlocking webs** of fear that make them even harder to track, trap, and contain.

1.1 Feeding Frenzy: Amplified Fear

Boogeymen are naturally drawn to fear, and when multiple entities gather, they can trigger a **feeding frenzy** that amplifies their power. This synergy between Boogeymen makes them bolder and more aggressive, leading to rapid escalation of supernatural activity. Understanding this dynamic is crucial, as failing to break this cycle can result in a runaway situation where the fear energy becomes too strong to control.

1.2 Hierarchies and Roles within Groups

In some cases, Boogeymen manifest in **hierarchies**, where a more dominant entity acts as the "leader," while others support its activities. Identifying the **dominant Boogeyman** is key to disrupting the group's synergy. By targeting the leader first, hunters can destabilize the entire group, making it easier to contain the lesser entities.

Conversely, there are situations where Boogeymen operate **cooperatively**, working in tandem to create fear traps for their victims. For example, one might act as a **distraction**, while another prepares to ensnare the target. This cooperative behavior requires hunters to remain vigilant and versatile in their approach.

2. Preparation: Building a Boogey-Hunting Team

To tackle multiple Boogeymen, a team of skilled hunters is necessary. Each member must have a **specific role** to ensure smooth operation during the encounter. The recommended team roles include:

1. **Lead Hunter:** The strategist who directs the team's movements and makes critical decisions on containment strategies. They must possess a thorough understanding of Boogeyman psychology and containment methods.
2. **Tracker:** Equipped with tools to identify and monitor Boogeymen's locations. This member uses **thermal sensors**, **fear gauges**, and **spirit detectors** to pinpoint supernatural activity.
3. **Bait Specialist:** The team member responsible for setting up **lures** and managing the emotional environment to attract and distract Boogeymen. They often use decoy traps and sound emitters.
4. **Containment Expert:** In charge of preparing and activating containment devices such as **shadow nets**, **mirror traps**, and **binding circles**. Their primary task is to ensure the captured Boogeymen remain immobilized.
5. **Warding Specialist:** Focuses on setting up **protective wards** and barriers around the encounter site to prevent Boogeymen from escaping and to limit their influence. This member uses salt lines, iron powder, and talismans to create protective zones.

Effective teamwork hinges on **clear communication**, quick adaptation to changing circumstances, and a thorough pre-encounter briefing to establish roles, strategies, and contingency plans.

3. Encounter Strategies for Multiple Boogeymen

When dealing with more than one Boogeyman, hunters must employ sophisticated tactics designed to **divide and conquer**. Here are several strategies tailored to different types of multi-Boogeyman scenarios:

3.1 Divide and Isolate

The primary goal when encountering multiple Boogeymen is to **divide and isolate** them, breaking the synergy that amplifies their power. Hunters can use **lures** and **decoy traps** to draw individual Boogeymen away from the group, creating opportunities for targeted containment.

- **Sound Decoys:** Place sound-emitting devices around the encounter area to mimic noises that attract Boogeymen. The team can use these sounds to lure Boogeymen into isolated zones, where pre-set traps like **shadow nets** await.
- **Mirror Traps:** Position mirror traps at key points in the environment to reflect the Boogeymen's forms. Since Boogeymen often avoid mirrors, these traps can serve as barriers that funnel the entities into containment zones.
- **Separation with Wards:** Use **iron powder** and **salt lines** to create paths and barriers that limit Boogeymen's movement. This setup allows the hunters to force the entities into separate rooms or areas, where they can be tackled one by one.

3.2 Focus Fire: Target the Leader First

If the Boogeymen appear to be organized under a dominant entity, the team should focus their efforts on **neutralizing the leader** first. Disabling the leader often weakens the remaining Boogeymen, making them easier to manage.

- **Fear Dampening:** Use **fear-dampening charms** and wards around the team to weaken the leader's influence. The reduction in fear energy disrupts the feeding frenzy, creating an opportunity to attack.
- **Containment Circles:** Deploy **containment circles** crafted with moonstone-infused powder to trap the leader. Once the leader is contained, other Boogeymen typically become disoriented, allowing the team to isolate and capture them.

3.3 Simultaneous Containment: Multi-Zone Trapping

In some cases, it is not possible to isolate Boogeymen, especially if they are cooperative entities working in tandem. The team must then execute **simultaneous containment** using advanced trapping techniques.

- **Double-Layer Traps:** Prepare **double-layered traps**, such as **binding circles** within **shadow nets**, to catch Boogeymen that attempt to escape after one layer of containment is triggered. This approach ensures that if one Boogeyman tries to free another, it becomes ensnared itself.
- **Lure Coordination:** The bait specialist coordinates the use of **emotional decoys**, such as feigned fear, across multiple zones to draw the Boogeymen into pre-defined trap zones simultaneously. Timing is crucial to ensure that all traps activate at once, preventing the Boogeymen from coordinating an escape.

3.4 Banishment Rituals: Group Dispersal

If containment proves too challenging, the team may need to resort to **banishment rituals** designed to **disperse** multiple Boogeymen at once.

- **Circle of Iron:** Create a **circle of iron powder** with moonstone crystals at the four cardinal points. This circle serves as a central hub for the banishment ritual, generating a field of repelling energy.
- **Chant of Severance:** The lead hunter performs the **Chant of Severance**, an incantation that breaks the connection between the Boogeymen and the fear energy they feed on. This chant forces the entities to lose their cohesion, weakening them enough for banishment.
- **Flame of Purification:** Light **binding candles** around the perimeter of the iron circle to burn away residual fear energy, cleansing the area of the Boogeymen's influence.

4. Advanced Containment Techniques for Multiple Boogeymen

Dealing with multiple Boogeymen requires **specialized containment devices** designed to handle multiple entities at once or in quick succession.

4.1 Multi-Chamber Containment Cubes

Multi-chamber containment cubes are designed to hold several Boogeymen simultaneously within separate compartments. Each chamber is reinforced with **runic etchings** and **binding oils** that create individualized containment fields, preventing the entities from interacting or feeding off one another.

- **Deployment:** Containment experts set up these cubes in key areas, using **attraction glyphs** to draw Boogeymen into the chambers. Once inside, the chambers automatically seal, separating the entities.
- **Maintenance:** The cubes require regular **purification rituals** to prevent the Boogeymen from gaining strength and attempting to break free.

4.2 Mirror Grid Traps

A **mirror grid** trap consists of interlocking mirrors arranged in a maze-like formation. Boogeymen are lured into this grid, where their reflections confuse and disorient them, making it difficult to escape.

- **Activation:** When a Boogeyman enters the grid, containment experts activate the mirrors, creating a web of reflective surfaces that trap the entities in an endless cycle of reflection.
- **Containment:** While the mirrors do not directly imprison the Boogeymen, they immobilize them long enough for hunters to set up secondary containment measures, such as **shadow nets** or **binding circles**.

4.3 Fear-Binding Talismans

Fear-binding talismans are **runes** or **amulets** crafted to siphon and store fear energy. When dealing with multiple Boogeymen, these talismans can be used to **drain** the entities' power, weakening them for capture.

- **Usage:** Place the talismans in locations where fear energy is most concentrated. As the talismans absorb the energy, the Boogeymen's hold on the environment diminishes, making them easier to ensnare.
- **Containment:** After capturing the Boogeymen, the talismans are stored alongside them in a **containment box** lined with silver and warded with binding runes.

5. Post-Encounter Protocols: Securing the Contained Entities

Once multiple Boogeymen have been captured, the team must perform **post-encounter protocols** to secure the entities and cleanse the environment of residual fear energy.

- **Containment Review:** The containment expert conducts an inspection of all traps and devices to ensure no breaches or weaknesses exist.
- **Environmental Cleansing:** The warding specialist performs a **cleansing ritual** using sage smoke and moonstone-infused water to purify the encounter area, preventing future Boogeyman manifestations.
- **Containment Storage:** Transport the captured Boogeymen to a **containment facility** designed for long-term storage. Multi-chamber cubes are placed in warded rooms, and mirror traps are covered and sealed with iron powder.

Conclusion: Mastering the Art of Multi-Boogeyman Encounters

Handling multiple Boogeymen at once requires a combination of **teamwork, strategy**, and **advanced containment techniques**. By understanding the dynamics of Boogeyman groups, hunters can develop plans that disrupt their synergy, isolate them, and neutralize their power. Successful encounters depend on careful preparation, clear communication among team members, and the effective use of specialized equipment.

As Boogeymen continue to adapt and evolve, hunters must remain vigilant, refining their tactics and expanding their knowledge to face these compounded threats. The strategies and methods outlined in this chapter form the foundation for **advanced Boogey-hunting**, equipping hunters to tackle the most complex and dangerous supernatural encounters. The next chapter will delve into the **long-term containment** and monitoring of captured entities, ensuring that these shadows remain securely imprisoned.

Chapter 27: Boogeyman Rebellion: When They Turn Violent

Capturing a Boogeyman is never a guarantee of total safety. These creatures are **masters of fear**, often harboring deep-rooted cunning and a relentless drive to regain freedom. At times, Boogeymen may attempt to **rebel**, turning violent as they seek to escape their containment. Such situations are extremely dangerous, as a rebelling Boogeyman not only threatens the safety of its captors but can also release an intense wave of fear energy that further destabilizes the environment around it.

In this chapter, we will explore the signs of a **Boogeyman rebellion**, the steps necessary to **manage containment breaches**, and the advanced techniques required to **subdue hostile entities**. Understanding and preparing for these eventualities is crucial to maintaining control over captured Boogeymen and preventing potentially catastrophic consequences.

1. Recognizing Signs of a Boogeyman Rebellion

Before a Boogeyman attempts an escape, it typically exhibits warning signs. Recognizing these signals early allows hunters to reinforce containment measures and implement calming strategies to prevent a full-scale rebellion.

1.1 Changes in Environmental Conditions

Boogeymen affect their surroundings, and a rebellion often manifests as **abrupt environmental changes**:

- **Temperature Drops:** A sudden, unnatural chill around the containment unit often indicates that the Boogeyman is gathering energy to break free.
- **Flickering Lights:** Electrical disturbances and flickering lights suggest the entity is exerting its influence on the physical realm, attempting to manipulate its surroundings to weaken containment.
- **Disturbing Noises:** Scratching, tapping, or low growls emanating from containment devices indicate a Boogeyman testing the integrity of its prison.

1.2 Containment Device Reactions

Advanced containment units are designed to **react** to changes in the Boogeyman's behavior:

- **Containment Cube Vibrations:** If a containment cube begins to hum, vibrate, or emit a high-pitched sound, it signifies that the Boogeyman inside is applying pressure on the inner seals of its chamber.
- **Runic Glow:** Runic inscriptions on binding circles or boxes may glow brighter when under stress, indicating that the entity is pushing against its restraints.

1.3 Emotional Feedback

Some Boogeymen have a psychic connection to their surroundings, particularly to the emotional state of those nearby. **Feelings of unease, dread, or sudden fear** among the team can indicate that the Boogeyman is attempting to provoke a reaction, thereby feeding off the fear to fuel its rebellion.

2. Immediate Actions: Reinforcing Containment

Upon noticing the signs of an impending rebellion, the priority is to **reinforce containment** to prevent the situation from escalating. Swift action is critical to subdue the Boogeyman before it can gain enough strength to break free.

2.1 Strengthening Physical Containment

- **Apply Iron Powder:** Sprinkle a fresh layer of **iron powder** around the containment unit. Iron is known to weaken Boogeymen, creating a physical barrier that limits their influence on the environment.
- **Salt Circles:** Surround the containment area with a **circle of salt** to further restrict the entity's movement and suppress its power. The salt circle acts as a protective barrier, reducing the Boogeyman's ability to manipulate objects outside its prison.

2.2 Reinforcing Runic and Mystical Wards

- **Runic Touch-Up:** Use **binding ink** to re-trace any fading runes on the containment unit. This reinforcement strengthens the seals, preventing the entity from exploiting weak points.
- **Talismans and Amulets:** Place **fear-binding talismans** and **moonstone amulets** around the unit to absorb the negative energy generated by the Boogeyman. These objects neutralize fear-based attacks and limit the entity's ability to project its power outward.

2.3 Deploying Calming Measures

- **Fear Dampening:** Activate **fear-dampening charms** to create a calming atmosphere around the containment area. These charms emit a soothing energy that counteracts the Boogeyman's efforts to provoke fear.
- **Burning Sage and Incense:** Light **sage bundles** and **frankincense** to purify the environment. The smoke disrupts the Boogeyman's connection to the physical realm, often calming its violent tendencies and forcing it into a dormant state.

3. Contingency Plans for Containment Breaches

In the event that a Boogeyman **escapes** or breaches containment, hunters must act quickly to **regain control**. Here's how to respond effectively to an escape attempt:

3.1 Immediate Containment Measures

- **Deploy Shadow Nets:** Keep **shadow nets** on standby for quick deployment. These nets are infused with moonstone dust and iron filaments, designed to ensnare the Boogeyman's shadow form if it manages to escape its primary containment.
- **Erect Binding Circles:** Use **portable binding circles** that can be placed around the Boogeyman's new location. These circles contain runes of power that restrict the entity's movement and bind it within a limited area, buying time for more permanent solutions.

3.2 Team Coordination: Role-Specific Responses

- **Lead Hunter:** Takes command, issuing instructions to the team. Their main focus is to **direct** the containment effort and make strategic decisions.
- **Tracker:** Uses **thermal imaging** and **spirit detectors** to locate the Boogeyman's new position, providing crucial information to guide containment measures.
- **Containment Expert:** Prepares and activates **secondary traps** and ensures that all available containment units are functional and ready for use.
- **Bait Specialist:** If necessary, uses **emotional decoys** to lure the Boogeyman into a controlled zone where it can be re-contained.
- **Warding Specialist:** Creates **temporary wards** to limit the Boogeyman's influence over its surroundings, reducing the risk of it manipulating objects or individuals during the containment process.

3.3 Emergency Re-Containment

- **Mirror Trap Deployment:** If the Boogeyman manifests visibly, use **mirror traps** to reflect its form and immobilize it temporarily. This action allows the team to reposition or repair primary containment devices.
- **Boogie Goo Application:** Use **Boogie Goo** on surfaces where the Boogeyman is likely to pass. The sticky substance ensnares the entity, preventing it from moving freely and allowing hunters to close in for containment.

4. Subduing a Hostile Boogeyman

When a Boogeyman turns overtly violent, it may launch psychic or physical attacks, creating a hostile environment. Subduing the entity requires a combination of **defensive spells**, **psychic shields**, and **counter-offensive measures**.

4.1 Defensive Measures

- **Psychic Barriers:** Activate **psychic shields** to protect the team from mental assaults. These shields, crafted from moonstone and obsidian, block psychic energy, preventing the Boogeyman from inducing fear or confusion among the hunters.
- **Counter-Chant:** Use **counter-chant incantations** to deflect the Boogeyman's offensive maneuvers. The **Chant of Reversal** can turn the entity's own fear energy back upon it, weakening its power and making it more susceptible to containment.

4.2 Counter-Offensive Measures

- **Binding Rituals:** For particularly aggressive Boogeymen, employ **binding rituals** using enchanted ropes or chains. These items are imbued with runes of binding and can physically and spiritually restrain the Boogeyman, forcing it into a state of dormancy.
- **Fear Draining:** Place **fear-draining talismans** near the Boogeyman's current location. These talismans siphon off the fear energy the entity has accumulated, reducing its strength and ability to resist containment efforts.

4.3 Forcing Dormancy

If subduing the Boogeyman proves difficult, hunters may need to resort to **forcing the entity into dormancy**:

- **Moonstone Light:** Shine **moonstone light** directly on the Boogeyman to drain its energy. Moonstone disrupts the creature's access to fear-based power, inducing a dormant state.
- **Freezing with Cold Iron:** Use **cold iron chains** to wrap around the entity, freezing its movements and suppressing its abilities. This method is risky and requires careful timing, but it effectively immobilizes even the most violent Boogeymen.

5. Reinforcing Long-Term Containment

After subduing a violent Boogeyman, hunters must **reinforce** the containment to prevent future rebellion attempts.

5.1 Multi-Chamber Reinforcement

For particularly resilient entities, transfer them into **multi-chamber containment cubes** with **layered wards** and **mirror linings**. The multiple chambers act as a failsafe, ensuring that if one layer is breached, the remaining chambers hold.

5.2 Runic Renewal

Perform a **runic renewal ritual** on the containment unit, inscribing **binding runes** using a mixture of iron powder, silver dust, and crushed moonstone. This ritual fortifies the containment's mystical seals, creating a nearly impenetrable barrier.

5.3 Fear Neutralization

Place **fear-binding talismans** within the containment unit to absorb and neutralize excess fear energy. These talismans act as **emotional dampeners**, preventing the Boogeyman from accumulating the energy needed for future rebellions.

6. Post-Rebellion Cleansing and Reflection

Once the situation is under control, a **thorough cleansing ritual** must be conducted to purify the area of residual negative energy. This process involves burning sage, sprinkling salt, and invoking protective chants to restore balance and reduce the risk of another rebellion.

The team should then **review the incident**, analyzing the Boogeyman's behavior, the effectiveness of their response, and identifying areas for improvement. This reflective practice is essential for refining techniques and adapting to the evolving nature of Boogeymen.

Conclusion: Mastering the Art of Subjugation

Dealing with a **rebellious Boogeyman** requires not only a deep understanding of its nature but also quick reflexes, strategic thinking, and the proper use of containment tools and rituals. While the threat of rebellion is ever-present, hunters who are vigilant, well-prepared, and adaptable can successfully manage and subdue even the most hostile entities.

By mastering these techniques, hunters ensure the **safety of their surroundings** and the continued containment of the Boogeymen. The knowledge gained from each rebellion further equips them to face future encounters, turning fear into a powerful ally in the endless battle against the shadows. The following chapter will explore **long-term containment and monitoring** strategies to ensure that captured Boogeymen remain securely imprisoned.

Chapter 28: Negotiating with Boogeymen: Friend or Foe?

Boogeymen are not mere mindless creatures of fear; they possess varying degrees of **intelligence**, **cunning**, and **sentience**. While they are primarily driven by a need to instill and feed off fear, there are instances where a hunter might find it beneficial—or necessary—to attempt **negotiation**. Whether driven by a desire to protect a larger community, gain critical information, or broker a temporary peace, striking a deal with a Boogeyman is a delicate and often dangerous process. This chapter delves into the complex art of **Boogeyman communication**, examining when negotiation is possible, the risks involved, and how to approach these shadowy entities with caution.

1. Understanding Boogeymen's Sentience and Motivations

Boogeymen come in various forms, ranging from primal manifestations of fear to intelligent, almost human-like entities capable of strategic thinking and speech. Recognizing a Boogeyman's level of **sentience** and its core motivations is the first step in determining whether negotiation is possible.

1.1 Levels of Boogeyman Intelligence

Boogeymen exhibit different levels of intelligence, which influences how they can be communicated with:

- **Primal Entities:** These are driven purely by instinct. They act solely to incite fear and chaos, with little to no capacity for reason or negotiation. Communication with primal Boogeymen is often futile, as they lack the self-awareness needed for meaningful dialogue.
- **Cunning Predators:** These Boogeymen exhibit strategic thinking, often setting traps and manipulating their environment. They may understand the concept of negotiation but are inherently distrustful and deceptive.
- **Sapient Entities:** The most advanced Boogeymen possess a high level of sentience, self-awareness, and even a form of morality. They can articulate their desires and, in some rare cases, recognize the benefits of negotiation. These entities are the most likely candidates for striking a deal.

1.2 Assessing Motivations

Before engaging in negotiation, hunters must identify the Boogeyman's **motivations**:

- **Fear Consumption:** Most Boogeymen seek fear as sustenance. If the Boogeyman is driven purely by a hunger for fear, negotiation might center around alternative sources or controlled feeding opportunities.
- **Territorial Control:** Some Boogeymen are protective of their territory. Negotiations in these cases may involve defining boundaries that allow both hunters and the Boogeyman to coexist.
- **Vengeance or Justice:** Certain Boogeymen are motivated by a sense of retribution or justice. Understanding their grievances can open the door to negotiation, offering a way to resolve their vendetta in exchange for peace.

2. Initiating Communication with a Boogeyman

Effective communication requires a mix of **ritual**, **psychic connection**, and **symbolic gestures**. Boogeymen are naturally suspicious and may see negotiation attempts as traps unless approached with caution and respect.

2.1 Creating a Safe Negotiation Space

A safe space for communication is essential to keep both the hunters and the Boogeyman on neutral ground:

- **Binding Circles:** Use a **binding circle** to contain the Boogeyman's influence while allowing it enough room to interact. The circle should be drawn with a mixture of iron powder and salt to prevent aggressive actions without provoking the entity.
- **Protective Wards:** Set up **protective wards** around the negotiation space to shield the hunters from psychic assaults. **Moonstone amulets** and **fear-dampening charms** should be worn by all participants to maintain emotional clarity.

2.2 Ritual Invocation

Boogeymen respond to rituals that signal intent. The **Invocation of Shadows** ritual can be used to summon the Boogeyman into the negotiation circle:

- **Shadow Words:** Recite the **Invocation of Shadows**, using words that appeal to the Boogeyman's nature. Phrases like "I call thee not to bind, but to bargain" signal that the interaction is not a trap but an invitation to converse.
- **Offering of Intent:** Place an **offering** within the circle that reflects the Boogeyman's desires. This could be an object imbued with fear energy (such as a **fear-binding talisman**) or a symbolic gesture, like a **broken mirror** to represent vulnerability. The offering serves as a token of good faith and a starting point for negotiation.

3. Conducting Negotiations: Rules of Engagement

Negotiating with a Boogeyman is akin to navigating a maze of **psychological traps**. Hunters must be vigilant, setting clear rules while remaining open to the entity's propositions.

3.1 Establishing Boundaries and Terms

- **Set Ground Rules:** Before delving into the negotiation, set explicit rules. For instance, "No physical or psychic harm during this negotiation," and "The circle shall remain unbroken until an agreement is reached." Boogeymen will test these boundaries, so enforce them strictly.
- **Define Objectives:** Clearly state the purpose of the negotiation. Whether it's to **establish a truce**, **define territorial boundaries**, or **exchange information**, outlining your objective helps frame the discussion and prevents the Boogeyman from steering the conversation into dangerous territory.

3.2 Listening and Understanding

- **Speak Sparingly:** Boogeymen are adept at twisting words and exploiting weaknesses. Keep dialogue **succinct** and **focused**. Use questions to guide the conversation, revealing the Boogeyman's desires and intentions.
- **Acknowledge Their Nature:** Boogeymen are aware of their dark nature and often take pride in it. Acknowledging this can build a rapport that makes negotiation possible. Phrases like "You have proven your strength here" can appeal to the Boogeyman's ego and open a path for discussion.
- **Offer Alternatives:** If the Boogeyman seeks fear, propose alternative sources that do not endanger innocent people. For example, hunters can offer **fear-binding talismans** filled with ambient fear energy harvested from haunted locations. This allows the Boogeyman to feed without direct harm.

4. The Nature of Deals: Common Agreements with Boogeymen

Boogeymen are driven by self-interest and will only agree to deals that offer them something they value. Here are some common types of agreements that hunters may strike:

4.1 Territorial Boundaries

In cases where a Boogeyman is protective of a specific area:

- **Establish Boundaries:** Hunters can negotiate a **territorial truce**, defining specific zones where the Boogeyman is allowed to roam, in exchange for leaving other areas unmolested. This agreement is usually marked by **warding stones** at the boundary lines, serving as both a reminder and a magical deterrent.
- **Safe Passage:** Hunters might secure **safe passage** through the Boogeyman's territory in return for regular offerings, such as fear-infused objects. This allows hunters to monitor and contain the entity without constant conflict.

4.2 Controlled Feeding Agreements

If a Boogeyman's primary drive is feeding on fear:

- **Fear Offerings:** Provide the Boogeyman with **fear-binding talismans** periodically, allowing it to feed without directly haunting humans. This arrangement often requires careful monitoring to ensure the entity does not grow too powerful.
- **Supervised Hauntings:** In rare cases, hunters might agree to allow the Boogeyman to manifest under controlled conditions, such as during **haunted house tours** or **ritual gatherings**, where fear is generated in a safe environment. The Boogeyman agrees to a code of conduct that limits harm to participants.

4.3 Information Exchange

Boogeymen, especially sapient ones, often possess **knowledge** about other supernatural beings, hidden realms, or the mechanics of fear. Hunters can leverage this information in exchange for favors or promises:

- **Trade for Secrets:** Offer to protect the Boogeyman's territory from rival entities in exchange for information about their weaknesses, locations, or plans.
- **Knowledge for Silence:** Boogeymen who prefer secrecy may provide information in exchange for hunters **disseminating false leads** or **concealing their presence** from other hunters.

5. Risks and Safeguards in Negotiation

Negotiating with a Boogeyman is inherently risky, as these entities are notorious for their cunning and treachery. Hunters must employ **safeguards** to protect themselves during and after negotiations.

5.1 Words of Power: Binding the Agreement

- **Contract Seals:** Inscribe **binding runes** into the negotiation circle to seal the agreement. This magical contract forces both parties to uphold the terms. Breaking the seal results in a backlash of energy that can weaken or even banish the Boogeyman.
- **Sworn Oaths:** Have the Boogeyman **swear an oath** using its true name, if known. A sworn oath holds immense power in the supernatural world, compelling the Boogeyman to honor the deal or face dire consequences.

5.2 Monitoring and Enforcement

After a deal is struck, hunters must **monitor the Boogeyman's behavior** to ensure compliance:

- **Ward Surveillance:** Place **warding stones** around the agreed-upon territory to detect breaches. The stones glow when the Boogeyman attempts to cross the boundaries, alerting the hunters.
- **Talisman Renewal:** Regularly provide **fear-binding talismans** to satisfy feeding agreements. If the Boogeyman grows too powerful or strays from the terms, use the talismans to drain its strength and reinforce the boundaries.

6. When Negotiations Fail: Preparing for Reprisal

Not all negotiations succeed, and some may end in hostility. Always have a **contingency plan** for immediate containment or banishment:

- **Emergency Circle Activation:** Keep a **secondary binding circle** ready to deploy at a moment's notice. This circle serves as a last-resort containment measure should the Boogeyman turn violent.

- **Seal the Portal:** If the negotiation occurs in a ritual space, prepare to **seal the portal** connecting the Boogeyman to the physical realm. This action cuts off its escape routes, forcing it to retreat into its realm or submit to containment.

Conclusion: The Art of Boogeyman Diplomacy

Negotiating with Boogeymen is an intricate dance of **power, respect, and cunning**. Success requires a deep understanding of the entity's nature, a careful balance of offering and demand, and a willingness to enforce the terms with supernatural safeguards. While the risks are high, a successful negotiation can lead to **valuable alliances**, **peaceful coexistence**, or critical insights into the supernatural world.

Hunters must approach these encounters with **confidence**, **clarity**, and **preparedness**, knowing that a misstep could spell disaster. Yet, with the right mix of diplomacy and firmness, even the most formidable Boogeyman can be made to listen, and sometimes, just sometimes, even cooperate. The next chapter will delve into the **psychological tactics** that hunters can use to outwit and manipulate Boogeymen, expanding on the delicate balance between fear and control.

- THE SPOOKY JOURNEY BEGINS

Part 9: *Boogeyman Lore and Research*

Chapter 29: Ancient Texts on Boogeymen

For centuries, the presence of **Boogeymen** has been chronicled in the pages of **ancient texts** and **scrolls**, serving as both warnings and repositories of knowledge about these fearsome entities. From the earliest cave paintings depicting shadowy figures to intricate manuscripts held in secret archives, humanity has long sought to understand, contain, and sometimes even wield the power of Boogeymen. This chapter will explore the most **significant ancient texts** that document Boogeymen's existence, their abilities, and the intricate rituals developed to interact with these beings. By delving into these texts, hunters gain insights into historical methods of **containment**, **negotiation**, and the cultural significance of Boogeymen across different societies.

1. The Shadow Codex (Egypt, c. 2500 BCE)

The **Shadow Codex** is believed to be one of the earliest known documents on Boogeymen, originating from the Old Kingdom of ancient Egypt. The papyrus scroll, now housed in a heavily guarded section of the Egyptian Museum in Cairo, contains a series of spells, diagrams, and instructions related to entities referred to as "Sha'kahet" or "Shadow-Dwellers."

1.1 Descriptions and Nature of Boogeymen

In the Codex, the Sha'kahet are described as **creatures of the Duat**, the Egyptian underworld. They were believed to be manifestations of the chaotic forces that Osiris, the god of the dead, sought to control. According to the text, these entities thrived in darkness and could traverse between the realms of the living and the dead.

The Codex notes that the Sha'kahet fed on **emotions**, particularly fear, and their presence was often heralded by the chilling of the air and the whisper of shadows. Unlike other spirits, they were not bound by the rites of the dead, making them especially dangerous to mortals.

1.2 Rituals and Containment

The Shadow Codex outlines several **rituals** for repelling and containing the Sha'kahet:

- **The Binding of Ma'at:** A ritual requiring the drawing of **hieroglyphic symbols** on the ground, invoking the power of Ma'at, the goddess of truth and order. This ritual creates a spiritual boundary that repels shadowy beings, preventing them from crossing into the mortal world.

- **Amulet of the Serpent:** The text describes an amulet carved from **serpent bones** and inscribed with protective symbols. When worn, this amulet creates a personal barrier around the wearer, rendering them invisible to the Sha'kahet's senses.

2. The Book of Nightmares (Sumer, c. 1800 BCE)

In ancient Sumer, fear and darkness were personified in the form of **Utukku**, spirits that haunted the night. The **Book of Nightmares**, a collection of clay tablets inscribed in cuneiform, provides some of the earliest detailed accounts of these Boogeyman-like entities. Fragments of this book are kept in the British Museum, though several tablets remain lost or hidden in private collections.

2.1 Utukku and the Realm of Night

The Book of Nightmares describes the Utukku as shadowy figures that could pass through walls and move unseen in the dark. They were believed to originate from the **Kur**, the underworld, and were said to slip into the mortal realm during the hours of twilight and darkness.

According to the text, the Utukku were agents of **Nergal**, the god of death and pestilence, sent to enforce the laws of the underworld upon mortals who had strayed from their path. Their power lay in their ability to **induce nightmares**, feeding on the terror they generated.

2.2 Rituals of Banishment and Protection

The Book of Nightmares outlines **protective measures** and **banishment rites** that remain influential in modern Boogeyman containment practices:

- **The Sealing of the Door:** Inscribing cuneiform symbols of protection on clay tablets and placing them above doorways and windows creates a barrier against Utukku. The text emphasizes the use of **lapis lazuli** in the inscriptions, as this stone was believed to channel the protective power of the gods.
- **The Rite of Salt and Fire:** A purification ritual involving the scattering of salt in a circle while invoking the names of the ancient gods. A flame is then passed over the salt to create a ring of protection, forcing the Utukku back into the Kur.

3. The Liber Tenebris (Rome, c. 200 BCE)

The **Liber Tenebris** ("Book of Shadows") is a Roman text that delves into the practices of **necromancy** and the summoning of shadowy entities. Although it primarily focuses on interactions with spirits of the dead, a significant portion of the text describes beings known as "Tenebrae," which exhibit characteristics similar to Boogeymen.

3.1 The Tenebrae: Spirits of Fear

The Tenebrae are depicted as shadowy forms capable of **shapeshifting** and **inducing paralyzing fear** in those who encounter them. According to the Liber Tenebris, they were ancient spirits who roamed the **crossroads** and **graveyards**, places believed to be doorways to the underworld.

The text warns that the Tenebrae are **deceptive** and thrive on the fear of mortals. They were often invoked by Roman sorcerers seeking to control others through nightmares and terror.

3.2 Spells and Protective Incantations

The Liber Tenebris offers several incantations for controlling and warding off the Tenebrae:

- **The Incantation of the Crossroads:** A spell performed at a **crossroads** at midnight, using symbols drawn in the dirt with a **silver dagger**. The incantation calls upon the gods of the underworld to bind the Tenebrae within the crossroads, limiting their movement.

- **The Shield of Pluto:** An inscription invoking **Pluto**, the Roman god of the underworld, is etched onto a **bronze disc** and worn as an amulet. The text claims that this amulet can repel the Tenebrae by creating a barrier of shadows that the entities cannot penetrate.

4. The Shiwa Manuscripts (Tibet, c. 600 CE)

The **Shiwa Manuscripts** are ancient Tibetan texts that explore the spiritual realm, including the nature of **nightmares** and the entities that dwell in darkness. The manuscripts, written on strips of paper and bound in silk, describe the **Namrö**—shadowy beings that feed on fear and suffering.

4.1 The Namrö: Weavers of Nightmares

According to the Shiwa Manuscripts, the Namrö are **spirit beings** that inhabit the **Bardo**, an intermediate state between life and death. They are attracted to negative energy, particularly fear, and use nightmares to weaken the spiritual defenses of humans.

The manuscripts highlight the Namrö's ability to **alter dreams** and induce sleep paralysis, rendering their victims vulnerable to spiritual attacks. The Namrö were believed to be agents of karmic retribution, acting upon the fears and negative karma of individuals.

4.2 Spiritual Remedies and Defensive Techniques

The Shiwa Manuscripts offer **spiritual practices** designed to protect against the influence of the Namrö:

- **Mantras of Clarity:** The text prescribes specific **mantras** to be chanted during meditation, creating a mental barrier against the intrusion of the Namrö into the dream state. The **Mantra of Vajrapani**, in particular, is said to invoke a fierce protective energy that repels shadowy spirits.
- **Dream Talismans:** The manuscripts describe the creation of **dream talismans** from inscribed stones wrapped in silk and blessed by monks. These talismans are placed under pillows to protect sleepers from nightmares and disrupt the Namrö's ability to alter dreams.

5. The Book of Dark Paths (Medieval Europe, c. 1200 CE)

During the Middle Ages, belief in the supernatural was pervasive, and numerous grimoires surfaced detailing methods for **summoning** and **controlling** dark entities. Among these, the **Book of Dark Paths** stands out for its detailed exploration of creatures referred to as "Dark Ones," which closely resemble modern Boogeymen.

5.1 The Dark Ones: Haunters of the Unseen

The Book of Dark Paths describes the Dark Ones as beings that exist between the **physical** and **spiritual realms**. They are often found lurking in the corners of dimly lit rooms, beneath beds, or within closets, striking fear into the hearts of those who sense their presence.

According to the text, the Dark Ones are **manipulative** and often employ illusions to disorient their victims. They have a particular affinity for haunting individuals struggling with grief, guilt, or inner turmoil, using these emotions to fuel their power.

5.2 Rituals for Binding and Banishment

The Book of Dark Paths contains complex **rituals** and **binding spells** for dealing with these entities:

- **The Circle of Warding:** A ritual involving the placement of **iron nails** and **sage bundles** around a room's perimeter, creating a protective circle that the Dark Ones cannot cross. The nails are inscribed with runes of protection, drawing upon both **Nordic** and **Christian** traditions to enhance their efficacy.
- **Banishment through Reflection:** The text details a **mirror banishment** ritual, where a **consecrated mirror** is used to reflect the Dark One's form back upon itself. The entity is then commanded, using specific words of power, to return to the shadow realms from whence it came.

6. The Necronomicon (Legendary, c. 700 CE)

Though its existence is debated, the **Necronomicon** is frequently cited in occult lore as an ancient tome that documents the secrets of the shadow realms. Within its supposed pages lie incantations for summoning and binding **shadowy horrors**, including Boogeyman-like entities.

6.1 The Nature of Shadow Entities

The Necronomicon allegedly describes the shadow entities as **primordial beings**, older than the earth itself. It attributes to them an understanding of fear that transcends human consciousness, suggesting that they feed not merely on individual fear but on the **collective dread** of humanity.

6.2 Forbidden Rituals

The book reportedly contains **forbidden rituals** for harnessing the power of these entities, warning that to do so comes at a great cost. Among these is the **Ritual of the Abyss**, which involves the use of **black candles, sacrificial offerings**, and invocations in ancient languages. While the details remain obscure, it is said that the ritual can summon a Boogeyman forth and bind it to the will of the summoner—though with potentially catastrophic consequences if not performed correctly.

Conclusion: The Legacy of Ancient Texts

The knowledge contained within these ancient texts has shaped our modern understanding of Boogeymen and their influence over the human psyche. From the **Shadow Codex** to the **Shiwa Manuscripts**, each document offers invaluable insights into the nature, power, and vulnerabilities of these elusive entities. While many of the rituals and incantations require adaptation to fit contemporary circumstances, the core principles of **containment**, **banishment**, and **negotiation** remain as relevant today as they were in ancient times.

Hunters who study these texts gain access to a vast reservoir of **arcane wisdom**, enabling them to approach Boogeymen encounters with both knowledge and caution. However, it is essential to remember that the use of ancient spells and rituals carries inherent risks. The next chapter will explore **modern adaptations** of these ancient techniques, providing hunters with updated tools and strategies for confronting the Boogeymen of the present era.

Chapter 30: Boogeyman Evolution: Are They Becoming Smarter?

Throughout history, **Boogeymen** have been perceived as shadowy figures lurking in the corners of our fears, instilling dread through primal, instinctual methods. Yet, recent findings indicate that Boogeymen may be undergoing a form of **evolution**, developing more sophisticated and **intelligent** methods of inducing fear. This evolution raises numerous questions: Are Boogeymen adapting to modern times? Is their increasing intelligence a reaction to humanity's changing fears? In this chapter, we explore the signs and implications of Boogeyman evolution, drawing on **recent case studies**, **hunter accounts**, and **psychological analyses** to build a comprehensive picture of this unsettling phenomenon.

1. Evidence of Boogeyman Evolution

To understand Boogeyman evolution, hunters have documented encounters that demonstrate a shift in these entities' behavior. From simple, repetitive scares to more complex and calculated methods, the evidence suggests an **increasing intelligence** among Boogeymen.

1.1 Advanced Scare Tactics

Historically, Boogeymen relied on basic scare tactics such as **noises, shadow movements**, and **nighttime ambushes**. However, recent encounters indicate that some Boogeymen now employ far more **nuanced strategies**:

- **Psychological Manipulation:** Modern Boogeymen have been observed utilizing psychological manipulation, targeting victims' personal traumas, fears, and insecurities. By replaying specific memories or manifesting fears in symbolic forms, they tailor their scares to the individual's psyche, maximizing the fear response.
- **Emotional Sabotage:** There are growing reports of Boogeymen exploiting **interpersonal relationships**, creating illusions or distorting perceptions to sow distrust, paranoia, and despair among family members or friends. By manipulating social dynamics, Boogeymen instill a lingering sense of fear that extends beyond the immediate scare.
- **Long-Term Haunting:** In contrast to traditional Boogeymen who struck and retreated quickly, evolving Boogeymen seem to take a **prolonged approach**, haunting their targets over weeks or even months. This extended presence not only increases the victim's fear over time but also suggests a calculated strategy to **break down mental defenses** gradually.

1.2 Learning from Mistakes

Recent hunter encounters suggest that Boogeymen may be capable of **learning** from past interactions:

- **Avoiding Traps:** Previously effective traps, such as **mirror grids** or **binding circles**, are now being circumvented by some Boogeymen. In some cases, hunters have observed entities **testing** these traps by sending decoy shadows to trigger them prematurely, allowing the Boogeyman to assess and exploit weaknesses in containment methods.

- **Resisting Rituals:** Certain Boogeymen exhibit an increased **resistance** to traditional banishment rituals. They disrupt the rituals by generating distortions in the environment (such as flickering lights, sudden temperature shifts, or loud noises), breaking the concentration of those performing the incantations. This behavior implies an awareness of how these rituals work and the ability to counteract them.

1.3 Adaptation to Technology

Boogeymen have historically thrived in dark, isolated spaces, but reports now indicate they are becoming increasingly comfortable with **modern technology**:

- **Digital Presence:** Some entities have been known to interact with electronic devices, appearing as **glitches on screens**, **distortions in audio recordings**, or **ghostly reflections** in video calls. These encounters reveal a newfound ability to adapt to digital environments, potentially using technology as a new medium to invoke fear.
- **Cyber-Luring:** In more extreme cases, Boogeymen have exploited **social media** and **messaging platforms** to target victims, sending cryptic messages, unsettling images, or mimicking familiar contacts. This evolution points to an understanding of how fear can be spread through virtual interactions, allowing Boogeymen to reach victims in previously inaccessible ways.

2. Why Are Boogeymen Evolving?

Understanding the potential reasons behind this evolution is key to devising effective countermeasures. Several theories offer insight into why Boogeymen are becoming more intelligent and adaptable.

2.1 Human Adaptation and Modern Fears

As humanity has progressed, our **collective fears** have shifted. Ancient people feared the wilderness, the darkness, and the supernatural; modern society, however, contends with more complex anxieties—mental health, social dynamics, technology, and the unknown future. Boogeymen, as **manifestations of fear**, may be evolving in response to these changes.

- **Sophisticated Fears:** Modern humans are less likely to be terrified by the mere **sound of creaking floors** or **shadowy movements** in the corner of a room. Instead, fears now encompass **psychological distress, existential dread**, and **loss of control** over one's reality. Boogeymen adapt to these new fears, employing more intricate methods to maintain their hold over human consciousness.
- **Desensitization:** With horror movies, video games, and haunted attractions becoming mainstream, people have become **desensitized** to traditional scare tactics. To continue eliciting fear, Boogeymen must adopt increasingly complex and subtle approaches, infiltrating the psyche rather than relying on overt scares.

2.2 Survival and Self-Preservation

Boogeymen feed on fear. As hunters become more adept at **detecting**, **capturing**, and **banishing** these entities, Boogeymen are forced to **evolve** to ensure their survival.

- **Avoidance of Capture:** Boogeymen that have learned to avoid traps and resist rituals are more likely to **survive** encounters with hunters. Over time, this natural selection results in a population of Boogeymen that are increasingly cunning, elusive, and capable of adapting to human countermeasures.
- **Exploiting New Territories:** With traditional haunts like forests and abandoned buildings dwindling due to urbanization, Boogeymen may be evolving to thrive in new environments, such as **urban settings** or **cyberspace**, where they can hide in the noise and complexity of modern life.

2.3 Influence of Collective Fear

The **collective unconscious** of humanity plays a role in shaping Boogeymen. As fears evolve, the psychic energy generated by these anxieties may drive Boogeymen to **mimic and embody** those fears in new ways.

- **Strengthening Through Modern Folklore:** Stories of **urban legends** and **internet horror** fuel the modern Boogeyman's evolution. Entities like **Slender Man** or **The Rake** have become cultural icons, lending power and form to Boogeymen that align with these new narratives. This interplay between cultural fear and Boogeyman evolution creates a feedback loop, reinforcing the entity's presence and intelligence.

3. Implications of Boogeyman Evolution for Hunters

As Boogeymen become more intelligent, hunters must **adapt** their strategies and deepen their understanding of these entities. Traditional methods of detection and containment may need to be revised or entirely reimagined in light of this evolution.

3.1 Enhanced Detection Techniques

- **Psychological Profiling:** Given that Boogeymen now employ more personalized scare tactics, hunters must develop **psychological profiles** of both the entity and its target. Understanding the victim's fears and how the Boogeyman exploits them can offer clues about the entity's behavior and weaknesses.
- **Digital Surveillance:** Since Boogeymen have adapted to interact with electronic devices, hunters should employ **digital surveillance** tools, including monitoring for **unusual patterns** in electronic communications, **audio distortions**, and **video feed anomalies**. Specialized software can analyze and detect these subtle disruptions, indicating a Boogeyman's presence.

3.2 Advanced Containment Strategies

- **Multi-Layered Traps:** The use of **multi-layered traps** combining physical, mystical, and digital elements is essential. For instance, a containment circle might now include **binding runes** encrypted within a virtual network, preventing the Boogeyman from escaping through technological means.
- **Psychic Wards:** As Boogeymen increasingly target the psyche, **psychic wards** must be fortified. Hunters can employ **mental shields** and **emotional dampeners** during encounters to block the Boogeyman's attempts at manipulation, maintaining focus and control over the situation.

3.3 Exploiting Evolved Traits

While their newfound intelligence makes Boogeymen more dangerous, it also presents opportunities:

- **Negotiation Leverage:** Intelligent Boogeymen are capable of **negotiation** and can be reasoned with if they see potential benefits in cooperation. Hunters can leverage this intelligence to broker temporary truces or gather information on other supernatural threats.
- **Baiting Complex Traps:** Knowing that Boogeymen learn from past encounters, hunters can set up **decoy traps** that appear flawed or easy to bypass, luring the entity into overconfidence. Once inside, a secondary, hidden trap can activate, catching the Boogeyman off-guard.

4. Case Studies of Evolved Boogeymen

Recent field reports provide concrete examples of evolved Boogeymen in action:

4.1 The Whisperer of Fallow Grove

This Boogeyman haunted a small village, gradually isolating individuals by **whispering lies** into their ears at night, turning neighbors against one another. Unlike traditional Boogeymen, the Whisperer used **emotional manipulation** rather than direct scares, breaking down community trust. Hunters successfully contained it by recognizing its **psychological tactics** and using **mirror grids** to reflect its whispers back upon itself, disorienting and trapping it.

4.2 The Digital Phantom

A modern Boogeyman, the **Digital Phantom**, manifested through social media platforms, sending cryptic messages and altering photos to sow fear. The entity proved adept at **cyber-luring**, using victims' personal information to target their deepest anxieties. Hunters employed **digital talismans**—software imbued with protective runes—to disrupt its presence in the virtual space and contained it by binding its essence to a specially crafted **hard drive amulet**.

5. Preparing for the Future: Evolving Hunting Methods

Given the evolving nature of Boogeymen, hunters must adopt a **dynamic approach** to their methods:

- **Ongoing Research:** Continuous research into **psychological** and **technological trends** will be vital in anticipating how Boogeymen might further evolve.
- **Interdisciplinary Collaboration:** Hunters should work with **psychologists, technologists**, and **folklorists** to develop more comprehensive containment strategies that address both the physical and mental aspects of Boogeyman encounters.
- **Training in Mental Fortitude:** With Boogeymen increasingly targeting the psyche, hunters must undergo **mental resilience training** to fortify their minds against psychological manipulation.

Conclusion: The Intelligence of Shadows

The evolution of Boogeymen presents both **new challenges** and **opportunities** for hunters. As these entities become more intelligent, cunning, and adaptable, they force humanity to confront the complexities of fear in the modern world. While their growing intelligence makes them more formidable, it also reveals their potential weaknesses—their dependence on psychological manipulation, their attraction to modern fears, and their susceptibility to technologically enhanced traps.

By staying vigilant, adaptable, and informed, hunters can not only keep pace with the Boogeyman's evolution but turn it to their advantage. As we move forward, the dance between hunter and shadow will continue, each step revealing more about the nature of fear and the darkness that thrives within and around us. The next chapter will delve into **modern adaptations of ancient rituals**, exploring how old-world knowledge can be integrated with new techniques to keep these evolving entities at bay.

Chapter 31: The Science of Fear: How Boogeymen Use It

Fear is one of the most **primal human emotions**, rooted in our biology as a survival mechanism. It triggers a complex array of physiological and psychological responses that prepare us to face danger. Boogeymen are **masters of fear**, harnessing its power to manipulate, control, and feed on human emotions. Unlike ordinary predators that rely on physical strength, Boogeymen utilize the subtleties of fear to assert dominance, break down mental defenses, and extend their influence over individuals and environments. In this chapter, we explore the **science of fear** and the sophisticated ways Boogeymen exploit it, delving into the mechanisms of fear response and the psychological strategies these entities employ to manipulate their victims.

1. Understanding the Biological Basis of Fear

Fear is a **biological response** triggered by perceived threats. It activates the **amygdala**, a small almond-shaped structure in the brain that processes emotions and coordinates the body's fight-or-flight response.

1.1 The Amygdala: The Epicenter of Fear

When the brain perceives a potential danger, the **amygdala** sends signals to the **hypothalamus**, initiating a cascade of physiological responses:

- **Fight-or-Flight Response:** The **sympathetic nervous system** releases adrenaline, increasing heart rate, blood pressure, and alertness. This prepares the body to either confront the threat or flee.
- **Heightened Senses:** Fear sharpens the senses, enhancing **vision**, **hearing**, and **smell** to detect potential dangers more acutely. This heightened state of awareness makes individuals more susceptible to subtle changes in their environment, which Boogeymen use to their advantage.
- **Freezing:** The **freeze response** occurs when an individual is so overwhelmed by fear that they become temporarily immobilized. Boogeymen often exploit this state, as it renders the victim unable to react or escape.

1.2 Memory and Fear Conditioning

Fear experiences are stored in the brain as **emotional memories**. The **hippocampus** plays a crucial role in encoding these memories, associating specific cues with fear responses. Boogeymen manipulate this conditioning by repeatedly exposing their victims to **fear triggers**, strengthening the association and making it more difficult for individuals to break free from the cycle of fear.

2. The Psychological Mechanics of Fear

Fear not only affects the body but also exerts a powerful influence on the mind. Boogeymen are adept at **psychological manipulation**, using fear to distort perception, heighten anxiety, and induce paranoia.

2.1 Fear as a Perceptual Distortion

Fear has the ability to **warp perception**, causing individuals to misinterpret harmless stimuli as threats. This phenomenon is known as **pareidolia**, where the brain sees patterns or familiar shapes—such as faces—in random objects. Boogeymen often manipulate this tendency by manifesting in **shadowy forms** or **faint outlines** that trigger the brain's fear response, leading victims to perceive their presence even when it might not be there.

2.2 The Feedback Loop of Anxiety

Fear can create a **feedback loop** with anxiety. When a person encounters something unsettling, their anxiety levels increase, which in turn makes them more sensitive to further fearful stimuli. Boogeymen exploit this loop by inducing **low-level scares** over an extended period. This tactic gradually heightens the victim's overall anxiety, making them more vulnerable to more intense scares.

- **Micro-Scares:** These small-scale disturbances—like faint footsteps, distant whispers, or fleeting shadows—trigger brief spikes of fear. Over time, these micro-scares accumulate, conditioning the victim to expect and fear the next occurrence, even if nothing happens.
- **Sleep Deprivation:** Boogeymen often disturb their victims' sleep through **nightmares**, **noises**, or **bedside apparitions**, leading to **sleep deprivation**. Lack of sleep impairs cognitive function and emotional regulation, leaving individuals more susceptible to fear and manipulation.

3. Boogeymen as Experts in Emotional Manipulation

Boogeymen do not rely solely on the biological aspects of fear; they are skilled at manipulating emotions to **heighten fear** and **weaken their victims' defenses**.

3.1 Exploiting Personal Fears and Traumas

Each individual has unique fears based on their personal experiences, phobias, and traumas. Boogeymen use their ability to **psychically sense** these vulnerabilities, tailoring their scare tactics to evoke maximum fear.

- **Manifesting Personal Fears:** If a person has a fear of drowning, for example, a Boogeyman might create illusions of water seeping into the room or simulate the sensation of being unable to breathe. By playing on specific phobias, Boogeymen bypass general fear responses and strike directly at the core of the victim's psyche.
- **Replaying Traumatic Memories:** Some Boogeymen can induce vivid, **hallucinatory flashbacks** of past traumatic events. By trapping the victim in a cyclical reliving of their trauma, they amplify the individual's fear, pushing them towards mental collapse.

3.2 Inducing Paranoia and Isolation

One of the most insidious tactics employed by Boogeymen is the **manipulation of perception** to foster **paranoia**. By subtly altering the environment, creating whispers, or shifting objects, Boogeymen make their victims question their reality.

- **Gaslighting:** The Boogeyman subtly influences the surroundings, moving objects or creating noises that the victim perceives but others cannot confirm. Over time, the victim begins to doubt their sanity, becoming increasingly paranoid and fearful.
- **Isolating the Victim:** Fear thrives in isolation. Boogeymen often use their tactics to estrange victims from friends and family, fostering feelings of abandonment and helplessness. By making the individual feel alone and unsupported, the Boogeyman deepens its hold over their psyche.

4. The Boogeyman's Feeding Process: Extracting Fear Energy

Boogeymen **feed** on fear, drawing energy from the heightened emotional state of their victims. This feeding process is not a simple consumption but rather a complex interaction between the Boogeyman and its prey.

4.1 Fear as an Energy Source

Fear generates a unique form of **psychic energy** that Boogeymen can absorb. This energy is most potent during moments of **intense terror** but can also be slowly extracted over time through persistent fear and anxiety.

- **Terror Peaks:** During moments of acute fear—such as when a Boogeyman reveals itself or induces a nightmare—the emotional energy released is at its peak. Boogeymen prefer to evoke these moments sparingly to avoid exhausting their prey too quickly, akin to a predator conserving its food source.
- **Lingering Dread:** By inducing a state of constant low-level anxiety, Boogeymen can extract a **steady stream of fear energy**. This method ensures a long-term supply of sustenance without driving the victim to total collapse or madness, which could render them useless as a source of fear.

4.2 Emotional Resonance: Amplifying Fear through Echoes

Some Boogeymen exhibit the ability to create **fear echoes**, psychic imprints that amplify and replay the emotional intensity of previous scares. By embedding these echoes into specific locations or objects, Boogeymen turn their environments into **reservoirs of fear** that continue to emanate distress long after the initial scare.

- **Haunted Objects:** The Boogeyman may anchor part of its essence to an object within the victim's home, such as a mirror or a toy. This object becomes a focal point for the fear echoes, radiating unsettling energy that keeps the victim in a state of anxiety.

- **Atmospheric Contamination:** Fear echoes can permeate the atmosphere of a room, making it feel **heavy** or **foreboding**. This atmospheric change increases the victim's apprehension and susceptibility to future scares, allowing the Boogeyman to feed more effectively.

5. Boogeymen's Mastery of Fear Cycles

Boogeymen understand the **cycles of fear** and how to manipulate them for maximum effect. By alternating between periods of **escalation** and **lulls**, they maintain control over their victims' emotional states.

5.1 The Build-Up and Release Method

Boogeymen are masters of building suspense. They use **small disturbances** to build tension gradually, creating a growing sense of unease. Just when the victim begins to feel on edge, the Boogeyman strikes with a more direct scare, releasing the accumulated fear in a **cathartic burst**.

- **Anticipatory Fear:** The knowledge that something terrifying might happen is often more unsettling than the scare itself. Boogeymen exploit this **anticipatory fear** by maintaining an aura of unpredictability, ensuring that the victim never knows when or how they will manifest next.
- **Lulls for False Security:** After a scare, Boogeymen often create periods of calm, allowing the victim to relax slightly. This lull lowers the individual's guard, making them more vulnerable to the next scare. The cycle of fear and relief keeps the victim emotionally destabilized and heightens the overall impact of each scare.

5.2 Conditioning and Fear Triggers

Through repeated exposure to specific stimuli, Boogeymen **condition** their victims to develop fear responses to particular **triggers**:

- **Sound Cues:** Whispering, scratching, or knocking sounds become cues for fear, conditioning the victim to react with anxiety whenever they hear similar noises, even in unrelated contexts.
- **Visual Triggers:** Shadows, reflections, or flickering lights become visual triggers associated with the Boogeyman's presence. These triggers activate the fear response automatically, making it easier for the Boogeyman to evoke fear without needing to manifest directly.

6. Countering Boogeymen's Fear Manipulation

Understanding how Boogeymen exploit the psychology and biology of fear allows hunters to develop **countermeasures**:

- **Breaking the Fear Cycle:** To disrupt the Boogeyman's control, hunters can use **fear-dampening charms** and **emotional support** to stabilize the victim's mental state, breaking the cycle of anxiety and reducing the Boogeyman's access to fear energy.
- **Desensitization:** By exposing the victim to **controlled scares** in a safe environment, hunters can help desensitize them to certain triggers, weakening the Boogeyman's influence.

- **Psychic Shields:** Hunters can teach victims to build **mental shields**, using techniques such as **visualization** and **mantras** to block out the Boogeyman's psychic intrusions and reduce their ability to manipulate the mind.

Conclusion: Fear as the Boogeyman's Weapon

Boogeymen are **experts** in the art of fear, using both **biological** and **psychological** mechanisms to manipulate, control, and feed on their victims. They understand the subtleties of human emotion, employing tactics that range from overt scares to the insidious sowing of paranoia and anxiety. This mastery of fear is what makes them so formidable and why they have haunted humanity's consciousness for millennia.

However, by unraveling the **science of fear** and recognizing the tactics Boogeymen use, hunters can devise strategies to counteract their influence. Armed with knowledge, resilience, and advanced techniques, hunters can break the chains of fear that bind their victims, diminishing the Boogeyman's power and reclaiming control over the shadows. The following chapter will delve into **modern adaptations of ancient rituals**, focusing on integrating psychological understanding into traditional methods of containment and banishment.

Chapter 32: Mystical Tools and Spells for Protection

Dealing with Boogeymen requires more than physical strength and mental resilience. These shadowy entities exist at the fringes of our reality, capable of manipulating fear and circumventing ordinary barriers. To protect against their influence, hunters and those facing Boogeymen must arm themselves with **mystical tools** and **spells** designed to ward off attacks, neutralize negative energies, and create barriers between our world and the shadow realm that Boogeymen inhabit. This chapter serves as an in-depth guide to the most **effective mystical tools** and **protective spells**, detailing their creation, use, and the underlying principles that make them powerful deterrents against Boogeymen.

1. Essential Mystical Tools for Protection

A well-prepared hunter's arsenal includes a range of tools, each designed to combat different aspects of a Boogeyman's attack, from physical manifestations to psychological manipulation.

1.1 Salt: The Universal Barrier

Salt is one of the most versatile and **potent mystical substances** for protection. It has long been used in various cultures as a purifying agent and a barrier against malevolent spirits.

- **Protection Circles:** To create a **protection circle**, sprinkle salt in a continuous line around the area to be protected. This circle forms a barrier that Boogeymen cannot cross. It is most effective when paired with **incantations** that charge the salt with protective energy.
- **Threshold Barriers:** Sprinkle salt across doorways, windowsills, and other entry points to prevent a Boogeyman from entering a room or building. For added strength, combine salt with **iron filings** to enhance its repellent properties.
- **Consecrated Salt:** For advanced protection, create **consecrated salt** by blessing it with moonlight or passing it through smoke from burning **sacred herbs** like sage or rosemary. Consecrated salt possesses enhanced energy and serves as a more powerful barrier.

1.2 Iron: The Metal of Banishment

Iron is traditionally known for its power to **repel** and **bind** supernatural entities, including Boogeymen. Its strength lies in its grounding properties, anchoring reality and disrupting the flow of otherworldly energies.

- **Iron Nails:** Place **iron nails** in the corners of a room or along windowsills to create a protective perimeter. The nails act as anchors that ground the area, making it difficult for Boogeymen to manifest or influence the environment.
- **Iron Chains:** Use **iron chains** to encircle objects or areas that need to be shielded. In some cases, hunters have used iron chains to **bind** physical manifestations of Boogeymen, trapping them in place until banishment can be performed.
- **Iron Talismans:** Carry an iron talisman inscribed with **binding runes** as a personal protective charm. When worn, it disrupts the Boogeyman's ability to psychically latch onto the wearer, creating a portable shield.

1.3 Mirrors: Reflectors of Shadows

Mirrors have a unique relationship with the supernatural, serving as **portals** to other realms as well as tools for **reflection** and **repulsion**.

- **Mirror Traps:** Position mirrors around the perimeter of a room to create a **mirror trap**. Boogeymen, which often rely on shadow and distortion, become disoriented when confronted with their own reflection. The mirrors reflect their energy back onto them, weakening their influence.
- **Consecrated Mirrors:** For increased potency, **consecrate a mirror** with moonlight and anoint its edges with **holy water** or **blessed oil**. This consecrated mirror can be used in rituals to **banish** or trap a Boogeyman, forcing it to confront its own essence.
- **Handheld Mirrors:** Carry a small, consecrated **handheld mirror** as a protective tool. When you sense a Boogeyman's presence, hold the mirror up to reflect the surrounding area. This action can reveal the entity's shadow form, giving you the upper hand in identifying and countering its influence.

1.4 Crystals and Gemstones: Amplifiers and Wards

Certain crystals and gemstones have inherent **protective properties** that can be harnessed against Boogeymen:

- **Black Tourmaline:** Known for its ability to **absorb negative energy** and provide a protective shield, black tourmaline is an essential tool. Place pieces of black tourmaline around your home, particularly in areas where the Boogeyman's presence is most strongly felt.
- **Amethyst:** Amethyst is associated with **spiritual protection** and **mental clarity**, making it effective against the psychological manipulation tactics of Boogeymen. Carry an amethyst stone with you to guard against nightmares and psychic attacks.
- **Moonstone:** Moonstone acts as a **gateway** between the physical and spiritual worlds, enhancing spells and tools used for protection. Create a **moonstone talisman** by setting the stone in silver and inscribing protective symbols on the back. Wear or place this talisman in strategic locations to strengthen the boundaries between your space and the Boogeyman's realm.

1.5 Sage and Incense: Purifiers of Space

Burning **sage** and **incense** is an ancient practice used to **purify** spaces and drive out negative energies.

- **Sage Smudging:** Use a **sage bundle** to smudge rooms, corners, and objects. The smoke acts as a purifying agent, disrupting the psychic resonance that Boogeymen rely on to manifest. As you smudge, recite protective incantations to enhance the cleansing effect.
- **Frankincense and Myrrh:** Burn **frankincense** and **myrrh** to create an environment hostile to Boogeymen. These incenses produce a scent and energy that disrupts the entity's presence, forcing it to retreat.

2. Protective Spells and Incantations

While mystical tools provide a physical barrier, **spells** and **incantations** offer the **spiritual and psychological power** necessary to repel Boogeymen, break their influence, and establish protective zones.

2.1 The Circle of Warding Spell

The **Circle of Warding** is one of the most powerful spells for establishing a **safe zone** impervious to Boogeyman incursions.

- **Materials Needed:** Salt, iron filings, a candle, and a piece of chalk.
- **Procedure:** Using the chalk, draw a large circle on the ground. Mix salt and iron filings together and sprinkle this mixture along the circle's edge. Place the candle at the circle's center and light it. As you do, recite the following incantation:

"By salt and iron, by flame and light,
I call forth a shield of might.
No shadow shall cross this sacred line,
Bound by power, fear entwined."

The incantation channels protective energies into the circle, creating an unbreakable boundary that Boogeymen cannot cross. The candle flame serves as the **anchor** for the circle's power, so it must remain lit for the duration of the protection.

2.2 The Banishment of Shadows
This spell is used to **expel** a Boogeyman from a space and sever its connection to the area.

- **Materials Needed:** A consecrated mirror, sage bundle, and an iron nail.
- **Procedure:** Begin by lighting the sage bundle and smudging the room. Hold the mirror up to the area where the Boogeyman's presence is strongest. Press the iron nail against the mirror's surface and recite:

"Shadow of fear, born of night,
I cast thee forth, retreat from sight.
By iron's might and mirror's grace,
Begone from this hallowed space."

Visualize the Boogeyman being drawn into the mirror and then expelled back into the shadows. Seal the spell by driving the iron nail into the ground near the entrance to the room, creating a ward that prevents the entity's return.

2.3 The Binding of Name
Knowing a Boogeyman's **true name** grants hunters a significant advantage. The **Binding of Name** spell is a means to **bind** a Boogeyman, restricting its movements and influence.

- **Materials Needed:** A piece of parchment, black ink, an iron dagger, and salt.
- **Procedure:** Write the Boogeyman's name on the parchment using the black ink. Surround the parchment with a circle of salt. Hold the iron dagger above the parchment and recite:

"By this name, I bind thee now,
By salt and iron, to this vow.
Bound in shadow, bound in night,
Yield thy power to this rite."

As you complete the incantation, use the dagger to make a small cut in the parchment, symbolically "cutting" the Boogeyman's power. Fold the parchment and bury it at a crossroads to finalize the binding, anchoring the entity to a point where its influence will dissipate.

2.4 Dream Shield Spell

Boogeymen often attack through dreams, inducing nightmares to instill fear. The **Dream Shield** spell creates a protective barrier around the dreamer, safeguarding them against psychic invasion.

- **Materials Needed:** Amethyst, moonstone, lavender oil, and a small pouch.
- **Procedure:** Place the amethyst and moonstone inside the pouch. Anoint the stones with a few drops of lavender oil, then hold the pouch in your hands and recite:

"Guard my mind as I sleep,
Seal my thoughts, shadows keep.
By stone and scent, this shield I weave,
No dream shall darken, no fear shall cleave."

Place the pouch under the pillow before sleeping. The combination of amethyst, moonstone, and lavender creates a soothing energy that repels negative influences, allowing the dreamer to rest without interference from Boogeymen.

3. Crafting Personalized Protective Amulets

Beyond spells and traditional tools, hunters can create **personalized amulets** tailored to their specific encounters with Boogeymen. These amulets serve as **constant sources of protection**, reinforcing one's mental and emotional defenses.

- **Choose a Base Material:** Use iron, silver, or black tourmaline as the core of the amulet, as these materials are naturally protective.
- **Inscription of Symbols:** Inscribe the amulet with protective symbols, such as the **pentacle** (symbolizing harmony and balance) or the **eye of Horus** (for watchfulness and psychic protection).
- **Charging the Amulet:** Hold the amulet in both hands and speak a personal incantation, invoking your intention for protection. Pass the amulet through sage smoke or place it under moonlight to charge it with mystical energy.
- **Wear or Carry:** Keep the amulet on your person or place it in areas where protection is needed. Its presence will act as a constant reminder of your safeguarded boundaries and deter Boogeyman attacks.

Conclusion: The Mystical Arsenal Against the Darkness

Boogeymen are formidable adversaries, skilled in the art of fear and manipulation. However, with the right **mystical tools** and **spells**, hunters and those threatened by these entities can establish powerful defenses, turning the tables on the shadows that seek to dominate our spaces and minds. From the simplicity of salt to the complexity of binding rituals, each protective measure serves as a bulwark against the Boogeyman's influence.

The mastery of these tools and spells requires practice, intention, and a deep understanding of the forces they engage. By wielding this mystical arsenal with knowledge and respect, individuals can carve out sanctuaries of safety and reclaim control over their environments and fears. The next chapter will explore **long-term containment strategies**, focusing on how to secure captured Boogeymen and prevent their return, providing a more permanent solution to these persistent haunters of the night.

Part 10: *Closing the Safari*

Chapter 33: After the Hunt: What to Do with a Captured Boogeyman

Successfully capturing a Boogeyman is a challenging and dangerous task, but the hunt doesn't end there. Once contained, the question arises: **What do you do with a captured Boogeyman?** While securing the entity is an achievement in itself, dealing with a captured Boogeyman presents a complex set of **ethical considerations, risks,** and **responsibilities**. Decisions made after capture impact not only the hunters but also the balance between our world and the shadowy realms Boogeymen inhabit. In this chapter, we explore the various **options** for handling a captured Boogeyman, delving into the **ethics** of containment, the potential consequences of releasing them, and the procedures for long-term storage in secure facilities.

1. Ethical Considerations in Handling Captured Boogeymen

The decision of what to do with a captured Boogeyman involves significant **ethical considerations**. These entities, despite their terrifying nature, are part of a larger mystical ecosystem. Hunters must weigh the consequences of their actions not just for themselves but for the **broader spiritual balance**.

1.1 Understanding the Nature of the Boogeyman

Not all Boogeymen are the same. Some are **primal entities**, driven by an insatiable hunger for fear, while others exhibit higher levels of **sentience**, capable of negotiation and even reason. Understanding the specific nature of the captured Boogeyman is crucial in making an informed decision.

- **Sentient Boogeymen:** More intelligent and communicative Boogeymen may possess an understanding of morality, suggesting the possibility of coexistence or even redemption. They might be trapped between realms or acting out of an intrinsic need rather than malice.
- **Primal Boogeymen:** These are often the most dangerous, driven solely by the desire to instill fear. They lack the capacity for negotiation and are inherently disruptive to the human world.

1.2 The Debate: Is Permanent Containment Ethical?

Some argue that **permanent containment** of Boogeymen is akin to a **life sentence** and disrupts the natural balance between realms. These entities, despite their fearsome nature, have their place in the mystical order. Forcing them into indefinite imprisonment could lead to unforeseen consequences, such as:

- **Ecological Imbalance:** Just as predators maintain balance in natural ecosystems, Boogeymen may play a role in regulating other supernatural activities. Removing them permanently could allow other, potentially more dangerous, entities to proliferate unchecked.
- **Energetic Repercussions:** The containment of a Boogeyman can create a **psychic disturbance**, as they often emanate residual fear energy that must be managed. Prolonged storage

of such energy can have negative effects on the surrounding environment, even in secure containment facilities.

1.3 The Risk of Release

On the other hand, releasing a captured Boogeyman back into the **Boogie World** or allowing it to roam free poses its own ethical and practical challenges:

- **Future Threats:** There is always the risk that the Boogeyman will return to haunt other individuals or attempt to reclaim its former territory.
- **Containment Break:** If the entity is released improperly or without the necessary protections in place, it may become more **aggressive** or **cunning**, having learned from its previous encounter with hunters.

Given these ethical dilemmas, hunters must carefully consider their next steps, keeping in mind both the **immediate safety** of humans and the **long-term spiritual balance**.

2. Option 1: Release into the Boogie World

Releasing a Boogeyman back into the **Boogie World**—its native dimension—is often seen as the most balanced solution. This option involves returning the entity to its original habitat, allowing it to exist in a realm more suited to its nature.

2.1 Preparing for Release

Releasing a Boogeyman is not as simple as opening its containment unit. The process requires careful planning and the execution of **rituals** to ensure a **safe transition**:

- **The Opening of the Veil:** To create a pathway between the physical realm and the Boogie World, hunters must perform a ritual known as the **Opening of the Veil**. This ritual involves creating a **temporary portal** using moonstone, iron powder, and a mirror consecrated under a new moon.
  - **Procedure:** Place the mirror on the ground within a salt circle. Sprinkle the iron powder in a spiral pattern leading to the mirror's surface. Light a candle and chant the following:

"Veil of shadow, realm of fright,
Open now to shadow's flight.
Bridge the gap, break the bind,
Let the darkness find its kind."

- The portal will shimmer briefly, signaling that it is ready for the Boogeyman to cross.

2.2 Risks and Safeguards

Releasing a Boogeyman poses inherent risks. The entity may **resist**, attempting to flee or attack during the process. To mitigate these dangers:

- **Binding Charms:** Equip the Boogeyman with **binding charms** that suppress its abilities during the transition, ensuring it cannot lash out or disrupt the ritual.
- **Containment Assistants:** Have other hunters ready with **containment tools** such as shadow nets and iron chains to subdue the Boogeyman if it becomes hostile.

2.3 The Aftermath

After releasing the Boogeyman, hunters should immediately **close the portal** by reversing the incantation and breaking the spiral of iron powder. It's essential to cleanse the area with sage to dispel any lingering fear energy. Monitor the area for signs of residual haunting, as echoes of the Boogeyman's presence may persist for a short period.

3. Option 2: Secure Long-Term Containment

In cases where releasing the Boogeyman poses too great a risk, **long-term containment** in a secure facility is the best option. This process involves placing the entity in a specialized containment unit designed to neutralize its powers and prevent escape.

3.1 Types of Containment Units

Different Boogeymen require tailored containment methods depending on their **nature** and **abilities**:

- **Multi-Chamber Containment Cubes:** These cubes consist of multiple compartments lined with **mirror surfaces**, iron plating, and runes of binding. The multi-layered approach ensures that even if the Boogeyman breaches one chamber, it remains trapped in the subsequent layers.
- **Shadow Spheres:** For Boogeymen that exhibit strong **shadow manipulation**, use **shadow spheres** crafted from obsidian and infused with moonstone powder. The sphere's dark, reflective surface absorbs and nullifies the Boogeyman's shadow form, trapping it within a pocket of darkness.

3.2 Long-Term Maintenance

Long-term containment requires **regular maintenance** to ensure the Boogeyman remains securely imprisoned:

- **Runic Renewal:** Perform periodic **runic renewals** on the containment unit, re-inscribing the symbols with **binding ink**. These runes degrade over time due to the Boogeyman's constant pressure, so frequent upkeep is necessary.

- **Energetic Cleansing:** Contained Boogeymen emit residual fear energy, which can accumulate in the environment and potentially lead to **containment breaches**. Use **sage smudging** and **fear-dampening crystals** to absorb and neutralize this energy.

3.3 Storing the Containment Unit

Secure containment units should be stored in a **dedicated facility** designed for supernatural entities. These facilities, often referred to as **warded vaults**, are equipped with multiple layers of protection:

- **Ward Stones:** Place **ward stones** at the vault's entrances and corners to create a protective barrier that prevents any psychic influence from leaking into the surrounding environment.
- **Guardianship:** Some facilities employ **spiritual guardians**—such as bound familiars or talismanic golems—that patrol the area, acting as an additional line of defense against escape attempts.

4. Option 3: Negotiated Release and Binding Agreements

For **sentient Boogeymen**, a **negotiated release** may be possible. This option involves striking a **binding agreement** with the Boogeyman, setting terms for its behavior post-release.

- **Contractual Binding:** Draft a **contract** using magical parchment inscribed with **binding runes**. The terms of the contract might include prohibitions against haunting specific individuals, requirements to remain within certain territories, or agreements to periodically return to the Boogie World.
- **Oath Ritual:** Have the Boogeyman **swear an oath** to abide by the contract. Binding oaths are powerful in the mystical realm, especially when enforced using the Boogeyman's **true name**.

4.1 Risks and Enforcement

Negotiating with a Boogeyman is inherently risky. There is always the possibility of **betrayal** or **deception**:

- **Enforcement Talismans:** Create **enforcement talismans** that serve as physical representations of the contract. If the Boogeyman violates the agreement, the talisman will activate, triggering a containment spell that traps the Boogeyman within the talisman itself.
- **Psychic Surveillance:** Periodically monitor the Boogeyman's activities through **psychic surveillance** to ensure it adheres to the contract's terms. Hunters skilled in **scrying** can observe the Boogeyman's movements remotely, providing an early warning if it begins to stray.

5. Choosing the Right Option

The decision of how to handle a captured Boogeyman depends on several factors:

- **The Nature of the Boogeyman:** Is it a sentient entity capable of reason, or a primal force of fear? Sentient Boogeymen may respond to negotiation, while primal ones often require containment or release.
- **Risk Assessment:** Evaluate the potential threat the Boogeyman poses if released. Does it have a history of violence, or is it bound to specific territories?
- **Long-Term Consequences:** Consider the impact of your choice on the spiritual balance and the environment. Will containment create a disturbance, or could release result in future harm?

Conclusion: Responsibility Beyond the Hunt

Capturing a Boogeyman is only the first step. What comes next is a matter of great **responsibility**, demanding wisdom, foresight, and respect for the mystical order. Whether choosing to release the entity into the Boogie World, contain it long-term, or negotiate a conditional release, hunters must act with caution and ethical consideration. Each option carries its own risks and benefits, shaping the dynamic between humanity and the shadows that lurk beyond the veil.

In the end, how a hunter deals with a captured Boogeyman reflects not only their **skill** but also their **understanding** of the balance between light and darkness. The next chapter will explore the **residual effects** of Boogeyman encounters on the psyche and environment, offering methods for cleansing, recovery, and healing after a confrontation with these enigmatic beings.

Chapter 34: Preventing Boogeyman Return: Long-Term Solutions

Successfully capturing or banishing a Boogeyman from a household is a triumph in itself, but the **battle isn't over**. Boogeymen, being persistent and cunning creatures, often attempt to return to places where they have previously thrived, especially if they have a **strong connection** to the location or the individuals within it. To ensure that a Boogeyman does not return, hunters and household members must take **long-term preventive measures**. This chapter provides a comprehensive guide to the most effective methods for preventing the reappearance of a Boogeyman, combining **mystical practices**, **psychological strategies**, and **environmental adjustments** to create a robust defense.

1. Cleansing the Environment

The first step in preventing a Boogeyman's return is to **cleanse the environment** of any residual negative energy or fear imprints left behind from its presence. Boogeymen are drawn to places with lingering fear energy, as it serves as a beacon for their return.

1.1 Purification Rituals

Cleansing rituals help to dispel the **negative energy** that Boogeymen thrive on and establish an atmosphere of protection.

- **Sage Smudging:** Burning **sage** is one of the most effective and accessible methods for purifying a space. As you smudge each room, focus on the corners, closets, and under the bed—areas where Boogeymen commonly hide. During the smudging, recite the following incantation:

"Smoke of sage, pure and bright,
Banish shadows, clear the night.
By this smoke, I cleanse this place,
No fear shall linger, no shadow's trace."

- **Salt and Iron Water Sprinkling:** Create a mixture of **consecrated salt** and **iron powder** dissolved in water. Using a sprig of rosemary or a similar herb, sprinkle this mixture around the perimeter of each room, especially doorways and windows. This mixture creates an **energetic barrier** that repels negative entities.

1.2 Sound Cleansing

Sound vibrations can disrupt lingering **fear energy** and reset the vibrational frequency of a space.

- **Bell Ringing:** Use a **bell** made of brass or bronze to ring in each corner of the room. The clear, sharp sound disrupts residual fear energy, scattering it and breaking the Boogeyman's hold on the environment.
- **Singing Bowls:** Tibetan singing bowls produce frequencies that resonate with the body's natural energy field. Play the bowl in each room, moving in a circular pattern to evenly disperse its sound waves, which cleanse the space of negative influences.

1.3 Crystalline Grid

Set up a **crystalline grid** throughout the household using **black tourmaline**, **amethyst**, and **clear quartz**.

- **Black Tourmaline:** Place pieces in the four corners of each room to **absorb negative energy** and prevent it from accumulating.
- **Amethyst:** Known for its protective and purifying qualities, amethyst helps neutralize fear energy and maintain mental clarity. Place a piece near entry points like doorways and windows.
- **Clear Quartz:** Position clear quartz in the center of the house. Its amplifying properties enhance the protective energy of other crystals and create a **harmonizing effect** throughout the space.

2. Establishing Protective Barriers

Once the environment is cleansed, the next step is to **establish protective barriers** that prevent the Boogeyman from returning. These barriers serve as both physical and spiritual fortifications.

2.1 Salt Lines

Salt is a **universal barrier** against negative entities. Maintain **salt lines** around the household's entry points to act as a first line of defense.

- **Threshold Barriers:** Sprinkle a line of salt across doorways, windowsills, and other potential entry points. For enhanced protection, mix the salt with **iron filings** or **ashes from a consecrated fire**. Replace these salt lines regularly, especially after adverse weather conditions, to ensure their integrity.
- **Salt Circles:** In the event of a heightened sense of Boogeyman activity, create a temporary **salt circle** around the bed before sleeping. This circle acts as a protective barrier that prevents the Boogeyman from approaching during the vulnerable hours of the night.

2.2 Warding Stones

Warding stones serve as **anchors** for protective energy and create a repellent field against dark entities.

- **Selection:** Choose stones with inherent protective qualities, such as **black onyx**, **obsidian**, or **hematite**. Cleanse the stones with sage smoke, then anoint them with **moon water** (water left to charge under the full moon).
- **Placement:** Bury the warding stones at the four corners of the property. As you bury each stone, recite the following incantation:

"Stone of earth, stone of might,
Guard this place both day and night.
By earth and stone, I set this seal,
No shadow shall cross, nor fear conceal."

These warding stones create an **energetic grid** that reinforces the household's boundaries, making it difficult for Boogeymen to penetrate.

2.3 Sigils and Symbols

Drawing **protective symbols** in strategic locations around the house strengthens spiritual barriers.

- **Protection Sigils:** Use **protective sigils** such as pentacles, runes of protection (like **Algiz** in Norse mythology), or the **Eye of Horus** to ward off negative energies. Draw these symbols above doorways, on windowsills, or under furniture using **chalk** or **essential oils** like frankincense.
- **Mirror Talismans:** Place small mirrors facing outward at key entry points. **Mirrors** have reflective properties that can bounce a Boogeyman's energy back at itself, disorienting it and preventing entry.

3. Personal Protection and Strengthening the Household's Psychic Defenses

While the environment is being fortified, household members must also work on **strengthening their own psychic defenses**, as Boogeymen are attracted to **vulnerability** and **fear**.

3.1 Personal Talismans

Personal talismans act as **portable protection** against Boogeyman attacks.

- **Iron and Moonstone Amulets:** Craft amulets using **iron** and **moonstone**, inscribed with protective runes. Iron repels negative entities, while moonstone strengthens the wearer's psychic defenses. Wear these amulets, especially during sleep, to ward off nightmares and psychic manipulation.
- **Fear-Binding Charms:** Create a small charm bag filled with **salt, lavender, amethyst**, and a piece of **hematite**. Anoint the bag with **lavender oil** and carry it in a pocket or place it un-

der the pillow. The combination of these elements binds fear energy, preventing Boogeymen from feeding on it.

3.2 Mental Resilience and Fear Management

Boogeymen are attracted to fear and mental vulnerability. Strengthening **mental resilience** is crucial in preventing their return.

- **Daily Affirmations:** Encourage household members to practice daily affirmations that promote **strength**, **clarity**, and **confidence**. Examples include:

"I am safe within this space; no fear shall find me here."
"My mind is strong, my spirit brighter than any shadow."

- **Mindfulness and Meditation:** Regular **meditation** helps cleanse the mind of negative thoughts and anxiety. Visualizing a **protective shield** around oneself reinforces personal boundaries, making it harder for a Boogeyman to establish a foothold.

4. Ritual Reinforcement for Continued Protection

Establish a routine for **ritual reinforcement** to maintain the household's defenses over time.

4.1 Monthly Cleansing Ritual

Perform a **monthly cleansing** using sage, sound, or incense to reset the energy in the home.

- **Procedure:** Burn sage or incense in each room, moving in a clockwise direction. As you cleanse, visualize negative energy dissipating and protective light filling the space. Reinforce salt lines and sigils where necessary.
- **Full Moon Charging:** On the night of the **full moon**, place warding stones, crystals, and amulets outside or on a windowsill to **recharge** them with lunar energy. This practice enhances their protective properties and keeps them effective against future Boogeyman incursions.

4.2 Seasonal Boundary Strengthening

As the seasons change, especially during **Halloween** (Samhain) or **Winter Solstice**, when the veil between worlds is thinner, perform a more intensive boundary strengthening ritual.

- **Iron and Salt Ritual:** Bury fresh iron nails at the property's corners and reinforce salt lines around the perimeter. Light candles at each corner of the property and recite an incantation to invoke the protection of elemental forces:

"Earth and fire, water and air,
Guard this home, by this prayer.

From shadowed realms and fearful plight,
Keep this place in blessed light."

- **Guardian Effigies:** Create small **guardian effigies** using natural materials like wood, stone, or clay, and place them at the main entry points. These effigies serve as symbolic protectors, reinforcing the household's defenses.

5. Environmental Adjustments

Boogeymen prefer environments that are **dark**, **cluttered**, and **neglected**, as these spaces are easier for them to inhabit. Making environmental changes can reduce the appeal of a household to these entities.

5.1 Decluttering and Organizing

Boogeymen often hide in cluttered areas. By keeping rooms organized and free of excess junk, you reduce potential hiding spots.

- **Closets and Under Beds:** Regularly clean and declutter **closets** and **under-bed spaces**. Store items in clear, sealed containers, allowing light to penetrate these areas and minimize shadowy recesses.
- **Open Spaces:** Arrange furniture and decor to create **open spaces** that are well-lit. Boogeymen struggle to manifest in areas where light and airflow freely move, as they rely on darkness and stagnation.

5.2 Light and Ventilation

Increasing **natural light** and **air circulation** makes the environment less conducive to Boogeyman activity.

- **Natural Light:** Open windows and curtains during the day to allow sunlight to flood the rooms. Sunlight purifies the atmosphere, dispelling lingering darkness.
- **Ventilation:** Use fans or open windows to circulate air. Stagnant air can create an oppressive atmosphere that Boogeymen can exploit.

Conclusion: The Path to a Boogeyman-Free Home

Preventing a Boogeyman's return requires a **multi-layered approach**, combining environmental cleansing, protective barriers, personal resilience, and regular ritual reinforcement. By creating an **inhospitable environment** for Boogeymen, both physically and energetically, households can maintain long-term safety and peace of mind.

The key to success lies in **consistency**. Regular maintenance of protective measures ensures that the household remains a **fortress** against the shadowy incursions of Boogeymen. In the next chapter, we will explore the **residual effects** of Boogeyman encounters on the psyche and environment, offering methods for **cleansing, recovery**, and **healing** after a confrontation with these enigmatic beings.

Chapter 35: Boogeyman and the Digital Age: Are They Online?

The Boogeyman has always thrived on fear, lurking in the shadows of closets, under beds, and within the recesses of the human psyche. However, in the **Digital Age**, our lives have expanded beyond the physical world and into the vast, interconnected realm of **cyberspace**. As the landscape of fear changes with modern technology, so too does the domain of the Boogeyman. This chapter explores the speculative concept of **digital Boogeymen**—whether these shadowy entities have adapted to the virtual world, what forms they might take online, and how they might use technology to interact with and instill fear in their victims.

1. The Evolution of Fear in the Digital Age

With the advent of the Internet, social media, and digital communication, human fears have evolved. Whereas old fears centered around **darkness**, **monsters**, and **the unknown** lurking in the physical world, modern anxieties often revolve around **cyberbullying, identity theft, privacy invasion**, and the **pervasiveness of digital surveillance**. This shift raises the question: **Have Boogeymen evolved to adapt to this new environment of fear?**

1.1 New Domains of Fear

In the digital world, fear manifests in various ways that differ from traditional forms:

- **Cyberstalking:** The fear of being watched or monitored online echoes the feeling of being observed by a Boogeyman in the dark. Digital Boogeymen might manifest through **phantom accounts**, eerie messages, or unexplained activities on social media.
- **Information Breach:** The fear of personal information being exposed or manipulated resonates with the Boogeyman's historical penchant for **exploiting vulnerabilities**. A digital Boogeyman could represent the fear of one's digital identity being invaded or controlled.
- **Online Anonymity:** The Internet's anonymity provides a fertile ground for a Boogeyman to hide and **shape-shift**, mimicking familiar contacts or appearing as an unknown entity to instill dread.

1.2 Digital Mythos and Urban Legends

In recent years, online myths and **urban legends** have given rise to new, digital forms of the Boogeyman:

- **Slender Man:** This fictional character, which originated as an Internet meme, has become a cultural symbol of the **digital Boogeyman**—an entity that lurks in cyberspace, watching and waiting to ensnare its victims. Such stories illustrate how the Boogeyman archetype has adapted to modern storytelling, suggesting an evolution into digital forms.

2. The Concept of Digital Boogeymen

While traditional Boogeymen inhabit the shadows of the physical world, the idea of **digital Boogeymen** suggests that these entities may have learned to traverse the **boundaries between physical reality and cyberspace**.

2.1 Manifesting in Cyberspace

If Boogeymen have indeed adapted to the digital age, they might manifest in various ways within the online realm:

- **Glitches and Distortions:** Boogeymen could influence **digital devices**, causing screens to glitch, audio to distort, or webcams to activate without cause. These disturbances mimic the uncanny sensations that occur during traditional hauntings—an unsettling presence that cannot be explained or seen.
- **Phantom Accounts:** A digital Boogeyman might create **phantom social media profiles** that mimic the appearance of real people, sending ominous messages or posting cryptic content. These phantom accounts could be used to spread fear, misinformation, or direct psychological attacks.
- **Haunted Emails:** There are reports of **emails** appearing in inboxes from unknown sources, often containing strange symbols, disturbing imagery, or unsettling content. Such emails may represent the Boogeyman's attempt to invade personal spaces through virtual means, creating a sense of exposure and vulnerability.

2.2 Manipulating Data and Perceptions

Boogeymen in the digital world may not have physical forms but could instead manipulate **data**, information, and **perceptions** to create fear:

- **Digital Mimicry:** Some accounts suggest that digital Boogeymen can mimic the writing style, tone, and behavior of familiar contacts, sending unsettling messages or making strange posts. This form of mimicry echoes the traditional Boogeyman's ability to change shape or voice, sowing confusion and fear.
- **Spreading Misinformation:** By exploiting the speed at which information spreads online, digital Boogeymen could incite fear on a larger scale, creating **panic** or **paranoia** among communities. False rumors, eerie stories, or doctored images might serve as tools for these entities to induce collective anxiety.

3. Can Boogeymen Physically Exist Within the Digital Realm?

The idea of Boogeymen existing **physically** within the digital realm is a complex concept, as it challenges the traditional boundaries of what these entities are and how they interact with reality.

3.1 Digital Imprints of Fear

Boogeymen are **manifestations of fear**, and the digital world is filled with fear-driven data—social media arguments, cyberbullying, privacy concerns, and horror stories. It's plausible that

Boogeymen could **anchor** themselves to these digital imprints, creating virtual counterparts that thrive in the networked shadows of cyberspace.

- **Data Parasites:** In this context, Boogeymen might behave like **data parasites**, feeding on the fear and anxiety present in digital interactions. They could attach themselves to disturbing stories, websites, or online experiences, creating a feedback loop that amplifies fear through repeated exposure.
- **Cyberphantoms:** Some theorize that Boogeymen could form as **cyberphantoms**, existing as clusters of corrupted data or malevolent code that haunt specific websites or platforms. They might manipulate their virtual surroundings to create experiences that evoke dread, similar to how they haunt physical spaces in the real world.

3.2 The Boogeyman as a Memetic Entity

A **memetic entity** is a being that exists and spreads through ideas, stories, and cultural symbols. In the digital world, where information can travel and evolve rapidly, Boogeymen might take on a **memetic** nature.

- **Viral Hauntings:** By becoming part of viral content—whether through eerie stories, unsettling images, or inexplicable glitches—digital Boogeymen spread from mind to mind, feeding on the fear they generate. This process is akin to how memes evolve and spread, suggesting that Boogeymen could exist as **living memes** that perpetuate themselves through digital interactions.
- **Self-Replicating Code:** Some believe that Boogeymen could encode themselves into digital environments, replicating their essence within files, websites, or programs. These self-replicating codes could trigger unsettling events on devices, such as sudden power fluctuations, screen flickering, or ghostly whispers through speakers.

4. How Boogeymen Use Technology to Instill Fear

Even if Boogeymen do not physically exist in cyberspace, there is evidence to suggest that they can **influence technology** to instill fear, using digital devices as tools for psychological manipulation.

4.1 Techno-Hauntings: Manipulating Devices

Boogeymen may use electronic devices to **project their presence** and incite fear.

- **Glitch Phenomena:** Hunters have reported instances of **glitches** occurring on devices during Boogeyman encounters, including scrambled text messages, distorted voices in recordings, and unexpected phone calls from blocked numbers. These glitches create an eerie sense of intrusion, suggesting that Boogeymen can manipulate digital signals.
- **Ghostly Reflections:** Some individuals have encountered ghostly reflections or shadowy figures in **webcam feeds** or **video calls**. While these could be tricks of light or software errors,

the timing and nature of these occurrences often align with Boogeyman activity, indicating a potential influence over visual mediums.

4.2 Digital Stalking and Harassment

Boogeymen have long used psychological pressure to weaken their victims, and in the digital world, they may adopt **cyberstalking** tactics.

- **Untraceable Messages:** Receiving cryptic, untraceable messages—whether via email, social media, or text—can create a profound sense of **invasion** and **fear**. Some hunters suspect that Boogeymen use these methods to plant seeds of doubt and paranoia in their targets.
- **Hijacking Online Presence:** In extreme cases, Boogeymen may attempt to **hijack** a person's online presence, posting eerie or disturbing content that the victim did not create. This tactic not only instills fear but also isolates the victim by creating distrust within their social circles.

5. Protecting Against Digital Boogeymen

If Boogeymen have indeed found a way to interact with the digital world, it becomes necessary to develop **new protection methods** that address the unique challenges of cyberspace.

5.1 Digital Warding Tools

Adaptations of traditional warding techniques can be applied to electronic devices and virtual environments.

- **Virtual Sigils:** Hunters have begun experimenting with **digital sigils**—coded symbols embedded within software or images—that act as barriers against negative entities. By setting these sigils as **wallpapers** or embedding them in files, users create a digital ward that repels malicious influences.
- **Firewall Charms:** Combine **firewall software** with **warding incantations** to create a **cyber-amulet** for your devices. Use the incantation while setting up the firewall to imbue it with protective intent:

"By code and key, I shield this space,
No shadow shall breach, nor fear embrace.
Guard the gate of data's flow,
Let no darkness in this realm grow."

5.2 Cleansing Digital Spaces

Just as physical spaces require cleansing, so too do digital environments.

- **Sound Frequencies:** Playing certain **sound frequencies** (such as 528 Hz or 432 Hz) through devices can disrupt digital disturbances. These frequencies create a calming and harmonious vibration that counteracts the disruptive energy associated with Boogeyman activity.

- **Digital Smudging:** Use an image or video of **burning sage** on your screen while reciting a traditional smudging prayer. Though this method is symbolic, it can serve as a psychological reaffirmation of boundaries and intent to keep the digital space clear of negative influences.

5.3 Strengthening Personal Cyber Boundaries
One of the best defenses against a digital Boogeyman is to maintain **strong cyber boundaries**.

- **Secure Accounts:** Regularly update passwords, enable **two-factor authentication**, and limit the sharing of personal information online. These measures not only protect against human threats but also reduce the entry points for Boogeymen attempting to infiltrate your digital life.
- **Mindful Interaction:** Be conscious of how you engage with disturbing content online. Avoid participating in or spreading fear-inducing media that could serve as a **magnet** for Boogeyman-like entities. By maintaining a positive digital environment, you make it less attractive for negative forces to latch onto your cyber presence.

6. Case Studies of Digital Boogeyman Encounters
Reports of digital Boogeyman encounters are growing, often involving unexplained technological disturbances, eerie communications, and psychological manipulation.

6.1 The Phantom Texter
A series of unsettling text messages sent from unknown numbers were reported by multiple individuals across different locations. The messages included cryptic phrases, distorted images, and personal information that the recipients had never shared online. Despite attempts to trace the source, the numbers were unregistered, and the messages ceased only after the recipients performed **digital warding rituals** on their devices.

6.2 The Glitching Apparition
In a documented encounter, a video call participant witnessed a **shadowy figure** appear and disappear in the background of their screen. The glitch was investigated, but no software errors or external sources could be identified. Subsequent technological disturbances persisted until the individual cleansed their digital environment with sound frequencies and **mirror talismans** placed near their computer.

Conclusion: The Boogeyman's Digital Domain
The possibility that Boogeymen have adapted to the digital age is a **disturbing yet plausible evolution** of these ancient entities. As human fears shift into the realm of cyberspace, Boogeymen may find new ways to manifest and exploit our anxieties. While it is unclear whether they can physically exist in the digital world, their influence over technology and use of virtual interactions to instill fear is becoming increasingly evident.

Protecting oneself from digital Boogeymen requires a blend of **modern cybersecurity** practices and **mystical adaptations** of traditional warding techniques. By remaining vigilant and strengthening both our digital and psychological defenses, we can mitigate the influence of these shadowy entities in the virtual realm. The following chapter will explore the **residual effects of digital**

hauntings, examining how exposure to digital Boogeyman activity can affect mental well-being and offering methods for **digital cleansing** and recovery.

Chapter 36: Becoming a Master Boogey Hunter

Boogeymen are some of the most elusive and complex supernatural entities, making the hunt for them both a dangerous and highly specialized pursuit. While novice hunters may rely on basic tools and techniques to repel or contain Boogeymen, **Master Boogey Hunters** employ advanced methods that require a deep understanding of the creatures' nature, behavior, and weaknesses. Mastery in Boogeyman hunting is not merely about learning tactics; it involves cultivating a heightened level of **awareness**, **mental fortitude**, **mystical knowledge**, and the ability to adapt to the evolving challenges these entities present. This chapter provides an in-depth guide to the advanced techniques, strategies, and skills necessary to become a Master Boogey Hunter, detailing the rigorous training, specialized tools, and psychological tactics involved in mastering the hunt.

1. The Path to Mastery: Cultivating the Hunter's Mindset

Before delving into advanced techniques, an aspiring Master Boogey Hunter must first cultivate the right **mindset**. Mastery in this field requires a balance of **fearlessness**, **strategic thinking**, and **emotional control**.

1.1 Embracing Fear as a Tool

Fear is the Boogeyman's primary weapon, but it can also be the hunter's greatest **ally**. Master Boogey Hunters learn to **harness their own fear**, using it to heighten their senses and sharpen their focus during hunts.

- **Fear Channeling:** During a confrontation with a Boogeyman, consciously channel the fear you experience into **awareness** and **clarity**. When fear arises, visualize it as an energy that spreads throughout your body, heightening your senses rather than clouding your judgment.
- **Meditative Exposure:** Regularly expose yourself to **fear-inducing environments** in a controlled manner. This could involve spending time in dark, enclosed spaces or deliberately inducing a fear response while maintaining composure. This practice builds **fear resilience**, allowing you to confront Boogeymen without being overwhelmed by their aura.

1.2 Mastering Emotional Boundaries

Boogeymen are experts in emotional manipulation, often exploiting a hunter's insecurities or fears to gain the upper hand.

- **Emotional Shielding:** Learn to erect **emotional barriers** through visualization techniques. Visualize a protective shield encasing your mind and emotions, blocking any intrusive thoughts or feelings that a Boogeyman might try to implant. This shield becomes a mental armor during hunts, safeguarding your psychological state.
- **Grounding Rituals:** Incorporate **grounding rituals** into your daily practice. These can include the use of grounding stones like **hematite** or performing grounding meditations. By keeping your emotional state stable, you remain less susceptible to the Boogeyman's influence during encounters.

2. Advanced Tools for the Master Hunter

Master Boogey Hunters have access to a sophisticated arsenal of mystical tools and artifacts that go beyond the basic salt lines and iron charms used by beginners. These tools are designed to **detect**, **trap**, and **neutralize** even the most cunning Boogeymen.

2.1 The Dimensional Key

One of the most powerful tools at a Master Hunter's disposal is the **Dimensional Key**, a mystical artifact used to open and close **portals** to the Boogie World.

- **Usage:** The Dimensional Key is forged from **obsidian** and **moonstone**, inscribed with ancient runes of opening and sealing. When turned clockwise within a containment circle, the key creates a temporary rift that draws the Boogeyman into a designated containment space, such as a shadow sphere. Turning it counterclockwise closes the rift, sealing the Boogeyman within its new prison.
- **Ritual Preparation:** Before using the Dimensional Key, perform a **cleansing ritual** to purify its energy. Anoint the key with **moon oil** and recite the following incantation:

"By this key, I turn the veil,
From shadowed realms, I shall not fail.
Close the breach, lock the door,
Let darkness haunt this world no more."

This preparation ensures that the key remains attuned to your intent and the task at hand.

2.2 Mirror Orbs

Mirror orbs are advanced containment devices designed to trap Boogeymen using their own **reflective essence**.

- **Crafting:** A mirror orb is made by hollowing out a **black tourmaline sphere** and lining its interior with a thin layer of **polished silver**. The orb is then sealed with a piece of **moonstone**, which acts as the locking mechanism.
- **Deployment:** During a hunt, place the orb in an area where the Boogeyman is most active. When the entity attempts to approach or interact with its surroundings, the orb reflects its essence inward, trapping it within the orb's reflective surface. To seal the orb, touch the moonstone cap and recite:

"Shadow caught within this glass,
Reflect, confine, and hold thee fast.
By silvered light and stone's embrace,
Bound thou art in this space."

Once sealed, the orb becomes a portable containment unit, allowing for safe transport of the captured Boogeyman.

2.3 The Shadow Net

A **Shadow Net** is a complex trapping tool woven from **iron wire** and **shadow thread**, a material that requires specialized crafting skills.

- **Crafting:** Shadow thread is made by soaking **black silk** in a mixture of **wormwood oil** and **moonwater** under a new moon. The threads are then woven with iron wire to create a net that resonates with both the physical and spiritual realms.
- **Usage:** The net is thrown over the Boogeyman when it manifests, binding it physically and metaphysically. The intertwined iron wire disrupts the Boogeyman's form, while the shadow thread anchors its essence, preventing it from shifting into the Boogie World.

3. Master Techniques for Boogeyman Detection

Master Boogey Hunters utilize advanced **detection techniques** that go beyond traditional methods, such as using salt lines or listening for strange noises. These techniques involve heightened **psychic awareness** and the use of specialized tools.

3.1 The Shadow Sight Ritual

The **Shadow Sight** ritual allows the hunter to perceive **shadows and auras** that are normally invisible to the naked eye, revealing a Boogeyman's presence and movements.

- **Preparation:** Prepare a mixture of **mugwort tea** and **hyssop**, then anoint your eyelids with the liquid. Light a candle and place it at eye level. Focus on the flame while chanting:

"Sight beyond sight, show me true,
Shadows hidden, now break through.
By fire's gaze and herb's embrace,
Reveal the haunt that hides its face."

- **Activation:** Once the ritual is complete, you will temporarily gain the ability to see **ethereal shadows** and **aura disturbances** within the environment. This heightened vision is crucial for locating a Boogeyman's hiding spots and understanding its patterns.

3.2 The Resonance Tuning Fork

A **Resonance Tuning Fork** is a mystical instrument that detects **vibrational anomalies** in the environment, indicating a Boogeyman's proximity.

- **Usage:** Strike the tuning fork against a piece of iron to activate it. As you walk through the suspected area, listen to the fork's resonance. If it emits a low, fluctuating hum, a Boogeyman is nearby, disrupting the natural vibrational field.

- **Interpretation:** A **stronger fluctuation** indicates the Boogeyman's location, while a **diminishing hum** suggests it is moving away. This tool is especially useful in large or labyrinthine environments where traditional detection methods might fail.

4. Advanced Containment and Banishment Tactics

Master Boogey Hunters employ **layered containment** and **banishment techniques** that provide redundancy and ensure the Boogeyman's capture or removal from the physical realm.

4.1 Multi-Layered Containment Circles

Unlike standard containment circles, **multi-layered circles** consist of several concentric rings inscribed with various runes and symbols, each serving a specific purpose in the containment process.

- **Outer Circle:** Drawn with **iron filings** and salt, this circle prevents the Boogeyman from escaping while weakening its physical form.
- **Middle Circle:** Inscribe this circle with runes of **binding** and **reflection** using chalk mixed with **moonwater**. This layer reflects the Boogeyman's essence inward, disorienting it and preventing it from focusing on escape.
- **Inner Circle:** The innermost circle is marked with **gold dust** and **obsidian powder**, symbols of finality and banishment. This circle seals the Boogeyman's essence and prepares it for capture in a mirror orb or shadow net.

4.2 The Ritual of Echo Severance

Boogeymen often leave behind **fear echoes** that can act as beacons, allowing them to return to a location. The **Ritual of Echo Severance** eliminates these echoes, cutting the Boogeyman's tether to the environment.

- **Preparation:** Place a **clear quartz crystal** at the center of the room and surround it with a circle of **silver candles**. Light the candles and pass a **scrying mirror** over the quartz while chanting:

"Echoes bound, now severed clean,
Fear's imprint fades, unseen.
By mirror's gaze and crystal's light,
Break the bond of shadow's might."

- **Completion:** The ritual disperses the fear echoes, creating a **spiritual blank slate** in the environment. This severance makes it extremely difficult for the Boogeyman to re-establish a foothold in the area.

5. Developing Strategic Adaptability

A Master Boogey Hunter must remain adaptable, as no two Boogeymen are alike. Strategies that work on one entity may fail against another, requiring the hunter to **improvise** and **adjust tactics** on the fly.

5.1 Psychological Profiling of Boogeymen

Master hunters study Boogeymen encounters to develop a **psychological profile** of the entity they are dealing with. This profile includes the Boogeyman's **preferred tactics**, **behavior patterns**, **feeding methods**, and **triggers**.

- **Weakness Identification:** By understanding the Boogeyman's psychological tendencies, hunters can exploit its **weaknesses**. For example, a Boogeyman that relies on inducing fear through auditory hallucinations may be vulnerable to **sound-cleansing techniques**.
- **Behavior Anticipation:** Profiling also allows hunters to anticipate the Boogeyman's moves during a hunt, setting traps and barriers accordingly.

5.2 Dynamic Containment Protocols

Master hunters employ **dynamic containment protocols**, adjusting their techniques in response to the Boogeyman's behavior during the encounter.

- **Trap Adaptation:** If a Boogeyman displays an unexpected ability, such as phasing through walls, hunters adapt by incorporating **barriers of reflective surfaces** or **shadow anchors** to pin it down.
- **Containment Reinforcement:** Use **sigil stones** to reinforce containment units if the Boogeyman shows signs of breaking free. Place the stones around the unit while invoking a binding incantation to strengthen the seals.

Conclusion: The Path to True Mastery

Becoming a Master Boogey Hunter is not just about learning advanced tools and techniques; it is a lifelong journey of **self-discipline**, **knowledge acquisition**, and **spiritual growth**. Master hunters understand that each Boogeyman encounter provides new insights into the nature of fear and the shadowy realms these entities inhabit. By refining their skills, maintaining their mental fortitude, and embracing the ever-evolving nature of Boogeymen, hunters can rise to the challenge of mastering the darkness that lurks just beyond the veil.

The following chapter will explore the **psychological impact** of long-term Boogeyman hunting, examining how exposure to these entities can affect a hunter's mind and offering methods for **mental cleansing** and **healing** after encounters.

Chapter 37: Boogeyman Myths Busted

The Boogeyman, shrouded in shadows and steeped in mystery, has been a source of fear and fascination for centuries. Throughout time, stories about Boogeymen have been told and retold, each adding layers of superstition, myth, and misunderstanding. While some of these tales hold kernels of truth, many others are fabrications born out of fear, cultural misunderstanding, or folk myths passed down through generations. As a Boogey Hunter, it is essential to distinguish fact from fiction in order to effectively confront and contain these entities. This chapter addresses and debunks common myths about Boogeymen, bringing clarity to what they truly are and how they operate.

1. Myth 1: Boogeymen Only Target Children

The Myth: A widely held belief is that Boogeymen exclusively target children, hiding in their closets, under beds, or in dark corners to terrify the young and innocent.

The Reality: While it is true that Boogeymen are often drawn to the fearful energy of children, they are not limited to this demographic. Boogeymen are opportunistic creatures that seek out vulnerable individuals of any age who exhibit signs of fear, anxiety, or unresolved trauma. Adults, especially those who are experiencing stress, grief, or fear, can become prime targets.

- Why This Myth Exists: The association between Boogeymen and children likely stems from the fact that children are more emotionally open and susceptible to fear. Their vivid imaginations and sensitivity to supernatural occurrences make them easier prey. However, Boogeymen can and do target adults, especially those whose fear has matured into complex anxieties.
- Fact Check: Boogeymen feed on fear, not age. They are attracted to environments and individuals that emanate the energy they need, regardless of whether their prey is a child or an adult.

2. Myth 2: Boogeymen Can Only Exist in Darkness

The Myth: It is commonly believed that Boogeymen can only manifest in the dark, hence their association with night, closets, and other shadowy places.

The Reality: Boogeymen prefer darkness because it amplifies fear and provides natural camouflage, but they are not confined to it. Advanced Boogeymen have been known to manipulate light, reflections, and even daytime shadows to conceal themselves. They can create unsettling phenomena in well-lit areas, such as flickering lights, shadow distortions, or ghostly reflections, to evoke fear.

- Why This Myth Exists: The human fear of darkness and the unknown has long been a fertile ground for the development of Boogeyman lore. Darkness naturally heightens the senses and breeds uncertainty, making it an ideal environment for these entities to thrive.
- Fact Check: Darkness is a preferred but not an exclusive domain for Boogeymen. They can operate in various environments as long as they can instill fear and doubt.

3. Myth 3: Salt and Iron Always Repel Boogeymen

The Myth: It is often said that creating lines of salt or using iron objects will always repel or trap a Boogeyman.

The Reality: While salt and iron are effective against many Boogeymen, they are not universal solutions. Different Boogeymen possess varying levels of resistance to traditional protective measures. For example, some Boogeymen have adapted to breach salt barriers or avoid contact with iron through clever manipulation of their surroundings. Others, especially those with elemental affinities, can neutralize these materials over time.

- Why This Myth Exists: Salt and iron are commonly used in folk traditions and magical practices as purifying and protective substances, leading to the assumption that they provide a catch-all defense.
- Fact Check: Salt and iron are tools in a hunter's arsenal but are not foolproof. Successful containment requires a combination of materials, rituals, and strategies tailored to the specific type and strength of the Boogeyman in question.

4. Myth 4: Boogeymen Cannot Cross Thresholds

The Myth: Some believe that Boogeymen cannot cross certain thresholds, such as doorways, windowsills, or boundaries marked with protective symbols.

The Reality: Boogeymen are not bound by the same rules that apply to traditional ghosts or vampires. While they might hesitate to cross well-warded thresholds out of caution, they are not inherently barred from doing so. Strong Boogeymen, particularly those that have fed on fear for an extended period, can breach these boundaries through ritual manipulation, psychic influence, or by exploiting gaps in the protective wards.

- Why This Myth Exists: The concept of thresholds as barriers against supernatural entities is deeply rooted in folklore and magic. However, Boogeymen, being masters of fear, can sometimes bypass these limitations if the protective barrier is weak or improperly maintained.
- Fact Check: Boogeymen can cross thresholds, especially if the household's defenses are compromised. Regular reinforcement and ritual cleansing of protective boundaries are essential to keep them at bay.

5. Myth 5: Boogeymen Can Be Permanently Destroyed

The Myth: Some stories claim that Boogeymen can be killed or destroyed using the right spell, weapon, or ritual.

The Reality: Boogeymen are energetic entities, not living creatures, so they cannot be "destroyed" in the conventional sense. They can be banished, trapped, or neutralized for varying lengths of time, but their essence remains connected to the realm of fear from which they originate. Even when a

Boogeyman is successfully captured or banished, it may eventually reform or another entity may emerge to fill its place.

- **Why This Myth Exists:** The desire to believe in a permanent solution to the Boogeyman problem is natural. Stories of "slaying" monsters are part of human culture, offering a sense of finality and victory over darkness.
- **Fact Check:** Boogeymen can be contained, banished, or rendered dormant, but they cannot be permanently destroyed. Their existence is tied to the concept of fear itself, which is a fundamental and enduring part of the human experience.

6. Myth 6: Naming a Boogeyman Gives You Power Over It

The Myth: The belief that knowing a Boogeyman's true name grants control over it is a common theme in many folklore traditions.

The Reality: While it is true that knowing the nature or type of a Boogeyman can provide insight into its weaknesses and behavior patterns, simply knowing its name does not necessarily give a hunter power over it. Some Boogeymen use false names to deceive hunters, and others change their names frequently to avoid being easily contained.

- **Why This Myth Exists:** Many cultural traditions emphasize the power of names in magic and ritual, leading to the idea that names confer dominance over supernatural beings.
- **Fact Check:** A name can be useful in identifying and classifying a Boogeyman, but it does not automatically confer power. Gaining control over a Boogeyman requires a deeper understanding of its nature, habits, and weaknesses, combined with the appropriate rituals and tools.

7. Myth 7: Boogeymen Are Only Found in Certain Cultures

The Myth: Some people believe that Boogeymen are exclusive to Western cultures or specific regions, where they appear in traditional forms like the "bogeyman" or "black man."

The Reality: Variations of the Boogeyman exist in nearly every culture around the world. While they may go by different names—such as Baba Yaga in Slavic folklore, El Coco in Spain, Namahage in Japan, and Jumbie in the Caribbean—they share common traits of lurking in shadows, inducing fear, and preying on human vulnerabilities.

- **Why This Myth Exists:** Cultural insularity and lack of cross-cultural knowledge have led to the misconception that Boogeymen are confined to certain regions or traditions.
- **Fact Check:** Boogeymen are a universal archetype, taking different forms and adopting characteristics unique to each culture's fears and beliefs. This universality suggests that they are manifestations of the collective human psyche rather than being limited to specific geographical or cultural contexts.

8. Myth 8: Boogeymen Are Always Malevolent

The Myth: It is widely believed that Boogeymen are inherently evil or malevolent entities that exist solely to harm humans.

The Reality: While many Boogeymen exhibit hostile or predatory behavior, not all are malevolent by nature. Some Boogeymen act as guardians of boundaries or as enforcers of moral lessons, appearing to those who stray into dangerous territory (both literally and metaphorically). Others may seek only to feed on ambient fear without causing direct harm. In rare cases, Boogeymen have been known to form pacts with individuals, exchanging protection for offerings or conditions.

- Why This Myth Exists: Boogeymen are traditionally associated with fear and danger, making it easy to label them as malevolent forces. However, their true motives and behaviors are often more complex.
- Fact Check: Boogeymen are primarily agents of fear rather than evil incarnate. Their actions are driven by their nature and purpose within the spiritual ecosystem, which can range from predatory to neutral or even protective, depending on the circumstances.

9. Myth 9: Boogeymen Can Be Summoned at Will

The Myth: Some believe that Boogeymen can be summoned using specific rituals, spells, or items, allowing a person to control them.

The Reality: Boogeymen cannot be summoned in the same way one might call upon a spirit or elemental. They are attracted by the emotional atmosphere of a place or person, particularly environments rich in fear, uncertainty, or trauma. Attempting to summon a Boogeyman using ritual is more likely to draw the attention of an unrelated malevolent entity than a true Boogeyman.

- Why This Myth Exists: Stories of summoning dark forces or spirits are common in folklore and occult practices, leading to the misconception that Boogeymen can be similarly invoked.
- Fact Check: Boogeymen are lured, not summoned. They gravitate toward situations that generate fear. Attempting to summon one without understanding its nature or intentions is both risky and ill-advised.

Conclusion: Separating Truth from Fiction

Understanding the true nature of Boogeymen requires separating fact from myth. Many of the stories and beliefs surrounding these entities are rooted in cultural fears, folklore, and the human desire to explain the unknown. By debunking these myths, hunters gain a clearer perspective on how Boogeymen operate, what their true limitations are, and how best to confront them. This knowledge is key to effective hunting, containment, and protection, transforming fearful superstition into informed strategy.

The next chapter will focus on advanced psychological techniques for resisting Boogeyman-induced fear, exploring how hunters can strengthen their minds to withstand the entities' attempts at emotional and mental manipulation.

Chapter 38: Advanced Psychological Techniques for Resisting Boogeyman-Induced Fear

Boogeymen thrive on **fear**, using it as both a source of sustenance and a weapon to weaken their victims. These entities employ psychological manipulation, inducing terror, doubt, and paranoia to break down a hunter's defenses. To successfully hunt or confront a Boogeyman, a hunter must possess more than mystical tools and rituals—they must have an **ironclad mind**. Advanced psychological techniques are crucial for hunters to resist the fear-induced tactics of Boogeymen and to remain grounded during encounters. This chapter explores these advanced techniques, offering strategies to build **mental resilience, emotional control**, and **cognitive clarity** in the face of a Boogeyman's attempts to infiltrate and manipulate the psyche.

1. Understanding Boogeyman-Induced Fear

Boogeyman-induced fear is unlike the natural fear response that one might feel when encountering danger. It is a **distorted**, **amplified** form of fear that affects not only the emotional state but also one's perceptions, thoughts, and behaviors. Boogeymen are adept at **triggering deep-seated fears**, exploiting personal insecurities, and using psychological techniques to induce a sense of dread and vulnerability.

1.1 The Fear Feedback Loop

Boogeymen often create a **fear feedback loop**: they induce small, seemingly innocuous disturbances that gradually escalate, causing the target to anticipate further scares. This anticipation creates a constant state of **heightened anxiety**, which the Boogeyman feeds on.

- **Technique:** The first step in resisting this loop is **awareness**. Recognize when the Boogeyman is using minor disturbances (such as unexplained noises, shadows, or feelings of unease) to build tension. Once you identify this pattern, you can begin employing psychological techniques to disrupt the feedback loop.

2. Building Mental Resilience: The Foundation of Psychological Defense

Mental resilience is the foundation of a hunter's defense against Boogeyman-induced fear. By fortifying the mind, hunters can withstand fear's assault and maintain control of their thoughts and emotions.

2.1 Fear Desensitization Training

Boogeymen capitalize on **unexpectedness** and **the unknown** to generate fear. Fear desensitization training involves exposing oneself to controlled fear-inducing stimuli to reduce sensitivity over time.

- **Method:** Create a safe environment where you can gradually expose yourself to **mild fear triggers**. For instance, spend time in a dimly lit room, listen to eerie soundtracks, or watch unsettling imagery. The key is to remain **calm** and **present** during these exposures, acknowledging the fear response without allowing it to control you.

- **Results:** Over time, this practice reduces the intensity of the fear response when encountering real Boogeyman manifestations. You become familiar with the physical sensations of fear, making it easier to separate **genuine danger** from psychological manipulation.

2.2 Cognitive Reframing

Boogeymen use **cognitive distortions** to manipulate a hunter's perception, often making small disturbances seem more significant or threatening than they are. Cognitive reframing is a technique that involves **consciously altering** your interpretation of fear-inducing events.

- **Technique:** When faced with a Boogeyman's disturbances (e.g., sudden noises, flickering lights), instead of interpreting them as direct threats, reframe them as **tricks** or **illusions** designed to provoke a reaction. This mental shift diminishes the Boogeyman's power over your emotions.
- **Example:** If you hear a knock on the wall, instead of thinking, "It's coming for me," reframe it as, "This is just an attempt to scare me. It's a trick that I do not need to react to."

2.3 Developing a Grounding Routine

Boogeymen often induce a sense of **dissociation** or **disorientation** to make their targets feel disconnected from reality. A grounding routine is a set of actions or mental exercises that **anchor** you to the present moment.

- **Method:** Create a simple routine that engages your senses:
    - **Visual:** Focus on an object in the room and describe it in detail to yourself. Notice its shape, color, texture, and size.
    - **Touch:** Hold a grounding object, such as a **smooth stone** or **metal talisman**, in your hand. Feel its weight, temperature, and surface texture.
    - **Auditory:** Listen to a **specific sound** (such as a tuning fork or a steady beat) that brings you back to the present. This sound becomes a mental anchor that can cut through the Boogeyman's psychological distortions.
- **Usage:** Practice this routine daily and employ it whenever you sense the Boogeyman attempting to manipulate your thoughts or surroundings. By focusing on tangible elements, you reaffirm your connection to reality, disrupting the Boogeyman's influence.

3. Enhancing Emotional Control: Mastery Over Fear Responses

Fear responses are **automatic**, but they can be **regulated** through emotional control techniques that help you manage your reactions to fear-inducing stimuli.

3.1 The Fear Box Technique

The **Fear Box** technique involves mentally containing your fear, giving you the ability to acknowledge it without letting it overwhelm you.

- **Visualization:** When fear arises, visualize a **small box** in your mind. Imagine placing your fear inside this box and closing the lid. Visualize the box becoming sealed and locked. Acknowledge that the fear is there, but it is now contained and separate from your immediate thoughts and actions.
- **Application:** Use this technique during Boogeyman encounters to prevent your fear from spilling over into panic. By containing the fear, you maintain emotional control, allowing you to think clearly and act strategically.

3.2 Breathing Techniques for Fear Regulation

Fear can trigger **shallow, rapid breathing**, which reinforces anxiety and panic. Using controlled breathing techniques can counteract this physiological response, promoting calmness.

- **Method:** Practice the **4-7-8 Breathing Technique**:
    - **Inhale** through your nose for a count of 4.
    - **Hold** your breath for a count of 7.
    - **Exhale** slowly through your mouth for a count of 8.
- **Benefits:** This technique activates the **parasympathetic nervous system**, helping to slow the heart rate and reduce the physical symptoms of fear. By controlling your breath, you assert dominance over your body's fear response, weakening the Boogeyman's hold on your psyche.

4. Strengthening Cognitive Clarity: Avoiding the Boogeyman's Mind Traps

Boogeymen often employ **mental traps**, such as planting false thoughts, inducing paranoia, or creating illusions. Maintaining cognitive clarity is vital to avoid falling into these traps.

4.1 Thought Auditing

Thought auditing is the process of **examining** and **questioning** your thoughts, especially when they are fear-based or irrational. Boogeymen thrive on **negative thinking** patterns, and thought auditing disrupts their influence.

- **Technique:** When a fear-inducing thought arises (e.g., "I'm not safe here"), ask yourself:
    - Is this thought based on evidence, or is it an **assumption**?
    - Is this thought **helpful** or **harmful**?
    - How would I perceive this situation if I were observing it from the outside?
- **Outcome:** By examining your thoughts critically, you identify **cognitive distortions** implanted by the Boogeyman, preventing them from taking root in your mind.

4.2 The Reality Check Protocol

Boogeymen manipulate perceptions, creating illusions or false sensory input to disorient and frighten their targets. The **Reality Check Protocol** is a mental exercise designed to verify the reality of your experiences.

- **Steps:**
    1. **Observe:** Take a deep breath and calmly observe your surroundings. Look for **inconsistencies** or **anomalies** that might indicate a distortion.
    2. **Engage Senses:** Touch an object, listen for ambient sounds, and pay attention to any scents in the air. Compare these sensations with what you would normally expect in your environment.
    3. **Cross-Check:** If possible, **cross-check** your perception with another person. Ask them to verify what they see, hear, or sense to ensure consistency.
- **Application:** Use this protocol whenever you suspect a Boogeyman is attempting to manipulate your reality. This method grounds your perceptions in **tangible reality**, weakening the Boogeyman's influence.

5. Advanced Visualization Techniques: Creating Mental Shields

Boogeymen often attack by infiltrating the mind, inducing fear and negative emotions. **Visualization** techniques can be used to create **mental shields** that protect your psyche from such assaults.

5.1 The Mirror Shield Visualization

The **Mirror Shield** is a mental construct that reflects the Boogeyman's psychological attacks back upon itself, preventing its fear-based projections from penetrating your mind.

- **Visualization:** Close your eyes and imagine a **large, circular mirror** forming in front of you. See its surface gleaming, smooth, and impenetrable. As the Boogeyman attempts to project fear or doubt toward you, visualize these emotions hitting the mirror and bouncing back toward their source.
- **Enhancement:** To strengthen the shield, visualize inscribing **protective runes** around its edge. These runes glow with a soft light, reinforcing the mirror's reflective power.
- **Practice:** Use this visualization daily to solidify the shield's presence in your mind. When facing a Boogeyman, conjure this shield to deflect its manipulations.

5.2 The Fortress Mind Technique

The **Fortress Mind** technique involves creating an inner sanctuary—a mental fortress that acts as a stronghold against external fear influences.

- **Visualization:** Picture a **fortress** within your mind, built of impenetrable stone walls. Inside this fortress is a tranquil, safe room filled with calming elements (soft light, gentle sounds, comforting scents). This room is your **mental refuge**, a place where the Boogeyman's fear-inducing efforts cannot reach.
- **Activation:** During encounters with a Boogeyman, mentally retreat to your fortress room. Imagine closing the doors behind you, sealing out all external disturbances. In this space, you regain composure, allowing you to think clearly and strategize.
- **Long-Term Benefits:** Regular use of this technique strengthens your mental defenses, reducing the Boogeyman's ability to affect your thoughts and emotions over time.

Conclusion: The Mental Battlefield

The confrontation with a Boogeyman is as much a **battle of the mind** as it is a physical encounter. By mastering advanced psychological techniques, hunters can build an inner fortress, grounding themselves in reality and maintaining emotional and mental clarity in the face of fear. These techniques do not eradicate fear but transform it into a **manageable** and **controllable** element, one that hunters can navigate and even use to their advantage.

Incorporating these advanced techniques into your daily practice will prepare you to withstand a Boogeyman's psychological onslaught, enabling you to confront these shadowy entities with confidence and resolve. The following chapter will delve into **post-encounter recovery**, exploring methods for cleansing the mind and environment after a Boogeyman confrontation to ensure complete restoration of balance.

Appendices

Appendix A: Boogeyman Field Guide Reference

This appendix serves as a **quick reference** for hunters in the field, providing essential information on various types of Boogeymen, their characteristics, weaknesses, and preferred habitats. Use this guide to identify the entity you're dealing with quickly and choose the most effective containment and banishment strategies.

1. Closet Stalker

Description: The **Closet Stalker** is the quintessential Boogeyman that lurks within closets, using the dark, confined space as a point of emergence. It preys primarily on those who fear enclosed spaces and the unknown depths of darkness. Known for its unsettling noises, rustling movements, and phantom whispers, the Closet Stalker is a master of hiding just beyond the edge of perception.

Preferred Habitat:

- Closets, wardrobes, and armoires.
- Enclosed storage spaces with limited lighting and visibility.

Behavior:

- Active primarily during nighttime or in darkness.
- Prefers to remain hidden and use noises or disturbances to induce fear in its target.
- Gradually opens closet doors or makes items within rustle to draw attention.

Weaknesses:

- **Light:** The Closet Stalker retreats when exposed to bright light sources. Flashlights, lanterns, and candles are effective deterrents.
- **Salt Lines:** Place a line of salt across the closet threshold. This creates a barrier the Closet Stalker is reluctant to cross.
- **Reflective Surfaces:** Mirrors placed inside the closet can disorient the entity, making it vulnerable to containment.

Containment Tips:

- Utilize **mirror traps** inside the closet to capture its essence.
- Line the closet with **iron nails** to prevent it from establishing a foothold within the space.

2. Underbed Creeper

Description: The **Underbed Creeper** resides in the dark, hidden space beneath beds. It thrives on the fear of unseen threats lurking just out of view. Its presence is often accompanied by cold drafts, a feeling of being watched, and the occasional movement or sound coming from beneath the bed.

Preferred Habitat:

- The dark, narrow spaces under beds.
- Areas with clutter or dust, which provide cover for its movements.

Behavior:

- Prefers to stay out of sight, only revealing its presence through subtle disturbances such as slight movements of bed skirts or scratching noises.
- Often targets individuals at the moment they are about to fall asleep, creating a sense of vulnerability.

Weaknesses:

- **Salt Circles:** Encircle the bed with a line of salt. This barrier prevents the Creeper from reaching out beyond the confines of its habitat.
- **Iron Rods:** Placing iron rods or bars underneath the bed disrupts its ability to manifest fully.
- **Sound Disruptors:** High-pitched frequencies or white noise generators disturb the Creeper's concentration, forcing it to retreat.

Containment Tips:

- Use a **shadow net** to trap it as it attempts to reach beyond the bed's edges.
- Employ **warding stones** placed under the four bedposts to create an energetic barrier.

3. Attic Dweller

Description: The **Attic Dweller** haunts attics, crawl spaces, and other seldom-visited areas of a house. It feeds on the fears associated with the unknown and the unexplored. Known for its unsettling noises—creaks, footsteps, or faint voices—it often induces paranoia and unease in its targets.

Preferred Habitat:

- Attics, crawl spaces, and lofts.
- Areas filled with clutter, old belongings, or forgotten items.

Behavior:

- Active during both day and night but prefers quiet periods when its noises are most noticeable.
- Remains elusive, rarely showing itself directly, relying on noises and disturbances to instill fear.

Weaknesses:

- **Bright Light:** Exposing the attic to bright lights, such as floodlights or lanterns, forces the Dweller to retreat into the farthest corners.
- **Incense Smoke:** Burning **frankincense** or **sage** in the attic purifies the space, making it less hospitable.
- **Chiming Bells:** The sound of chimes or bells disrupts its concentration, weakening its hold on the environment.

Containment Tips:

- Set up **sound decoys** that mimic normal household sounds to lure it into a trap.
- Use **iron-bound containment boxes** within the attic to capture its essence.

4. Night Terror Wraith

Description: The **Night Terror Wraith** is one of the most dangerous forms of Boogeyman, known for inducing sleep paralysis and feeding off nightmares. It manifests through dark, shadowy forms that loom over its victims, often instilling an intense sense of dread and helplessness.

Preferred Habitat:

- Bedrooms, particularly those where individuals experience frequent nightmares or disturbed sleep.
- Dark corners and ceiling spaces near sleeping individuals.

Behavior:

- Attacks during sleep, inducing nightmares or paralysis to immobilize its target while it feeds on their fear.
- Occasionally leaves behind a lingering sense of dread or anxiety in its target.

Weaknesses:

- **Amethyst Crystals:** Placing amethyst stones near the bed weakens the Wraith's influence and helps protect against nightmares.
- **Moonlight:** Exposure to **direct moonlight** disrupts the Wraith's ability to manifest fully.
- **Lavender:** Burning lavender incense or applying lavender oil near the sleeping area creates a calming effect that repels the Wraith's presence.

Containment Tips:

- Use **mirror traps** to capture the Wraith during its manifestation. Place mirrors at angles around the bed to reflect its shadowy form inward.
- Perform **dream-shielding rituals** nightly to prevent it from accessing the dream realm.

5. Mirror Phantom

Description: The **Mirror Phantom** resides within reflective surfaces, often appearing as distorted or shadowy figures in mirrors. It preys on the fear of altered perceptions and distorted reality. These entities use reflections to create illusions, instilling a sense of paranoia and unease.

Preferred Habitat:

- Mirrors, windows, and other reflective surfaces.
- Rooms with multiple reflective surfaces, which allow it to move and manipulate reflections.

Behavior:

- Active during both day and night but is more prominent in dimly lit environments.
- Capable of creating illusions, making reflections appear distorted or causing movement within mirrors.

Weaknesses:

- **Breaking Reflection:** Disrupting the reflective surface (e.g., covering the mirror or turning it to face the wall) forces the Phantom to retreat temporarily.
- **Consecrated Mirrors:** Mirrors anointed with **moonwater** or **holy oil** can repel or trap the Phantom within their confines.
- **Candles:** Burning candles around mirrors creates a fluctuating light source that disorients the Phantom, disrupting its influence.

Containment Tips:

- Use a **specially consecrated mirror** to trap the Phantom. Once it manifests, turn the mirror toward it while reciting a binding incantation.
- Encase captured mirrors in **black silk** and **iron frames** to prevent the Phantom's escape.

6. Shadow Lurker

Description: The **Shadow Lurker** is an ethereal Boogeyman that melds with shadows, moving seamlessly through darkened areas. It uses its amorphous form to intimidate its targets, creating the sensation of being watched or followed.

Preferred Habitat:

- Areas with shifting light, such as hallways, stairwells, or rooms with curtains that cast shadows.
- Corners and edges of rooms where shadows naturally accumulate.

Behavior:

- Relies on stealth, moving through shadows undetected.
- May cause temperature drops, flickering lights, or the sense of a looming presence.

Weaknesses:

- **Sunlight:** Exposure to direct sunlight forces the Lurker to dissipate temporarily.
- **Obsidian:** Obsidian stones placed in shadowy areas absorb its energy, weakening its form.
- **Sound Clarity:** Ringing **brass bells** or using tuning forks disrupts the Lurker's ability to meld with shadows.

Containment Tips:

- Use **shadow nets** to ensnare it when it manifests.
- Place **obsidian stones** in the room's corners to reduce its influence and movement.

7. Corner Watcher

Description: The **Corner Watcher** resides in the peripheries of a room, particularly in corners where two walls meet. It is known for creating the unsettling sensation of being watched from the edges of vision, often seen as a fleeting shadow when glanced at directly.

Preferred Habitat:

- Room corners, stairway landings, and narrow passageways.
- Low-lit areas with deep shadows and visual obstructions.

Behavior:

- Remains stationary, focusing its energy on inducing feelings of being observed.
- Appears briefly when looked at directly but vanishes when fully confronted.

Weaknesses:

- **Crossed Candles:** Placing candles in a **crossed pattern** in the corner disrupts its ability to gather shadows.
- **Hematite:** Carrying hematite repels the Watcher's influence, preventing it from establishing a link with its target.
- **Movement and Light:** Keep the area around corners well-lit and free of clutter to minimize its hiding spots.

Containment Tips:

- Use **warding symbols** marked in chalk around corners to seal its presence.
- Set up **mirror traps** angled toward corners to capture its shadowy essence.

8. Hallway Strider

Description: The **Hallway Strider** is a Boogeyman that haunts long corridors, often manifesting as faint footsteps, whispers, or shadowy figures glimpsed from a distance. It capitalizes on the fear of the unknown, using the liminal nature of hallways to induce unease.

Preferred Habitat:

- Long, narrow hallways, especially those with limited visibility at the far end.
- Passageways with numerous doors or branching paths.

Behavior:

- Moves slowly and subtly, creating an atmosphere of suspense.
- Avoids direct confrontation, preferring to lurk at the edge of perception.

Weaknesses:

- **Barrier Lines:** Drawing chalk lines or placing iron nails across hallway thresholds prevents it from crossing.
- **Sound Disruption:** Loud, continuous noises like ringing bells or white noise generators break its focus and cause it to retreat.
- **Reflective Barriers:** Setting up reflective surfaces at hallway ends disorients the Strider, disrupting its path.

Containment Tips:

- Use **sound decoys** placed at hallway ends to lure it into a trap.
- Employ **multi-layered containment circles** in the hallway to capture its form.

Conclusion

This quick reference guide is designed to provide essential information on various types of Boogeymen, their behaviors, habitats, and weaknesses. Effective hunting and containment rely on a hunter's ability to **identify** the type of Boogeyman they're dealing with and to use the **right tools and techniques** for the situation. Keep this field guide on hand during hunts to navigate encounters with Boogeymen confidently and efficiently. The next appendix will delve into **containment rituals** and **binding incantations** for different types of Boogeymen, offering hunters detailed methods for securing captured entities.

Appendix B: Boogey Safari Gear Checklist

Every Boogeyman hunt requires meticulous preparation and the right gear. Without the proper equipment, even the most seasoned hunter risks being outmaneuvered or overpowered by these elusive creatures. This appendix provides a **complete checklist** of essential tools, devices, and mystical items that every Boogey Hunter should carry on a safari. From basic necessities to specialized equipment, this guide ensures that hunters are well-prepared for any situation. Each item includes a brief description and tips for its effective use in the field.

1. The Boogey Book

Description: The **Boogey Book** is the most crucial item in any hunter's arsenal. This ancient tome contains invaluable knowledge on Boogeymen, including their types, behaviors, weaknesses, and containment rituals. Its pages are filled with incantations, field notes, and diagrams essential for identifying and confronting various Boogeymen.

- **Why You Need It:** The Boogey Book serves as both a **reference guide** and a **ritual manual**. Use it to quickly identify the Boogeyman you're dealing with and select the appropriate containment or banishment strategy.
- **Pro Tip:** Bookmark key sections with colored tabs for quick access during hunts. Always keep the book protected with a **leather binding** and store it in a **waterproof pouch** to prevent damage from environmental elements.

2. Light Sources

Boogeymen often lurk in darkness, so having multiple light sources on hand is essential for both visibility and protection.

- **Flashlight (High Lumen):** A high-powered flashlight is essential for illuminating dark spaces, such as closets, under beds, and attics. Choose a flashlight with adjustable brightness settings and a **strobe function** to disorient certain Boogeymen.
- **UV Light:** Some Boogeymen leave behind **ethereal residues** that are visible under ultraviolet light. A compact UV flashlight helps detect these traces, providing clues to the entity's movements and hiding spots.
- **Lanterns:** Battery-operated lanterns provide a wide spread of light, ideal for lighting up larger areas like attics and basements.
- **Candles:** Traditional candles are useful during rituals, particularly for creating **protection circles** or purifying spaces. Include windproof candles for outdoor use.

3. Reflective Surfaces

Boogeymen often fear their own reflection, making mirrors and other reflective surfaces essential for trapping and disorienting them.

- **Compact Hand Mirror:** A small, **consecrated hand mirror** is versatile for quick reflections to reveal hidden Boogeyman forms.

- **Mirror Traps:** Specialized **mirror traps** are designed with inscriptions around the edges to capture and contain a Boogeyman when it attempts to interact with its reflection.
- **Reflective Foil Sheets:** Lightweight and foldable, these sheets can be quickly placed around a room to create a makeshift reflective barrier.

4. Containment Tools

Proper containment is key to a successful hunt. Always carry the necessary tools to trap and secure a Boogeyman once identified.

- **Shadow Net:** A net woven from **iron wire** and **shadow thread**, specifically crafted to ensnare Boogeymen. Use this as your primary containment tool when confronting a physical manifestation.
- **Iron-Bound Containment Boxes:** These boxes, lined with **iron** and **runes**, are designed to trap Boogeymen once they are captured. Include a variety of sizes to accommodate different types of entities.
- **Mirror Orbs:** Hollow spheres lined with polished silver on the inside, used to capture Boogeymen that rely on reflective surfaces to move or manifest.
- **Salt Bags:** Small cloth bags filled with **consecrated salt** for creating containment circles or reinforcing protective boundaries on the fly.

5. Protection and Warding Items

Boogeymen often attempt to manipulate hunters' emotions and surroundings. Use protective gear to safeguard yourself from psychological and spiritual assaults.

- **Amulets (Iron and Moonstone):** Wear an **iron and moonstone amulet** for personal protection. Iron repels the Boogeyman's influence, while moonstone strengthens mental resilience.
- **Warding Stones:** Small stones inscribed with protective runes. Place them in the **four corners** of a room to create an energetic barrier.
- **Salt (Bulk Supply):** Keep a jar or pouch of **consecrated salt** for drawing protective lines, circles, and barriers. Salt is a universal purifying agent that repels many types of Boogeymen.
- **Sound Disruptors (Bells, Tuning Forks):** Carry a **brass bell** or **tuning fork** to create sound vibrations that disorient Boogeymen and disrupt their manifestations.
- **Candles (White, Black, and Red):** Include candles of various colors for different purposes:
    - **White** for purification.
    - **Black** for banishment rituals.
    - **Red** for sealing and binding.

6. Sensing and Detection Devices
Identifying a Boogeyman's presence is critical for strategic planning during a hunt.

- **Resonance Tuning Fork:** Used to detect vibrational anomalies in the environment, indicating a Boogeyman's proximity.
- **Thermal Imager:** A handheld thermal imaging device helps detect **cold spots** or **energy fluctuations** caused by the presence of a Boogeyman.
- **UV Flashlight:** As mentioned earlier, a UV flashlight is indispensable for spotting **ethereal residues** left by certain Boogeymen.
- **Digital Voice Recorder:** Used to capture **EVP (Electronic Voice Phenomena)** that Boogeymen may emit. Listening to these recordings can provide insight into the entity's intentions and movements.

7. Cleansing and Purification Supplies
After confronting or containing a Boogeyman, it's vital to cleanse the area to remove lingering fear energy and prevent the entity's return.

- **Sage Bundles:** For smudging rooms, closets, and attics. Sage smoke purifies spaces and neutralizes negative energy.
- **Frankincense and Myrrh Incense:** Burn these incenses to create an environment hostile to Boogeymen and to purify rooms after an encounter.
- **Holy Water or Moonwater:** Keep a small vial of **holy water** or **moonwater** for use in rituals and purifying objects that have come into contact with a Boogeyman.
- **Spray Bottle:** Fill a small spray bottle with **saltwater** for quick purification of objects or spaces.

8. Ritual and Binding Supplies
For advanced Boogeyman hunting, you may need to perform specific rituals to banish or bind an entity.

- **Chalk (White and Red):** For drawing **containment circles** and inscribing symbols on floors or walls. Include both white and red chalk, as different Boogeymen may respond to different types of symbols.
- **Herbs (Mugwort, Wormwood, Lavender):** Carry dried herbs for use in ritual work. **Mugwort** enhances psychic sight, **wormwood** weakens a Boogeyman's defenses, and **lavender** promotes calm and protection.
- **Binding Thread:** Black silk thread soaked in **moonwater** and **wormwood oil**, used to bind objects or mirrors that contain Boogeymen.
- **Runic Stamps:** Small stamps inscribed with protective and binding runes. Use these to mark doors, windows, or containment items.

9. Communication Tools

Boogeymen occasionally communicate indirectly, requiring tools for interpretation and negotiation.

- **Pendulum:** Use a pendulum to ask **yes/no questions** when attempting to communicate or understand a Boogeyman's intentions.
- **Scrying Mirror:** A **black mirror** used for observing the Boogeyman's realm or seeking guidance from the spirit world during a hunt.

10. Personal Care and Resilience Items

Hunting Boogeymen is physically and mentally taxing. Carry these items to maintain your strength and focus during prolonged encounters.

- **Water Bottle:** Staying hydrated is essential for maintaining mental clarity. Consider using a **water bottle infused with crystals** like amethyst or clear quartz for additional spiritual protection.
- **Energy Bars:** Quick snacks to keep your energy levels up during an extended hunt.
- **Hematite Stone:** A **grounding stone** that helps maintain focus and clarity during high-stress situations.
- **Lavender Oil:** Apply to temples and wrists to calm nerves and resist Boogeyman-induced anxiety.

11. Documentation Supplies

Recording your encounters is crucial for learning and refining hunting techniques.

- **Journal (Field Notebook):** A waterproof, pocket-sized journal for recording observations, incidents, and findings during the hunt. Include a pencil and waterproof ink pen.
- **Camera (With Night Vision):** A camera equipped with night vision capabilities is useful for capturing evidence of Boogeyman manifestations and identifying patterns in its behavior.

Conclusion: Preparing for the Hunt

The **Boogey Safari Gear Checklist** covers everything a hunter needs to successfully identify, contain, and protect against various Boogeymen. Proper preparation and the right gear can mean the difference between a successful hunt and a dangerous encounter. Always double-check your equipment before setting out on a hunt to ensure you are fully equipped for any situation you may face. The following appendix will provide a comprehensive guide to **containment rituals**, including incantations and gestures necessary for sealing and trapping a Boogeyman effectively.

Appendix C: Rituals and Spells for Boogeyman Containment

This appendix presents a comprehensive collection of **incantations**, **symbols**, and **rituals** tailored for trapping, containing, and warding off Boogeymen. The methods outlined here encompass a range of mystical practices, from quick containment spells to elaborate rituals requiring specific materials and preparation. These tools form the backbone of every Boogey Hunter's strategy in the field, providing the necessary means to not only subdue Boogeymen but also to fortify the environment against future incursions. Each ritual includes detailed instructions, symbols, and incantations to ensure their proper execution.

1. Basic Containment Circle Ritual

The Containment Circle is the foundational spell for trapping Boogeymen. This ritual creates a **barrier of energy** that restricts a Boogeyman's movement, allowing the hunter to proceed with further binding or banishment.

Materials Needed:

- White chalk or salt
- Four candles (one for each cardinal direction: North, South, East, West)
- Iron nail (to reinforce the circle)

Steps:

1. **Draw the Circle:** Use white chalk or salt to draw a circle around the Boogeyman's suspected location. Ensure that the circle is **unbroken** and extends at least six feet in diameter.
2. **Place the Candles:** Set a candle at each of the four cardinal points of the circle. Light them in a **clockwise** direction, starting from the East.
3. **Reinforce with the Nail:** Place the iron nail at the circle's northernmost point to fortify the boundary.
4. **Chant the Incantation:** Stand just outside the circle, facing inward. Hold your hands palm-out toward the circle and chant:

"Circle of salt, iron, and light,
Bound in shadow, trapped by night.
By candle's flame and earth's cold steel,
I seal thee now, break thy will."

1. **Observe:** If the Boogeyman attempts to breach the circle, the candles' flames will flicker. This indicates that the containment is working.

Pro Tip: Keep a piece of **moonstone** in your pocket while performing this ritual to enhance your psychic focus and protect your mind from the Boogeyman's influence.

2. Mirror Trap Ritual

The Mirror Trap ritual captures Boogeymen that use **reflective surfaces** for movement or manifestation. This spell binds the Boogeyman within a mirror, containing it until a more permanent solution can be employed.

Materials Needed:

- A consecrated hand mirror
- Black silk cloth
- Chalk or white paint
- A piece of clear quartz

Steps:

1. **Prepare the Mirror:** Cleanse the mirror by passing it through sage smoke or sprinkling it with moonwater. This removes any residual energies and readies the mirror for containment.
2. **Draw the Containment Symbol:** Use chalk or white paint to draw a **binding sigil** (a circle with interlocking triangles) on the back of the mirror.
3. **Set the Trap:** Place the mirror face-up in the Boogeyman's known habitat (e.g., closet, under the bed). Position the **clear quartz** on top of the mirror to amplify its reflective power.
4. **Chant the Incantation:** Stand over the mirror, focusing your intent on trapping the Boogeyman within its surface. Chant:

"Silver glass, reflection's snare,
Capture shadow, hold it there.
Bound by light, confined in space,
Trapped within this mirrored place."

1. **Cover the Mirror:** Once the incantation is complete, cover the mirror with the black silk cloth to seal the Boogeyman inside. This prevents it from escaping and neutralizes its power.

Pro Tip: Store the captured mirror in a **locked, iron-bound box** to further restrict the Boogeyman's influence.

3. Shadow Net Binding Ritual

This ritual utilizes the **shadow net** to ensnare a Boogeyman in its physical or ethereal form. The net disrupts the Boogeyman's ability to phase or shift between dimensions, allowing for its containment.

Materials Needed:

- Shadow net (woven from iron wire and shadow thread)

- Black candle
- Wormwood oil
- Small silver bell

Steps:

1. **Anoint the Net:** Apply a small amount of **wormwood oil** to the shadow net, focusing on each knot or intersection. This enhances the net's binding properties.
2. **Set the Ambush:** Wait until the Boogeyman begins to manifest. Remain hidden until the entity is within reach.
3. **Throw the Net:** As the Boogeyman moves into the designated space, throw the shadow net over it with a decisive motion.
4. **Light the Candle:** Immediately light the black candle to signify the start of the binding process.
5. **Ring the Bell:** Ring the silver bell three times to disorient the Boogeyman and sever its connection to the surrounding shadows.
6. **Chant the Incantation:** While holding the net taut, chant:

"By thread and wire, bind thee tight,
No more shadows, no more night.
Caught in net, bound by spell,
Locked in place where shadows dwell."

1. **Secure the Net:** Once the Boogeyman is ensnared, secure the net's edges with iron clips to reinforce the binding.

Pro Tip: Keep a **salt pouch** nearby to create a protective circle around the net if the Boogeyman struggles.

4. Warding Sigil Inscription

Drawing **warding sigils** is an effective way to fortify a space against Boogeymen. This ritual creates a protective barrier that repels Boogeymen and prevents them from crossing into the protected area.

Materials Needed:

- White chalk or paint
- Iron nail (optional, for inscribing on hard surfaces)
- Lavender oil

Steps:

1. **Choose Your Symbol:** The most effective warding sigil for Boogeymen is a **pentacle** surrounded by a circle, with **protective runes** inscribed along its perimeter.
2. **Draw the Sigil:** Use chalk or paint to draw the sigil on the floor, wall, or door of the space you wish to protect. If inscribing on a hard surface, use an iron nail to etch the symbol.
3. **Anoint with Oil:** Dab a small amount of **lavender oil** at the center of the sigil to empower it with calming and protective energy.
4. **Chant the Activation Spell:** Place your hand over the sigil and chant:

"By mark and line, this ward I place,
Keep shadows out, deny their space.
Bound by oil, sealed by might,
No darkness cross this warding light."

1. **Final Step:** Visualize the sigil glowing with a soft white light. This light represents the barrier's active state, ready to repel any Boogeyman that attempts to approach.

Pro Tip: Redraw the sigil monthly or whenever the ward's strength seems to wane.

5. Binding Ritual with Binding Thread

For advanced hunters dealing with sentient or particularly powerful Boogeymen, a **binding ritual** using **binding thread** is an effective containment strategy. This ritual ties the Boogeyman's essence to a physical object, restricting its movements.

Materials Needed:

- Binding thread (black silk soaked in moonwater and wormwood oil)
- Small iron box
- Red candle
- Hematite stone

Steps:

1. **Wrap the Object:** Choose a small, personal object that the Boogeyman has interacted with (e.g., a toy, trinket). Wrap the binding thread around the object tightly.
2. **Light the Candle:** Light the **red candle** to symbolize control and dominance over the Boogeyman's energy.
3. **Place in the Box:** Put the wrapped object into the iron box, placing the **hematite stone** inside to ground the Boogeyman's essence.
4. **Chant the Incantation:** Hold your hand over the box and chant:

"Thread of night, bind thee fast,
Essence caught, this bond shall last.
By iron's hold and stone's embrace,
Tethered now, sealed in place."

1. **Seal the Box:** Close the iron box, securing it with a lock. Anoint the lock with wormwood oil to enhance the binding.

Pro Tip: Store the sealed box in a **warded vault** or **iron-bound chest** to prevent accidental release.

6. Banishment Ritual: The Final Release

When containment is insufficient or temporary, a **banishment ritual** forces the Boogeyman back into the Boogie World, cutting its ties to the physical realm.

Materials Needed:

- Circle of salt
- Black and white candles
- Iron nail
- Amethyst crystal
- The Boogey Book (for reference)

Steps:

1. **Create a Banishment Circle:** Sprinkle salt to form a circle around the Boogeyman or its manifestation point. Place the black candle at the northern edge and the white candle at the southern edge of the circle.
2. **Set the Amethyst:** Place the **amethyst crystal** in the circle's center to focus the banishment energy.
3. **Chant the Banishment Spell:** Open The Boogey Book to the **Banishment Incantations** page. Hold the iron nail in your dominant hand and chant:

"From whence you came, return ye now,
Shadows deep, to dark you bow.
By salt and flame, by earth and stone,
I cast thee out, leave this home."

1. **Drive the Nail:** Push the iron nail into the ground (or floor) within the circle's boundary to anchor the banishment.
2. **Snuff the Candles:** Simultaneously snuff out the black and white candles to finalize the ritual, symbolizing the severance of the Boogeyman's link to this realm.

Pro Tip: After the ritual, cleanse the space with **sage smoke** or **frankincense** to remove residual fear energy and to seal the dimensional rift.

Conclusion

This collection of rituals, incantations, and symbols provides a comprehensive toolkit for **trapping**, **binding**, and **banishing** Boogeymen. While these practices are powerful, their success depends on the hunter's **focus**, **intent**, and adherence to each step. Always ensure that your rituals are performed within a **protected space** and with a **clear mind**. With practice and careful execution, these spells will serve as a formidable defense against the entities that lurk in shadows. The next appendix will delve into **advanced magical symbols** for fortifying spaces and objects against Boogeyman influence.

Message from the Author:

I hope you enjoyed this book, I love astrology and knew there was not a book such as this out on the shelf. I love metaphysical items as well. Please check out my other books:

-Life of Government Benefits

-My life of Hell

-My life with Hydrocephalus

-Red Sky

-World Domination:Woman's rule

-World Domination:Woman's Rule 2: The War

-Life and Banishment of Apophis: book 1

-The Kidney Friendly Diet

-The Ultimate Hemp Cookbook

-Creating a Dispensary(legally)

-Cleanliness throughout life: the importance of showering from childhood to adulthood.

-Strong Roots: The Risks of Overcoddling children

-Hemp Horoscopes: Cosmic Insights and Earthly Healing

- Celestial Hemp Navigating the Zodiac: Through the Green Cosmos

-Astrological Hemp: Aligning The Stars with Earth's Ancient Herb

-The Astrological Guide to Hemp: Stars, Signs, and Sacred Leaves

-Green Growth: Innovative Marketing Strategies for your Hemp Products and Dispensary

-Cosmic Cannabis

-Astrological Munchies

-Henry The Hemp

-Zodiacal Roots: The Astrological Soul Of Hemp

- **Green Constellations: Intersection of Hemp and Zodiac**

-Hemp in The Houses: An astrological Adventure Through The Cannabis Galaxy

-Galactic Ganja Guide

Heavenly Hemp

Zodiac Leaves

Doctor Who Astrology

Cannastrology

Stellar Satvias and Cosmic Indicas

Celestial Cannabis: A Zodiac Journey

AstroHerbology: The Sky and The Soil: Volume 1

AstroHerbology:Celestial Cannabis:Volume 2

Cosmic Cannabis Cultivation

The Starry Guide to Herbal Harmony: Volume 1

The Starry Guide to Herbal Harmony: Cannabis Universe: Volume 2

Yugioh Astrology: Astrological Guide to Deck, Duels and more

Nightmare Mansion: Echoes of The Abyss

Nightmare Mansion 2: Legacy of Shadows

Nightmare Mansion 3: Shadows of the Forgotten
Nightmare Mansion 4: Echoes of the Damned
The Life and Banishment of Apophis: Book 2
Nightmare Mansion: Halls of Despair
<u>Healing with Herb: Cannabis and Hydrocephalus</u>
<u>Planetary Pot: Aligning with Astrological Herbs: Volume 1</u>
Fast Track to Freedom: 30 Days to Financial Independence Using AI, Assets, and Agile Hustles
<u>Cosmic Hemp Pathways</u>
How to Become Financially Free in 30 Days: 10,000 Paths to Prosperity
Zodiacal Herbage: Astrological Insights: Volume 1
Nightmare Mansion: Whispers in the Walls
The Daleks Invade Atlantis
Henry the hemp and Hydrocephalus

10X The Kidney Friendly Diet
Cannabis Universe: Adult coloring book
Hemp Astrology: The Healing Power of the Stars
Zodiacal Herbage: Astrological Insights: Cannabis Universe: Volume 2
<u>Planetary Pot: Aligning with Astrological Herbs: Cannabis Universes: Volume 2</u>
Doctor Who Meets the Replicators and SG-1: The Ultimate Battle for Survival
Nightmare Mansion: Curse of the Blood Moon
<u>The Celestial Stoner: A Guide to the Zodiac</u>
Cosmic Pleasures: Sex Toy Astrology for Every Sign
Hydrocephalus Astrology: Navigating the Stars and Healing Waters
Lapis and the Mischievous Chocolate Bar

Celestial Positions: Sexual Astrology for Every Sign
Apophis's Shadow Work Journal: : A Journey of Self-Discovery and Healing
Kinky Cosmos: Sexual Kink Astrology for Every Sign
Digital Cosmos: The Astrological Digimon Compendium
Stellar Seeds: The Cosmic Guide to Growing with Astrology
Apophis's Daily Gratitude Journal

Cat Astrology: Feline Mysteries of the Cosmos
The Cosmic Kama Sutra: An Astrological Guide to Sexual Positions
Unleash Your Potential: A Guided Journal Powered by AI Insights
Whispers of the Enchanted Grove

Cosmic Pleasures: An Astrological Guide to Sexual Kinks
369, 12 Manifestation Journal

Whisper of the nocturne journal(blank journal for writing or drawing)
The Boogey Book
Locked In Reflection: A Chastity Journey Through Locktober
Generating Wealth Quickly:
How to Generate $100,000 in 24 Hours
Star Magic: Harness the Power of the Universe
The Flatulence Chronicles: A Fart Journal for Self-Discovery
The Doctor and The Death Moth
Seize the Day: A Personal Seizure Tracking Journal

| 226 | – THE SPOOKY JOURNEY BEGINS

If you want solar for your home go here: https://www.harborsolar.live/apophisenterprises/

Get Some Tarot cards: https://www.makeplayingcards.com/sell/apophis-occult-shop

Get some shirts: https://www.bonfire.com/store/apophis-shirt-emporium/

Instagrams:
@apophis_enterprises,
@apophisbookemporium,
@apophisscardshop
Twitter: @apophisenterpr1
Tiktok:@apophisenterprise
Youtube: @sg1fan23477, @FiresideRetreatKingdom

Podcast: Apophis Chat Zone: https://open.spotify.com/show/5zXbr-CLEV2xzCp8ybrfHsk?si=fb4d4fdbdce44dec

Newsletter: https://apophiss-newsletter-27c897.beehiiv.com/

Milton Keynes UK
Ingram Content Group UK Ltd.
UKHW010924131024
449482UK00010B/53